ARCHAEOLOGICAL SURVEY OF WESTERN INDIA, VOL. IX.

THE ARCHITECTURAL ANTIQUITIES OF NORTHERN GUJARAT

MORE ESPECIALLY OF THE

DISTRICTS INCLUDED IN THE BARODA STATE.

ARCHAEOLOGICAL SURVEY OF WESTERN INDIA, VOL. IX.

THE ARCHITECTURAL ANTIQUITIES OF NORTHERN GUJARAT

MORE ESPECIALLY OF THE

DISTRICTS INCLUDED IN THE BARODA STATE.

BY

JAS. BURGESS, C.I.E., LL.D., F.R.S.E.,

AND

HENRY COUSENS, M.R.A.S.,
SUPERINTENDENT ARCHAEOLOGICAL SURVEY,
WESTERN INDIA

GYAN

Published by

GYAN

Gyan Publishing House
5, Ansari Road
Daryaganj, New Delhi-110002
Phone: 011-47034999, 9811692060
E-mail: books@gyanbooks.com

Distribution Network
gyanbooks.com
India, USA, Canada, UK, Australia, France

ISBN : 978-81-212-2718-6 (HB)
First Published, 1903

2nd Impression 2021

Printed at: Gyan Press, Delhi.

The
Architectural Antiquities
of
Northern Gujarat
Author: Jas. Burgess

ARCHÆOLOGICAL SURVEY OF WESTERN INDIA, VOL. IX.

THE

ARCHITECTURAL ANTIQUITIES

OF

NORTHERN GUJARAT,

MORE ESPECIALLY OF THE

DISTRICTS INCLUDED IN THE BARODA STATE.

BY

JAS. BURGESS, C.I.E., LL.D., F.R.S.E.,

HON. A.R.I.B.A.; HON. M. IMP. RUSS. ARCHÆOL. SOC., AND AMER. OR. SOC.; F.R.G.S.; M.R.A.S.; M. SOC. AS. PARIS
HON. COR. M.R. PHILOS. SOC. GLASGOW, BERLIN SOC. ANTHROP. ETHNOL., AND BATAVIAN SOC. ARTS AND SC.;
LATE DIRECTOR-GENERAL OF THE ARCHÆOLOGICAL SURVEY OF INDIA.

AND

HENRY COUSENS, M.R.A.S.,

SUPERINTENDENT ARCHÆOLOGICAL SURVEY, WESTERN INDIA.

LONDON:

BERNARD QUARITCH; KEGAN PAUL, TRENCH, TRÜBNER, & Co.; LUZAC & Co.
CALCUTTA: THACKER, SPINK, & Co. BOMBAY: THACKER & Co., LIMITED.

1903.

PLATE I.

OLD HINDU TEMPLE AT MODHERÁ FROM THE SOUTH-WEST.

PREFACE.

THE present volume of the Archæological Survey of Western India is devoted to the description of the antiquarian remains in Northern Gujarât, principally within the dominions of His Highness the Gaikwâḍ of Baroda. The antiquities of Dabhoi in the west of the same territory were illustrated and described in a separate work published in 1888 by order of His Highness, and subsequently translated and republished in Gujarâti.

The remains now dealt with were surveyed by Mr. Henry Cousens during two tours made in the cold seasons of 1886-87 and 1889-90, when the drawings and photographs illustrating this volume were prepared.

For the letterpress I have had the use of the notes and descriptive outlines collected by Mr. Cousens and partly engrossed in the *Revised Lists of Antiquarian Remains in the Bombay Presidency* (1897). I had also personal local knowledge of the principal places surveyed, obtained during two private tours in December 1869 and December 1872, of which the materials collected were partly embodied in *Notes of a Visit to Gujara* (1870) and in the text of a volume of *Photographs of Architecture and Scenery in Gujarat and Rajputana* (1874). Again, in 1875, I visited the western area of the district on a tour through Râdhanpur viâ Jhinjhuwâḍa and Viramgâm to Ahmadâbâd.

The materials thus accumulated have been arranged and supplemented by historical, geographical, mythological, and other information from various sources, to which references have been made throughout the volume.

The chapter prefixed, on the ancient geography and history of Gujarât, is an attempt to condense the results of the discoveries made by epigraphical and other research during the last thirty years. There are still difficulties to be solved and lacunæ to be supplied in the chronology; but so much has already been accomplished that we may reasonably expect most of these to be cleared up in the near future, if only inscriptional records continue to be sought for and interpreted with the same energy and success as during the recent past.

The paragraphs where native architectural technical terms have been introduced (pp. 22-28, 67, 76-79, 84, and 104-5) are from the notes supplied by Mr. Cousens, to which I have only added occasionally an equivalent Sanskṛit synonym; but few of these technical terms are to be found in our lexicons, and their precise forms can hardly be controlled out of India.

The concluding pages may be useful in pointing out the localities that still call for more careful examination.

Finally, as has been indicated elsewhere, much of the value of such a volume as this lies in the illustrations—valuable in proportion as they are judiciously selected, complete, and trustworthy; and those now published have been carefully laid down on the spot from accurate measurements, and represent the subjects architecturally and in a style that surely does credit to Mr. Cousens and the members of his native staff, trained and superintended by him.

JAS. BURGESS.

Edinburgh, 20th September 1902.

CONTENTS.

LIST OF PLATES.

ILLUSTRATIONS IN THE TEXT.

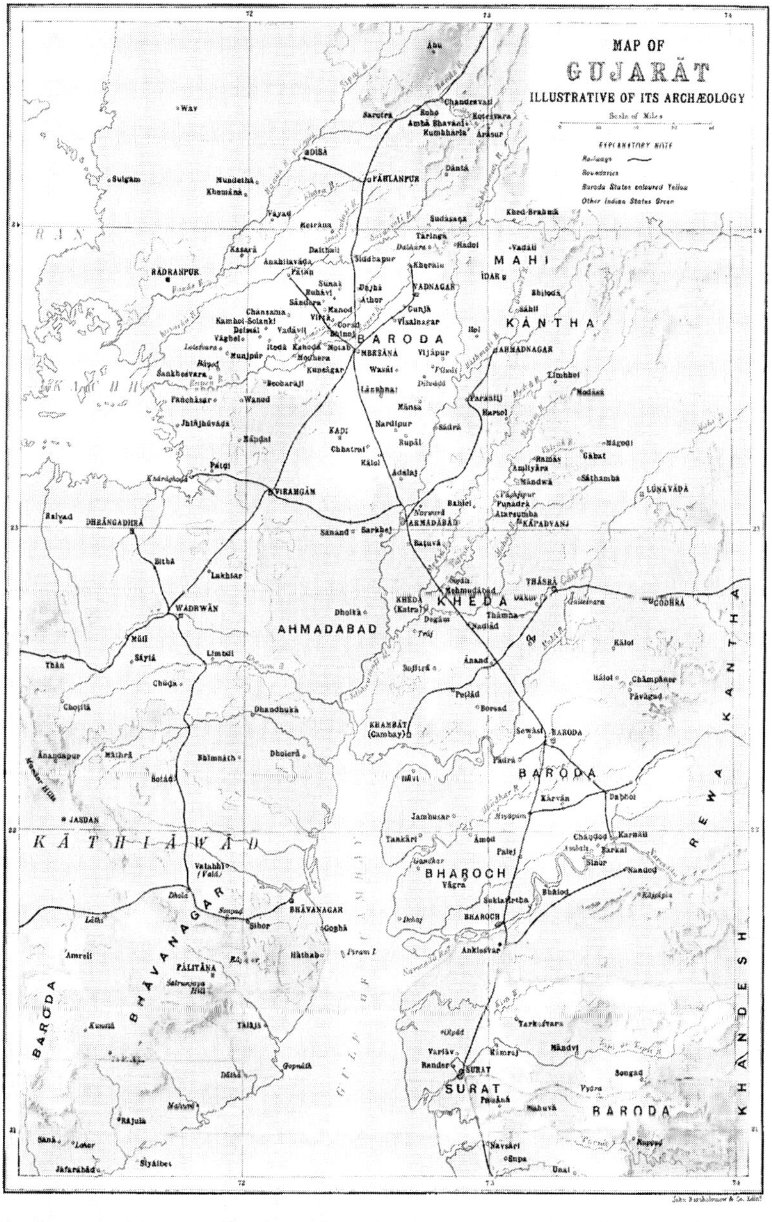
MAP OF
GUJARĀT
ILLUSTRATIVE OF ITS ARCHÆOLOGY
Scale of Miles
EXPLANATORY NOTE
Railways
Boundaries
Baroda States coloured Yellow
Other Indian States Green
Abu
Chandravati
Sarutra
Roho
Ambā Bhavāni
Kumbhariā
Koteśvara
Ārāsur
Wav
DISĀ
PĀHLANPUR
Dāntā
Suigām
Mundethā
Khemānā
Vāyad
Sudāsaṇa
Ked-Brahmā
Kotrāna
Tāringa
Kasarā
Dalthali
Anahilavāda
Pātan
Siddhapur
Kheralu
Vadāli
MAHI
ĪDAR
RĀDHANPUR
VADNAGAR
Bhiloda
Chansama
Vīsalnagar
Kāmhol-Solanki
KĀNTHA
BARODA
Hol
Vāghel
Modhera
MESSĀNĀ
Vijāpur
AHMADNAGAR
Sankhesvara
Kunsāgar
Wasāi
Limbhoi
Modāsa
Panchāsar
Wanod
Lānghnaj
Parantij
Harsol
Jhiñjhuvāda
KADI
Mānsā
Nardipur
Sādrā
Māndal
Chhatral
Rupāl
Māgodi
Pātdi
Kālol
Adalaj
Ramās
Gabat
Amliyāra
Māndwā
Sāthamba
LŪNĀVĀDĀ
VIRAMGĀM
Bahiel
Raiyad
DHRĀNGADHRĀ
Sānand
Sarkhej
AHMADĀBĀD
KAPADVANJ
Batuvā
Bithā
Lakhtar
Mehmudābād
THĀSRĀ
WADHWĀN
Dholkā
KHEDA
(Kaira)
KHEDA
GODHRA
Mūli
AHMADABAD
Thāmna
Nadiād
Limbdi
Thān
Sāyla
Od
Kālol
Chūda
Ānand
Hālol
Chāmpāner
Pāvāgad
Chotila
Dhandhuka
Petlād
Borsad
KHAMBĀT
(Cambay)
Sewāsi
BARODA
Ānandpur
Māthra
Bhimnāth
Dholerā
Pādrā
Botād
BARODA
Kārvān
Dabhoi
JASDAN
Jambusar
KĀTHIĀWĀD
Tankāri
Āmod
Chāndod
Karnāli
Palej
Barkal
Sinor
Vatabhi
(Vala)
BHAROCH
Nāndod
Vāgra
Sukla Tirtha
Bhālod
BHĀVANAGAR
BHĀVANAGAR
Sihor
BHAROCH
Goghā
Ankleśvar
Amreli
Hāthab
PĀLITĀNA
Satrunjaya Hill
REWA KĀNTHA
BARODA
Tālājā
Tarkeśvara
Variāv
Kāmrej
Māndvi
Rander
SURAT
SURAT
Songad
Gopnāth
Vyāra
Mahuva
BARODA
Rājulā
Navsāri
Supa
Unai
KHANDESH
Jāfarābād
Siyālbet
GULF OF CAMBAY
John Bartholomew & Co. Edin

ARCHITECTURAL ANTIQUITIES OF NORTHERN GUJARAT.

CHAPTER I.

GEOGRAPHICAL AND HISTORICAL.

THE antiquities described in this volume are included generally in the geographical area covered by the modern state of Barodâ, which lies within the limits known as the province of Gujarât or Gujarâshṭra. The districts belonging to H.H. the Gaikwâḍ of Barodâ are much intermixed with British areas in the same province, but need only be defined generally for the present purpose. Exclusive of portions of territory lying further west, in the peninsula of Kâṭhiâwâḍ, the Barodâ possessions fall roughly into three areas, corresponding to three administrative prânts,—viz. (1) the districts included in the Nausâri prânt lying to the south of the Narmadâ river; (2) those of the Barodâ or Vaḍodrâ prânt, to the north of that river and south of the British district of Kairâ or Khêḍâ; and, (3) the Kaḍi-Pattan prânt, which is the largest, and, archæologically, by far the most important,—extending from the parallel of Aḥmadâbâd (23° N.) to the borders of Pâhlaṇpur (26° 6′ N.). This district lies in the northern plain of Gujarât and covers an area of about 3160 square miles, the larger part of it being to the west of the Sâbhramatî river and extending about 75 miles from north to south and 66 miles from east to west. It touches the Baṇâs (the ancient Parṇâśâ) river on the north-west, and is watered by its affluents and those of the Sâbhramatî, and by the Sarasvatî or Kuvarkâ and the Rupen. It is mostly pretty well wooded, fertile and populous.

What are now the southern prânts belonged in early times to the province then called Lâṭa or Lâṭadeśa, the Λαρικὴ of Ptolemy,[1] in which was the great mart of Barygaza—the modern Bharoch. To the early Arab writers the district was known as Lâr, and the gulf of Khambay they called the sea of Lâr, whilst the language spoken on its coast was Lâri.[2]

---

[1] Ptolemy, *Geog.* bk. VII, c. i, §§ 4, 62. In the *Periplus of the Ærythræan Sea*, it is called Arabikē or Ariakē. The Sanskrit name Aparântikâ, in Prâkṛit—Abarâtikâ or Avarâikâ—has been suggested as the origin of the Greek form Aburatikē (*Ind. Antiquary*, vol. VII, pp. 259, 263). By Ptolemy Ariakē (*loc. cit.* § 82) is placed to the south of Larikē but stretching much farther inland than the native Aparânta.

[2] Mas'ûdi, tom. I, pp. 330, 381; Yule's *Marco Polo*, vol. II, p. 353; Reinaud, *Relation des Voyages, dans l'Inde*, &c. tom. II, p. 5.

The Greek writers do not supply much clear information on the early geography of Gujarât. They knew about the great emporium of Barygaza or Bargosa—the Bharukachchha or Bhṛigukshetra of Indian literature—and the modern Bharoch or Barûch on the Narmadâ[1]—exporting to Egypt and the West, cottons of all sorts, silk, ivory, spikenard, bdellium, onyx-stones, porcelain, &c., and importing wines, metals, sashes, sandarach, stibium, unguents, silver vases, handsome young women, &c.[2]

Both Ptolemy and the author of the *Periplus Maris Erythræi* mention Astakapra, and the latter says it is opposite to Barygaza. Now a grant of Dhruvasena I of Valabhî, belonging to the first half of the sixth century, mentions Hastakavapra, which is satisfactorily identified with Hâthab, once a port, about 8 miles south of Goghâ.[3] Ptolemy's Nausaripa also is easily located as the modern Nausâri, 53 miles south of Bharoch; and as the Kammōni of the *Periplus* corresponds to the Kamanē which Ptolemy places to the south of the mouth of the Namados or Narmadâ, we might with some probability place it about the mouth of the Kim river.

Besides these, Ptolemy mentions quite a number of other towns to which he assigns positions that should lie within the limits of Gujarât; in one list of places on the coast, we have the mouth of the Mōphis or Mahi, Pakidarē—a village, Cape Maleō, Kamanē, mouth of the Namados, Nausaripa, and Pulipula; in another, of inland cities, from north-east to south-west—Auxoamis, Asinda, Orbadaru or Ordabari, Theophila, and Astakapra; and in a third—Bammogura, Sazantion and Zērogerei. Colonel Sir H. Yule and Prof. Kiepert have tried conjecturally to locate these places, but with small confidence. Pulipula Col. Yule places at Sâñjân, to the south of Nausâri, and it may probably have been there or nearer Balsâḍ; Theophila he interpreted as "Dewaliya" and suggested its position to be east of Wadhwân, while Kiepert assigned it a place on the Baṇâs near Râdhanpur. Orbadaru was identified conjecturally by Yule with Arbuda or Âbû; Kiepert placed it near Chitalwâna on the Loṇî. Yule supposed Sazantion might have been at Sojitrâ—north of Khambay, and Kiepert near Pâṭaṇa, with the Minnagar of the *Periplus* (c. 41) at Ahmadâbâd[4]; but all these are mere conjectures.

The province of Gujarât or Gurjarâshṭra, lying to the north of Lâṭa, takes its name from the Gurjjara tribe, who appear to have come from the Panjâb, and,

---

[1] Barûch appears in a Pâli inscription at Junnar under the form Bhârukachha (*Arch. Sur. W. Ind.* vol. IV, p. 96); in Sanskrit it is Bharukachchha and Bhṛigukachchha or Bhṛigukshetra, from the locality being the traditional residence of the sage Bhṛigu (*Bṛih. Saṅh.* v, 40; xiv, 11; xvi, 6; *Mahâbhârata*, ii, 1830; *Kâśîkhaṇḍa*, vi, 25; *Bhâg. Pur.* viii, 18, 21; *Pariśishṭa Ath. Veda*, in Berlin *Cat. S. MSS.* p. 92; *As. Res.* vol. IX, p. 184; *Jo. Amer. Or. Soc.* vol. VII, pp. 32, 33; *Oxford Cat. Sansk.* MSS. pp. 67*a*, 338*b*, 339*b*; Lassen, *Ind. Alt.* Bd. I, Ss. 113, 136; also Ptolemy, *Geog.* lib. vii, c. 1, 62; *Periplus Mar. Eryth.* c. 42, 49, &c. The Bhârgava Brâhmaṇs of Bharûch are the representatives of an early colony of the school of Bhṛigu. It was from Bharûch the Śramana came who burnt himself at Athens. (Strabo, *Geog.* lib. xv, c. 1, 73.) Conf. my note in Beal's *Si-yu-ki*, vol. II, p. 259, n. 54.

[2] *Peripl. Mar. Eryth.* c. 49.

[3] *Ind. Antiquary*, vol. V, pp. 204, 314.

[4] Conf. Kiepert's Map of Ancient India (1853), in Lassen's *Ind. Alterthum.*; Yule's Map of India, in Murray's *Cl. Atlas* (1874); and Kiepert, *Carta delle cogn. Greche sull' Indie* (1875) in *Studi Italiani di Filol. Indo-Iranica*, vol. IV (1901).

before the fifth century of our era, had established themselves in the south of Râjputâna, and even to the south of the Loṇî river, where they seem to have formed a state or kingdom. Hiuen Tsang, about 640 A.D., states that 1800 *li* or so, north of Valabhî, lay the kingdom of Kiu-che-lo, of which the capital was Pi-lo-mo-lo; and these Chinese forms represent respectively Gurjjara and Bhillamâla. M. Vivien de Saint-Martin suggested that the capital was to be identified with the modern Bâlmêr or Bârmêr in the Mallani district of western Râjputâna, and General Cunningham, taking the rough distance as exactly 1800 *li* from Valabhî, adopted this identification.[1] Major John W. Watson, with more local knowledge, pointed out that Bhinmâl—formerly known as Bhillamâla and Śrîmâla—must correspond to the old Gurjjara capital,[2] and still retains some indications of early greatness. It lies about 83 miles north of Aṇhilawâḍa-Pattana and 40 miles north-west from Mount Âbû, in lat. 25° 0′ N., long. 72° 20′ E., and in the plain forming the southern portion of the basin of the Loṇî with its tributary the Sukrî river. What area Hiuen Tsang's estimated circumference of about 870 miles may have included, it would be futile to attempt tracing: it might perhaps cover about 30,000 square miles.

The capital of Bhillamâla is mentioned by Albiruni, circa A.D. 1030, as the birthplace of the astronomer Brahmagupta, the son of Jishṇu, who was born in 598, and who, as he himself tells, wrote the *Brahmasphuṭa Siddhânta* "in the reign of Śrî Vyâghramukha of the Śrî Châpa dynasty, 550 years after the Śaka king," or in A.D. 628.[3] This mention of the Châpa dynasty suggests the question whether the Châpotkaṭa or Châvaḍâ dynasty of Gujarât in the ninth century may not have been an offshoot of these earlier Gurjjara rulers.

Bhillamâla had at an early date borne the name also of Śrîmâla, and from it came the Śrîmâlî Brâhmaṇs, who are now chiefly votaries of Vishṇu and are widely scattered throughout Râjputâna, Kachh, Gujarât, and Central India. They are largely either mendicants or *gurus*—officiating priests to merchant Vâṇiyâs and Sonîs or goldsmiths. Their favourite Kuladevi, or family goddess, is Mahâlakshmî—a notable image of whom was brought from Bhinmâla to Aṇhilapura in the times of the Gujarât kings.

The famous Sanskṛit poet Mâgha, the author of the *Śiśupâlavadha*, was a Śrîmâlî Brâhmaṇ, whose date has not yet been ascertained, though he probably lived about the end of the ninth century; one tradition, however, makes him a contemporary of Bhoja-râja of Dhârâ, who belongs to the first half of the eleventh century.[4]

Of the Gurjjara or Châpa dynasty of Bhillamâla we have no records. At an early date, however, they, or a branch of them, appear to have ruled at

[1] In lat. 25° 46′ N., long. 71° 23′ E. Stan. Julien *Mémoires sur les Contr. Occident.* tom. II, pp. 166, 407 f.; Beal, *Si-yu-ki*, vol. II, pp. 269 f.; Reinaud, *Mém. sur l'Inde*, p. 337; Tod, *Râjasthan*, vol. II, p. 209; and Cunningham, *Anc. Geog.* p. 312 f.

[2] *Ind. Antiq.* vol. VI, p. 63; vol. XIX, pp. 235-36, 240; conf. *Bomb. Gazetteer*, vol. I, pt. i, p. 3.

[3] Albîrunî's *India*, Sachau's transl. vol. I, pp. 153, 267; *Jour. R. As. Soc.*, N.S., vol. I, p. 410; Duff, *Chronology of India*, pp. 44, 48; Reinaud, *Mém.* p. 337.

[4] Duff, *Chronology of India*, pp. 70, 84; Wilson, *Indian Caste*, vol. II, pp. 111, 167.

Bharoch as contemporaries of the Valabhî kings in Saurâshṭra or Kâṭhiâwâḍ, whose sway probably extended northwards round the head of the gulf of Khambâyat. About A.D. 630, or soon after, Praśâutarâga-Dadda, the Gurjjara king of Bharoch, claimed to have protected the Valabhî ruler from Harshavardhana of Thâṇeśvara[1]; but about twenty years later Dharasena IV of Valabhî seems to have occupied Bharoch itself. It was a period of disturbance and upheaval: Harshavardhana or Śrî-Harsha, between A.D. 606 and 640, had overrun and subjugated northern India; the Valabhî prince was allied to him by marriage and possibly was his vassal when he took Bharoch; but on Harsha's death the subject kings revolted, and the more powerful conquered the feebler chiefs.[2]

The Gurjjaras appear in Bharoch till the early part of the eighth century, when Jayabhaṭa III was probably overthrown by the Arabs, his last inscriptional date being in A.D. 736.[3] About this period the Arabs were making frequent incursions from Sindh into Western India: in A.D. 724 Junaîd ibn 'Abdu-*l* Raḥman, governor of Sindh made a foray towards Bharoch and Mâlwâ, and in 739 the Arabs seem to have overrun "Kachh, Saurâshṭra, Châvoṭaka, the Maurya and Gurjjara kings," and turning southwards they advanced to the Navasârikâ or Nausâri district in Lâṭa, where they were met and repulsed by the feudatory Chalukya chief Avanijanâśraya-Pulikeśin—a son of Dharâśraya-Jayasiṁha-varman, the younger brother of Vikramâditya I of Bâdâmi (655–680 A.D.). This occurred in the reign of Vikramâditya II (733-4—746-7), and it seems probable that Pulikeśin, after the victory, annexed the Gurjjara territory to the Chalukya dominions. The Gurjjara ruler overthrown by these Tajikas or Arabs was probably Jayabhaṭa III, while the Châvoṭaka refers to the Châpotkaṭa prince of Bhillamâla.[4]

The Valabhî copper-plate grants bring down that dynasty to Śîlâditya VII Dhruvabhaṭa, in whose reign we have one dated in A.D. 766, and it was probably soon after that the dynasty finally disappeared. Recent research enables us to discard the conjectural chronologies of Tod, Wathen, and others, and to show that Valabhî was not overthrown either by Skythians or Baktrians in the sixth century, nor by Nâshîrwân the Great, but by some Muhammadan expedition from Sindh, sent perhaps by 'Amrû ibn Jamâl, the general of Hashâm ibn 'Amrû-a*l* Taghlabî the governor. The ruin of Valabhî may have been partly effected even somewhat earlier, for its power had previously begun to decay; but after A.D. 766 we learn no more of it.

The Gujarât bards relate that about the end of the seventh century,[5] Vacharâja, a Châvaḍâ or Parmâr Râjput, had set up a principality at Divakoṭa or Divapaṭṭana, now Diu, and was succeeded by his son Venirâja. After they

---

[1] *Ind. Ant.* vol. XIII, pp. 74, 79.

[2] *Ind. Ant.* vol. VI, p. 12; vol. XVII, p. 195 f.; *Epigraphia Indica*, vol. I, p. 69; *Śrîharshacharita* (Kâśmir ed.) p. 274.

[3] *Ind. Ant.* vol. VII, p. 62; vol. XIII, pp. 70-90; vol. XVII, pp. 192, 220; vol. XVIII, p. 176; *Epig. Indica*, vol. II, p. 19.

[4] Duff, *Chron. of India*, pp. 59, 62, 64 and refs.

[5] One version gives A.D. 730, or only fifteen years before the reputed date of the founding of Aṇahilawâḍa; but chronology is the weakest point in the native chronicles. *Ind. Ant.* vol. IV, p. 146.

had ruled 71 years, Venirâja was drowned by an inundation of the sea, which converted Diva into an island, and his queen escaping first to Pañchâsar in northern Gujarât, after the destruction of that town by the sovereign of Kanauj, fled to the forests, and finally at Chandur gave birth to a son named Vanarâja.

The version of the story contained in the *Ratnamâlâ*[1] of Kṛishṇaji, makes Pañchâsar on the Rupen river (lat. 23° 27′ N., long. 71° 45′ E.) the capital of a chief named Jasarâja or Jayaśekhara of the Châvaḍâ clan. In 696 he was attacked by a king Bhûyaḍa or Bhûvaḍa of Kalyâṇakaṭaka (Kanauj ?) and slain; but his brother-in-law Sûryapâla managed to escape with his sister, the wife of Jasa, into the forests where her son Vanarâja was born.[2] He is said to have been reared at Wanod, to the east of Pañchâsar, by a Jaina monk named Śîlaguṇasûri, and when a lad he was taken out by his uncle to share in his freebooting raids.[3]

In the eighth and ninth centuries the Râṭhors or Râshṭrakûṭas held southern Gujarât with Bharoch as its capital; but the north of the province appears to have owned the suzerainty of Kanauj. In A.D. 731, Yaśovarman was the ruler of Kanauj, and we learn that he sent a Bauddha priest (*bhadanta*) on an embassy to China, apparently to ask assistance against the Arabs; and, again, we find him at a later date attacked by Muktâpîḍa-Lalitâditya of Kaśmir.[4] Of his successors, we have as yet but meagre information. From inscriptions the names of probably most of the princes of Kanauj or Mahodaya during the eighth century have been recovered, and again from 862 to 950 A.D.[5] The Gujarât Jaina chroniclers, however, mention a different list of kings—Bhûyaḍa, Kamâditya, Chandrâditya, Somâditya, and Bhuvanâditya, as ruling in succession at Kalyâṇakataka or Kanauj during this period. These differ so entirely from the epigraphical names that we might suppose they were only feudatories or governors in Râjputana, under the Kanauj kings, or else that Kalyâṇakaṭaka represents some other capital than Kanauj. It is useless, however, to attempt to solve difficulties of this sort by hasty assumptions; some epigraphical discovery may at any time clear it up.

The Kanauj sovereign, Merutuṅga tells us, had settled the revenues of Gujarât on his daughter Mahaṇikâ, as her dowry, and the officer sent to collect the tribute appointed the young Vanarâja to be his *sellabhṛit* or spear-bearer—perhaps deputy. When the tribute was ready to be sent away, Vana killed the officer and escaped with the wealth to a forest fastness. Collecting followers he succeeded in establishing his authority, and is said to have built the city of Aṇahilapura, where he was crowned in V. Saṁvat 802 (A.D. 746). But the chronicles represent him as being then 50 or 56 years of age and his early Jaina protector still alive, whilst afterwards he reigned for fully 50 years, dying at the age of 109 years. This is

[1] Translated by A. K. Forbes, 1849, in the *Jour. Bom. B. R. As. Soc.* vol. IX, pp. 20–100.

[2] Forbes, *Râs Mâla*, vol. I, pp. 25-37; *Prabandha chintâmaṇi* of Merutuṅga, Tawney's transl. pp. 16–18; *Âin-i-Akbari*, vol. II, pp. 259, 261; Bayley, *Hist. of Gujarât*, p. 24; Tod, *Western India*, p. 153; *Ind. Ant.* vol. IV, p. 147.

[3] *Ratnamâlâ* in *Jour. Bom. B. R. As. Soc.* vol. IX, p. 100.

[4] Pauthier, *Examen des faits rel. au Thien-tchu*, p. 66, or *Jour. Asiat.* 1839, p. 322; conf. *Jour. A. S. Beng.*, vol. VI, p. 71; *Jour. As.* IXme ser. tom. VI, p. 353; *Râja Taranginî*, bk. IV, 133–36.

[5] *Epigraphia Indica*, vol. I, pp. 170, 186; vol. V, p. 208; *Ind. Ant.* vol. XV, pp. 112, 140.

hardly credible; but Merutuṅga, in another work—the *Vichâraśreṇi*—gives Saṁ. 821 (A.D. 765) as the date of the founding of Aṇahilapura, after which he reigned 60 years,[1] to 825 A.D. Here is a difference of 19 years in the statements of the same author—showing that the chronology had got hopelessly into error by the fifteenth century.

The date Saṁvat 802 for the foundation of Aṇahilapura by Vanarâja, plays a prominent part in Gujarât history, and probably it marked some local event. In the Gandharovâḍâ ward of Pattana, the writer was shown, in 1869, a couple of old images in a ruined cell—Gaṇapati and Umâmaheśvara—the first of which bore an inscription dated "Saṁvat 802, Chaitra śuddha, 2, Friday" and stated that "Vanarâja installed the image of Umâmaheśvara at Aṇahillavâḍipattana." The alphabet, however, indicates that it must have been inscribed several centuries after its date. Again, at the temple of Sindhvâi Mâtâ, just outside the walls, on the east, a Brâhmaṇ possessed a copper-plate grant, purporting to have been issued by Vanarâja on the 3rd day of Vaiśhâkha śuddha, Saṁ. 802, settling upon a Brâhmaṇ named Jaṅguli a subsistence, raised as an octroi, and "assented to by Śrîmâlis, Uswâlas, Pauravatas, Nâgaras, Moḍhas, Hobadas or Deḍvas," &c. But the very language as well as the alphabet prove this to be a late forgery for an obvious purpose. Whether Aṇahilavâḍa was founded in Saṁ. 802, and whether Vanarâja was installed then, or only one of those events occurred at that date and the other in Saṁ 821, is quite uncertain. He may have reigned 59 or 60 years, or that period may indicate his age: it is hardly probable that in so turbulent a period he ruled a kingdom till he was 109 years of age.

Vanarâja, we are told by the Jaina chroniclers, after being established on the throne, sent for his old protector Śîlaguṇasuri from Pañchâsar and built a *chaitya* or Jaina temple for him at Aṇahilapura, which was called Pañchâsara-Pârśvanâtha, with an image of the Tîrthakara or Jina, and also a statue of himself as a worshipper. This temple founded by Vanarâja, or dating from his time, has long since disappeared, together with all the great temples of the early city—swept to destruction in the various Musalman sacks of this place. The present temple of Pañchâsara-Pârśvanâtha is one of the largest in the city and may perhaps date from the fifteenth or sixteenth century. In one of the cells of the *bhamti*, or series of twenty-four small shrines surrounding this *chaitya*, are still shown the images of Vanarâja and of Jamba—a merchant who became his *diwân* or prime minister—standing against the returning wall to his right.[2] These figures are said to have been brought from the old city, but may not be of great age: indeed the inscription under the figure of Vanarâja is dated Saṁ. 1524 (A.D. 1467), and though neither inscription is very legible, that under Jamba seems to bear a different date.[3]

---

[1] *Jour. B. B. R. As. S.* vol. IX, p. 155. But the *Vichâraśreṇi* is of doubtful accuracy; R. G. Bhandarkar, *Search for Sansk. MSS*, 1883-84, p. 12.

[2] See below p. 45.

[3] Tod, *Travels in Westn. India*, p. 230, gives what professes to be a substantial translation of these inscriptions, and dates one of them at least in Saṁ. 1352, a year before the sack of Aṇahilavâḍa by the forces of 'Alâu-*l*-din Muḥammad Shâh, and yet mentioning him as "Śrî Khuni Allam Muhammad." We can only suppose that Colonel Tod was imposed upon by some of the Jaina Yatis with a story, in place of a copy of the inscriptions.

The Jainas claim that—

"This kingdom of the Gurjaras, even from the time of king Vanarâja, was established with Jaina *mantras*, its foe indeed has no cause to boast."[1] This sect seems always to have been very influential in Gujarât; they were numerous and wealthy, and frequently held high posts in the state; and they impressed their character and tastes upon the rest of the population. Vanarâja was a Hindu and built a Hindu temple of Kaṇṭheśvarî near his palace, but he was also sufficiently liberal as well as politic to encourage substantially his Śrâvak subjects.

The chronology of the Châuḍâ or Châpotkaṭa dynasty is related by different writers with constant variations and contradictions, and it is perhaps impossible to arrange the names in their real order. The chroniclers were probably misled by different *birudas* or titles of the same prince, and, careless in verifying the dates by the years of each reign, they are at discord both as to the order and durations of the reigns. They mostly assert that the dynasty lasted 196 years, from A.D. 746 to 942, and some divide this period among seven rulers, but other *patâvalis* or registers add two more names: one class of them place Ratnâditya and Vairisiṁha in the third and fourth places, and another in the fifth and sixth.

The principal differences will best be understood by a comparison of some of the lists:—(1) from Arisiṁha's *Sukṛitasaṁkîrtana* and Merutuṅga's *Therâvali;* (2) from Merutuṅga's *Prabandha-chintâmaṇi;* and (3) from the *Ratnamâlâ* and others."[2]

1. Arisiṁha and Merutuṅga's *Therâvali* corrected.	2. Merutuṅga's *Prabandha-chintâmaṇi*.	3. Kishnaji's *Ratnamâlâ*, &c.
Vanarâja. S. 821–862	Vanarâja, 59 y. S. 802–862.	Vanarâja, 802.
Yogarâja. 862–891.	Yogarâja, 17 y. 862–878.	Yogarâja, 862.
Ratnâditya. 891–894.	Ratnâditya, 3¼ y. 878–881.	
Vairisiṁha. 894–905.	Vairisiṁha (881–898).	
Kshemarâja. 905–930.	Kshemarâja, 38¼ y. 898–925.	Kshemarâja, 897.
Châmuṇḍa. 930–951.	Châmuṇḍa, 13¼ y. 925–938.	Bhûyaḍa, 922.
		Vairisiṁha, or Vijayasiṁha, 951.
Râhaḍa, Thaghaḍa. 951–979.	Âkaḍadeva, 26 y. 938–965.	Ratnâditya, or Râvatasiṁha, 976.
Bhûbhaṭa or Puâḍa. 979–998.	Bhûyagaḍa, 27¼ y. (965)–991.	Sâmantasiṁha, 991–998.

[1] *Prabandha-chintâmaṇi*, p. 19; *Râs Mâlâ*, vol. I, p. 39.

[2] Bhâu Dâjî in *J. B. B. R. As. S.* vol. IX, p. 155. It is evident that the dates are mostly, if not all, increased by 19 years. The *Vichâraśreṇi*, however, has the same dates.

[3] Tawney's *Prabandha-chintâmaṇi*, pp. 19-21; Bhandarkar, *Search for Sansk. MSS.*, 1883-84, pp. 10, 150; *J. B. B. R. A. S.* vol. IX, p. 157.

The *Âin-i-Akbari* follows the chronology of the *Ratnamâlâ*, calling the third prince Bhîma-râja instead of Kshemarâja. The discrepancies are not to be got over by interposing another reign or an interval between Vanarâja and Yogarâja. The traditions had apparently become confused perhaps before they were committed to writing, and the manuscripts have been carelessly copied and vitiated. There is, however, a consensus among them which yields a chronology that may be accepted as fairly trustworthy.

According to most sources Vanarâja began his reign in Saṁvat 802, Vaiśakha (A.D. 746); some accounts place the founding of Aṇahilapâṭaka in V.S. 821; and his reign, according to the *Prabandha-chintâmaṇi* lasted 59 years 2 months 21 days, or to Ashâdha V.S. 861 (A.D. 806). That he lived fully 109 years may be discarded.

He is represented as succeeded by his son Yogarâja, to whom is ascribed a reign of 35, 32, and 17 years by different texts: the *Prabandha-chintâmaṇi* assigns to him 17 years 1 month 1 day, terminating in Śrâvana 878 V.S. (A.D. 822). The *Ratnamâlâ* carries it down to V.S. 897, and transfers the reigns of Ratnâditya and Vairisiṁha to a much later period. Yogarâja built a temple of Yogîśvarî at Aṇahilapura.

Merutuṅga ascribes to Ratnâditya a reign of 3 years 3 months and 4 days, ending in Kârtikâ 881 V.S. (A.D. 825); but from this date the *Prabandha-chintâmaṇi* passes over a period of fully 15½ years, where Arisiṁha and others place the reign of Vairisiṁha, with a duration of 11 or more years.

Kshemarâja, in some accounts said to have been a son of Yogarâja, then ascends the throne in Jyeshṭha 897 (A.D. 841) and rules till Bhâdrapada 922, which the *Prabandha-chintâmaṇi* misstates as 38 years 3 months 10 days, whilst it makes the next reign begin in 935 and, after 13 years, end in V.S. 938. There must be two errors of 10 years each here, compensating one another. If Kshemarâja's reign began in Jyeshṭha 897 and lasted 28 years 3 months 10 days it would end in Bhâdrapada 925 (A.D. 869).

Next follows his son Châmuṇḍa's reign of 13 years 4 mts. 16 days, which would thus end in Mâgha 938 (A.D. 881). Dr. Bühler considered this prince a transference back from the Solaṅki dynasty, and it is curious that the latter had a reign of very nearly the same length; but Châmuṇḍa has a place in both Arisiṁha's and Merutuṅga's lists of the Châvaḍâs.

Âkaḍadeva succeeds, in the *Prabandha-chintâmaṇi* list, apparently called Râhaḍa and Thâghaḍa by others. "He caused to be built in the city of Karkarâ the temple of Âkaḍeśvarî and Kaṇṭheśvarî." He reigned 26 yrs. 1 m. 20 days, that is, till Chaitra 19, V.S. 965, but the text says till Pausha 9, or nearly nine months longer, and making the reign last 26 yrs. 10 mts. 10 days.

The next is Bhûyagaḍadeva or Bhûbhaṭa, who built "the temple of Bhûyagaḍeśvara in Pattana and a rampart"; he reigned 27 yrs. 6 mts. 5 days, or till Âshâdha 993 (A.D. 936).[1] But in one place we read Âshadha 991, and this

[1] *Prabandha-chintâmaṇi*, trans. by C. H. Tawney, pp. 18-23; at p. 21 we find the date V.S. 991; and from p. 29 and 30, note it is to be inferred that Mûlarâja's reign of 55 years ended in 1052-53, and hence began V.S. 998 conf. Bühler, *Das Sukṛitasaṁkîrtana des Arisiṁha*, S. 8-10.

is the date usually given for the accession of Samantasiṁha, the last Châvaḍâ prince, who ruled till Saṁ. 998 (A.D. 941-42).

This differs from the chronology adopted by Forbes in his *Râs Mâlâ* from Kṛishṇabhaṭṭa's *Ratnamâlâ*, but it is quite as well supported; and the text of the *Ratnamâlâ* has not been critically edited. Better manuscripts may correct the details or even modify some of them, but the chroniclers must be our guides. These, however, seem to follow two different traditions:—the one—that which is outlined above with variations which seem due to manuscript errors; the other gives Yogarâja a reign of 32 to 35 years, succeeded immediately by his son Kshemarâja, and places Bhuyaḍa, Vairisiṁha or Vijayasiṁha, and Ratnâditya or Râvatasiṁha in succession to him. This makes up the seven kings of tradition, which number may have been based on seven generations during the 196 years of the dynasty; and such is possibly the origin of the second form of the list.[1]

We have, as yet, but few side lights or contemporary information to help us for the history of these two centuries of Châvaḍâ rule in north Gujarât. And we have to beware of confounding them with their perhaps more powerful neighbours the Châpas of Bhillamâla. We meet with the rule of Kanauj, too, in the time of Vanarâja, without any hint as to how they were related. Sulaimân, an Arab merchant from the Persian gulf, who had made several voyages to the west coasts of India and to China, wrote some account of what he had learnt in A.D. 851, which was at least partly incorporated, sixty years later, by Abu Zaidû-l-Ḥasan in his *Salsalat-al-Tewarikh* or "Catena of Events."[2] Now Sulaimân remarks[3] that "round the Balharâ are other princes with whom he is at war, but whom he greatly surpasses. Among these is the prince called the king of al-Jorz (Gurjara). This king has a numerous army and no other Indian prince has so fine cavalry. He has a dislike, however, to the Arabs. No Indian prince hates Islam more than he." And Abu Zaid speaks of Kanauj as belonging to the large empire of Jorz or Gurjara.[4] Mas'ûdi, who visited western India in A.D. 912-16 had met with Abu Zaid and derived from him part of the information,[4] which he incorporated in his "Prairies of Gold," and he also speaks of the frontiers of the Balharâ as exposed to the attacks of the king of Jorz (Gujarât). This king, he adds, was rich in cavalry, in camels, and had a numerous army with many elephants.[5] These notices cannot refer to the Gujarât of the Châvaḍâs, and hardly even to the princes of Bhilmâl; but they may easily apply to Kanauj, if that kingdom held Bhilmâl as a subordinate state. The Balharâ or Râshṭrakûṭa kings, holding Bharoch, would then be their rivals.

Valabha-râja[6] or Balharâ was the distinctive title of the Râshṭrakûṭa sovereigns, who, till the end of the Châvaḍâ dynasty, ruled from Bharoch over the south of Gujarât and up to the Mahî, if not to the Sâbhramatî river; and Idrisi, on the

---

1 Any attempt to arrange the chronology so arbitrarily as is proposed in the *Bombay Gazetteer* (vol. I, pt. i, pp. 151-55) is to be deprecated: it can only introduce more confusion. We must wait for some epigraph or other evidence turning up that may correct and adjust our information.

2 Reinaud, *Relation des Voyages, dans l'Inde et à la Chine*, tom. I, p. 26.

3 *Ib.* tom. I, p. 133, and tom II, p. 17; conf. Renaudot, *Ancient Accounts of India*, &c., p. 87*a*.

4 Reinaud, *ut sup.* tom. I, p. xvii f.

5 Barbier de Maynard et Pavet de Courteille, *Maçoudi*, tom. I, p. 383.

6 This in Prâkrit takes the form of Ballaharâya, which gives the Arabic form of Balharâ. Conf. *Ind. Ant.* vol. VI, p. 64, and see below, p. 34.

authority of Obud allah ibn Khordadbeh (circa 930 A.D.), as well as Mas'ûdî, states so much; but the latter distinguishes between his realm and that of Jozr.[1] We can only suppose that Idrisi was misled by the proximity of their possessions in Gujarât, and ascribed the Châvaḍâ kingdom to its more powerful neighbour.

About A.D. 757 the Râshṭrakûṭas dispossessed the western Chalukyas of their dominions in southern Gujarât. In 766 the Kaira or Khêḍa district and the country round Godrâ belonged to Śilâditya VII. of Valabhi.[2] About 784, or soon after, Govinda III. took Lâṭa from his relatives, who had ruled it for a short time, and placed it in charge of his brother Indrarâja. Two Râshṭrakûṭa grants show that, by 812, they had extended their territory at least to the Mahî, and in A.D. 835 Khêḍâ was a Râshṭrakûṭa town,[3] whilst in 910 the country round Kâpaḍwaṇaj was part of the dominions of Kṛishṇa II. But in 914 A.D. the country to the west of the Sâbhramatî was in the possession of a king Mahîpâla, who had a local representative, Dharaṇîvarâha of the Châpa family at Wadhwân.[4] Was this Mahîpâla the successor of Mahendrapâla of Kanauj and patron of Râjaśekhara, and was Dharaṇîvarâha one of the Châpas of Bhillamâla or an officer of the Châpotaka prince of Aṇahilawâḍa?

However this may be, the above details indicate pretty clearly that the Châvaḍâs held but a portion of Gujarât, and that possibly as feudatories of a greater power.

The Châvaḍâ dynasty came to an end in V.S. 998 (A.D. 941). The legends say that Râja, Bija, and Ḍaṇḍaka, sons of Muñjaladeva or Bhuvanâditya who was the fourth in descent from Bhûyagaḍa, king of Kalyâṇakaṭaka or Kanauj, came to Aṇahilapura on their way from Somanâtha, and, finding favour at the court, Râji married Lîlâdevî the king's sister.[5] She died in childbirth, but the child—named Mûlarâja—grew up at the court; and the last Châvaḍâ—Sâmantasiṁha—proving a weak, vacillating ruler, Mûlarâja raised a rebellion and killed him.[6] This is the substance of the story; the details may be set aside as bardic embellishments. If Sâmantasiṁha reigned only seven years, it must have been to the court of a predecessor that prince Râji came: as Merutuṅga states[7]—it may have been to that of Bhûyaḍa, who ruled for fully 27 years.[8] In a copper-plate grant by Mûlarâja, dated V.S. 1043 (A.D. 986–7), he claims to be—"the son of the Mahârâjâdhirâja Râji—who belongs to the Chaulakika family—who has conquered with his own arm the province watered by the Sarasvatî."[9] From this it would seem that Râji

---

[1] *Geog. d'Édrisi*, trad. Joubert, tome I, p. 172; *Maçoudi*, tr. par Barbier de Meynard et Pavet de Courteille, tome I, p. 382 f.; Reinaud, *Relation des Voyages, faits par les Arabes et les Persans dans l'Inde et à la Chine*, tome I, pp. 24 ff.

[2] Fleet, *Gupta Inscriptions*, p. 173; *Ind. Ant.* vol. VI, p. 16; *Bomb. Gaz.* vol. I, pt. ii, p. 383 f.

[3] *Ind. Ant.* vol. XII, p. 156; conf. vol. V, p. 145; *Epig. Ind.* vol. III, p. 53; *Ind. Ant.* vol. XIV, p. 196.

[4] *Epig. Indica*, vol. I, p. 52; *Ind. Ant.* vol. XII, p. 192; vol. XVIII, p. 90; Duff, *Chronology of India*, p. 84.

[5] Conf. Tod, *Travels in West. India*, p. 166; K. Forbes, *Râs Mâlâ*, vol. I, p. 49; Jarrett's *Âin-i-Akbari*, vol. II, p. 262.

[6] This story is supported by the copper-plate grant of Trilochanapâla Chaulukya, A.D. 1050. *Ind. Ant.* vol. XII, p. 198.

[7] *Prabandha-chintâmaṇi*, Tawney's tr., p. 22.

[8] Bühler's *Sukṛitasaṁkîrtana des Arisiṁha*, p. 9.

[9] *Ind. Ant.* vol. VI, pp. 191, 192; vol. XVIII, p. 186.

was a sovereign prince, but whether of Kanauj,[1] of Bhillamâla, or of some other district, may be uncertain; he had married a Châvaḍâ princess, and his son asserted successfully in arms his pretensions to Gujarât. Other two grants of his are dated in V. Saṁvat 1030 and 1051,[2] the latter making a grant of land in the vicinity of Sâchor in Marvâd, to a Brâhmaṇ, Srî Dirghâchârya who had emigrated from Kanyakubja.

Mûlarâja thus, at the age of twenty-one, became the founder of the Chaulukya or Solaṅkî dynasty. He appointed as his Purohita or family priest a member of the Gulecha family named Sola, belonging to the Vasishṭhagotra and of the Nâgara division of the Gujarât Brâhmaṇs, and whose descendants held the office under successive princes at least till the time of Vîradhavala (A.D. 1311), to whom Someśvara, the author of the *Kirtikaumudi*, was domestic priest. Sola is credited with performing the Vâjapeya sacrifice,[3] and attained great influence over the king.[4]

Mûlarâja was a Śaiva in religious profession, and brought colonies of Audichya Brâhmaṇs to Gujarât, settling them at Siṁhapura or Sihor in the east of Kâṭhiâwâḍ, at Stambhatîrtha or Khambay, and in various villages between the Baṇâs and Sâbhramatî rivers.[5] At Maṇḍalî or Mâṇḍal, to the north-west of Viramgâm he built a Śaiva temple called Mûliśvara or Mûlanâthadeva, with a monastery attached to it. To this he assigned the village of Kamboika, now Kamboî, to the north-west of Moḍherâ. At a later period he also began the great Rudraprâsâda or Rudramahâlaya "the palace of Rudra" at Siddhapura, to be noticed below.

He soon set about extending his kingdom by annexing Kâṭhiâwâḍ and Kachh, but his dominions were invaded by Bârava—variously described as the general of the ruler of Lâṭadeśa, that is, of Tailapadeva the western Chalukya prince who had recently defeated the Râshṭrakûṭa ruler Kakkala[6] and held Lâṭa. This invasion Mûlarâja seems to have successfully repelled, as well as another about the same time (A.D. 974) by Vigraharâja the Sapâdalaksha king of Eastern Râjputâna.[7] His invasion of Soraṭh was directed against the chief of Vâmanasthalî, now Vanthalî, and probably took place about A.D. 952. In this expedition he was successful, taking the chief himself prisoner, and, it is said, killing his ally Lâkhâ Phulâni of Kachh in battle. Other legends place the death of Lâkhâ on a different occasion; he had harboured Râkhaich, a younger relative of Mûlarâja, as a rival for the throne of Aṇahilapura, and had been long at strife with Mûlarâja, who at length besieged him in Kapilakoṭi, and finally slew him.

At Pattana Mûlarâja built a *vasahikâ* or temple and monastery, called after himself, and the temples of Muñjâladevasvâmin and the Tripurushaprâsâda.[8] Towards the end of his long reign of fifty-five years he is said to have devoted himself to

[1] It has been suggested (*Bomb. Gaz.* vol. I, pt. i, p. 156 n.) that the Kanyakubja to which Mûlarâja's ancestors belonged might be Karṇakubja, which occurs in the *Girnâr Mâhâtmya* as a name of Junâgaḍh. *Arch. Sur. W. Ind.* vol. II, p. 156. There is no ground for such a conjecture.

[2] A.D. 973-74 and 994-95. *Vienna Oriental Journal*, vol. V, p. 300.

[3] *Sac. Bks. of East*, vol. XLI, pp. xi, xxiii f., 1-41.

[4] Bhandarkar, *Rep. on the Search for Sanskrit MSS.*, 1883-84, p. 20.

[5] Forbes, *Râs Mâlâ*, vol. I, p. 64 f.

[6] *Ind. Ant.* vol. XII, p. 199.

[7] Conf. *Epig. Ind.* vol. II, p. 118; *Vienna Or. Jour.* vol. VII, p. 191; *Ind. Ant.* vol. VI, p. 184.

[8] *Prabandha-chintâmaṇi*, pp. 23–29.

asceticism, or at least to religious performances, devolving his royal duties on his son Châmuṇḍa. He died in V.S. 1052.

Of Châmuṇḍa we are told that he caused to be built at the capital the temple of the god Chandanâtha and of the god Châchineśvara, and that he ruled 13 years 1 month and 24 days, dying on the 5th Âśvina sudi V.S. 1065 (A.D. 1009). He had three sons—Vallabha, Durlabha and Nâga, of whom the first succeeded him, but after a reign of six months, while engaged in the siege of Dhârâ in Mâlava, he died of small-pox.

His brother Durlabha succeeded A.D. 1010, and built, for the welfare of the soul of his brother, the temple of Madanaśaṅkara. He also built a palace and excavated a lake called Durlabhasarovara. After a reign of twelve years, he placed on the throne the son of his brother Nâgarâja, called Bhîma,[1] and set out on pilgrimage to Banâras, V.S. 1077. But in passing through Mâlava, he is said to have been deprived of his umbrella and other insignia of royalty by king Muñja, and obliged to continue his journey in the dress of a pilgrim. The same story is told of Châmuṇḍa; but as Muñja or Vâkpati II probably died before Mûlarâja, if the story have any basis, the Mâlava sovereign must have been either Sindhurâja or more probably Bhoja. After this, Merutuṅga says, there was rooted enmity between the kings of Gujarât and Mâlava.

Bhîmarâja ascended the throne in A.D. 1022 (V.S. 1078) and ruled for forty-two years. Early in his reign Maḥmûd of Ghazni made his tenth raid into India, directed against the great Śaiva shrine of Somanâth, or Prabhâsa Pattana. The Muhammadan writers differ as to the date of this invasion; Ibn Asîr, whose account is the earliest, gives A.H. 414, but others give 416, or October 1025 as the date of starting, and January 1026 as that of the sack of Somanâth. On his way south, Bhîmadeva, being unprepared to resist so powerful an enemy, hastily retreated for safety and to prepare himself for attack, to a fort called Kandahat or Kandaba, which may be almost certainly identified with Kanṭhâ or Kanṭhkôt in Kachh. Maḥmûd pressed on, sacking the towns and temples on the way, eager to reach the shrine whose wealth he had learnt was almost fabulous and the booty in which would enrich his fanatic army. Ibn Asîr tells that whenever there was an eclipse the Hindus flocked to the temple at Somanâth to the number of a hundred thousand. Everything most precious was brought here; its attendants received the most valuable presents, and the shrine was endowed with more than ten thousand villages. In the temple were amassed jewels of the most exquisite quality and incalculable value. Between the Ganges and Somanâth is a distance of 200 parasangs, but water was daily brought from it with which the idol was washed.[2] A thousand Brâhmaṇs attended daily to perform the worship, and to introduce visitors. Three hundred persons were employed in shaving the heads and beards of the pilgrims. Three hundred and fifty sang and danced at the gate of the temple. Every one

---

[1] *Prabandha-chint.* p. 29; the writer in the *Bombay Gazetteer*, vol. I, pt. i, p. 163, has either misunderstood the chronicler or had a different text. See *Navasâhasâṅkacharita*, by Bühler and Zachariae, p. 47; conf. *Ind. Ant.* vol. IV, p. 114.

[2] At the great temples in Southern India this practice still continues.

of these received a settled daily allowance.[1] Maḥmûd, on reaching the place, immediately assaulted and took the town and temple, slaying and massacring more than fifty thousand Hindûs. "The worth of what was found in the temple of jewels, gold and silver exceeded two millions of dînârs,[2] all of which was taken."

Maḥmûd, hearing that Bhîma had taken refuge in the fort of Kandahat—or Kaṇṭhkoṭ in Kachh—marched thither, taking advantage of the ebb of the tide to cross the Rann, and drove the enemy out; or probably the Hindûs escaped before he reached them. He then returned by Mansura in Sindh and Bhâtiâ to Ghazni, which he reached 2nd April 1026.[3]

No sooner had the enemy left Gujarât than Bhîmadeva returned to his capital and began to retrieve the injuries that had been inflicted. He is said to have made war on Sindh and to have formed a treaty with Karṇadeva the king of Chedi (A.D. 1042 seqq.), and was at war with Bhoja of Dhârâ.

In his reign Vimala Śâ was his *dandapati* or governor at Âbu, which had previously belonged to the Parmâra chiefs of Chandrâvatî. Whilst in this position Vimala Śâ erected one of the superb marble temples at Devalwâḍâ, on mount Âbû, which he dedicated to Ṛishabhanâtha the first Tîrthakara. He also erected splendid temples at Kumbhâriyâ on the Ârâsur hill, near to the celebrated Brahmanical shrine of Ambâ Bhavânî.

Udayamatî the consort of Bhîma is said to have constructed the Râṇî's Wâv or step-well at Aṇahilawâḍa; and Bhîma built the temples of Tripurushaprâsâda, of Bhîmeśvaradeva, and of the goddess Bhîruânî.

Karṇadeva succeeded his father Bhîma in A.D. 1063–64, and had the *biruda* or alias of Trailokyamalla. According to the *Dvyâśrayakosha* of Hemachandra, he married Mayaṇalladevî daughter of Jayakeśin of Chandrapura,[4]—probably the Kadamba king of Goa who was reigning in A.D. 1052. His was on the whole a peaceful reign, his chief conquest being that of Âśâ a Bhilla chief at Âśâpalli, now Âshâval, close to Aḥmadâbâd. He built there temples to Kocharaba, on the west of the Sâbhramatî, and to Jayantîdevî. He also founded a new capital called Karṇâvatî possibly at Aḥmadâbâd. In Pattana he built the temple of Karṇameru; but his greatest work was the Karṇasâgara lake, which he formed on the Rupên river near the town of Modherâ. It survived for centuries as a great irrigation lake; but in 1814, after a very heavy fall of rain, the river broke through the great dam and reduced the extensive "ten mile tank" to a waste.

On Karṇa's demise in 1093–94, he was succeeded by his son Siddharâja Jayasiṁha then a minor, the government being carried on by Mayaṇalladevî with the assistance of the ministers Udayana—a Śrîmâli Vâṇiyâ, Sântû and Muñjâla. Udayana had built a temple at Karṇâvatî called Udayavasahi containing

[1] Ibn Asîr says the temple was built on fifty-six pillars of teak wood covered with lead. The idol rose five cubits above the basement, and was sunk two cubits into it. It had no appearance of having been sculptured. Maḥmûd burnt part of it, and part he carried away to Ghaznî, where he made it a step at the entrance of the Jâmi' Masjid. Elliot, *History of India*, vol. II, p. 471.

[2] If the dînâr be taken at 64·8 grains, this would be about 270,000 ounces troy of gold, or fully £1,050,000 of our present money.

[3] Elliot, *Hist. Ind.* vol. II, p. 249.

[4] *Prabandha-chint.* p. 79; *Ind Ant.* vol. IV, p. 233.

images of the seventy-two Jaina Tîrthakaras of the past, present and future ages. Sântû was also a Jaina and founded a temple at Pattana; and another minister is said to have built a Jaina temple, called Mahârâjabhuvana, at Siddhapur, whilst the king was restoring the Rudramahâlaya or temple of Rudramahâkâla there.

Early in his reign Siddharâja, at his mother's request, remitted the duties on Śaiva pilgrims to Somanâth, which were levied at Bâhulod, now Bhâlod, on the Narmadâ, and he proceeded with her to the shrine at Prabhâs Pattana. While then absent from his capital, it is said, Yaśovarman of Mâlava began to overrun Gujarât. But as Yaśovarman did not come to the throne till A.D. 1133, it is more probable that it was his father, Naravarman of Dhârâ (A.D. 1104–1133). The Paramâra invader was bought off by Sântû, but a long war with Mâlava ensued in which Siddharâja was ultimately victorious. He also made war on Khaṅgar the son of Navaghana III, the Chuḍâsamâ prince of Girnâr, and after a severe struggle subdued the country.[1]

During his absence in Mâlava the great Sahasraliṅga tank at Aṇhilapattana was finished, and after his return he completed, or perhaps rebuilt on a much enlarged scale, the temple of Rudra at Siddhapur, which had been founded by Mûlarâja about a hundred and seventy years before. The *Prabandha-chintâmaṇi* says:—"Then, in course of time, the temple, twenty-three cubits in height, was completed, and the king caused to be made figures of distinguished kings, lords of horses, lords of elephants, and lords of men,[2] and so on, and caused to be placed in front of them his own statue, with his hands joined in an attitude of supplication, and so entreated that, even if the country were laid waste, this temple might not be destroyed. On the occasion of setting up the flag on that temple, he had the flags of all the Jaina temples lowered, as in the country of Mâlava,—when the banner of Mahâkâla is displayed, no flag is hoisted on any Jaina temple."[3]

The Jains, however, were protected and even favoured—especially by the ministers: a temple was erected to Neminâtha at Ujjayanta or Girnâr and endowments made to the Śatruñjaya shrines. In A.D. 1124 a famous Digambara disputant from Karṇâṭa, named Kumudachandrâchârya, the religious adviser of Mayaṇalladevi's father, arrived at Karṇâvatî and sought to draw Śrîdevasûri (A.D. 1087–1170), the famous Śvetâmbara logician and pupil of Munichandra, into a public discussion as to the merits of their respective sects. Śrîdevasûri accordingly offered to meet him at Pattana; and Siddharâja, having consulted with Hemachandra, the great Jaina scholar (A.D. 1089–1163), summoned a *râjasabhâ*, or disputation before his court. The Śvetâmbara, if worsted, was to adopt the Digambara doctrines; the Digambaras if defeated were to leave Gujarât. Śrîdeva proved the victor and was rewarded by a land-grant of villages, a shawl and other presents.[4]

Jayasiṁha Siddharâja, the hero-king of Gujarât, reigned forty-nine years and died A.D. 1142–43, leaving no son to succeed him. Śrîpâla, author of the *Vairochanaparâjaya*, was poet-laureate to him and his successor.

---

[1] *Târikh-i Sorath*, Eng. vers. pp. 103 f.; *Râs Mâlâ*, vol. I, pp. 154 ff.

[2] Aśvapati, Gajapati, and Narapati, see below, p. 62.

[3] *Prabandha-chintâmaṇi*, p. 90.

[4] *Ib.* pp. 97–104; *Ind. Ant.* vol. XI, p. 254.

Merutuṅga relates that Bhîmadeva had taken into his harem a *hetaera* named Chaulâdevî or Chakulâdevî, by whom he had a son Haripâla; Tribhuvanapâla was Haripâla's son and the father of Kumârapâla.[1] Jayasiṁha, jealous of Kumârapâla, sought to compass his death; but being protected and concealed, chiefly by the Jainas, he escaped to Khambay, where he met with the minister Udayana and the Jaina teacher Hemâchârya, to whom he promised—if he should attain rule—that he would be devoted to the law of Jina. Kumârapâla had two brothers—Mahipâla and Kîrttipâla, and two sisters of whom Premal was married to Kâṇhaḍadeva a general of Siddharâja. On the death of the king this officer brought the three princes in succession before the people to choose their sovereign, and Kumârapâla, then fifty years of age, manifesting his martial spirit, was at once selected.

At first he had some trouble with the courtiers who had served Jayasiṁha Siddharâja, and his firmness in dealing with them perhaps led to the revolt of Bâhaḍa, one of the sons of the minister Udayana, who had been a special favourite with Siddharâja. Corrupting the officers of Kumârapâla, this Bâhaḍa or Wâhaḍa incited the Sapâdalaksha or Śâkambharî râja Âna or Ânâka to invade Gujarât. When the armies joined battle, Kumârapâla saw his captains were deserting him, but driving his elephant into the lines, he encountered and captured Bâhaḍa, killed Ânâka with an arrow, and thus turned the fight into a victory.

Hemachandra the Jaina gained great influence over Kumârapâla, but used it adroitly. At the request of Bhâva Bṛihaspati, the *gaṇḍa* or temple priest of Somanâtha, Kumârapâla had undertaken the restoration of the famous temple at Prabhâsa-pattana or Devapattana, built by Bhîmadeva I, fully a century before, and which was in a state of decay.[2] Hemachandra affected to approve of the work but suggested that the king's merit would be thereby still further increased by his abstaining during the restoration from eating flesh and drinking liquor. Then, at the dedication of the temple, he got him to take the vow of abstinence for the rest of his life.

After this Vâghbhaṭa, the son of Udayana, founded the town of Vâghbhaṭapura, near the Śatruñjaya mountain, and erected a Jaina temple on the sacred hill, A.D. 1164–65, whilst his brother, Âmrabhaṭa, built another at Bharoch. The king also built a Jaina temple called the Kumâravihâra, at Somanâthapattana, and others at Girnâr, Śatruñjaya, Khambâyat or Stambhatîrtha, Aṇahilavâḍa, and Dhandukka. With the exception of the repulse of the Sapâdalaksha or Śâkambharî prince at the beginning of his reign, the defeat of Ballâla of Dhârâ, and an invasion of the Koṅkaṇa, it was a period of general peace and prosperity, and the wealthy Jainas built temples in all the principal towns as well as at their tîrthas. Kumârapâla's reign lasted thirty-one years till V.S. 1230 (A.D. 1173–74),

---

[1] Forbes says Kshemarâja was Bhîmadeva's son by Bâkuladevî; Devaprasâd was the son of Kshemarâja and father of Tribhuvanapâla. *Râs Mâlâ*, vol. I, p. 180.

[2] For the Somanâthapattan *praśasti* of Bhâva Bṛihaspati of A.D. 1169, see *Vienna Orient. Jour.* vol. III, pp. 1–19; *Jour. Bom. B. R. As. Soc.* vol. VIII, pp. 59 f.; and Tod, *Trav. West. Ind.* p. 504; conf. *Ind. Ant.* vol. IV, p. 268 f.; vol. XI, p. 241 f.; and vol. XVI, pp. 147 ff.

the great Jaina scholar and courtier, Hemachandra, having died a few months before the king.

On Kumârapâla's demise without male issue, his nephew, Ajayadeva or Ajayapâla, the son of Mahîpâla, came to the throne. The Śankarâchârya, the Śaiva pontiff, had come to Gujarât before Kumârapâla's death, and had doubtless stirred up the zeal of his sect against the Jainas. Ajayadeva may have been influenced by this movement, but whether or not, he began his reign by a merciless persecution of some of the prominent Śrâvaks. Their leader, Râmachandra, was tortured to death, Âmrabhaṭa and Kapardin, favourite nobles of his uncle, were destroyed by the king. But his career was a short one; he was stabbed by a doorkeeper named Vayajaladeva, after a reign of three years, in A.D. 1176.[1]

Ajayadeva was succeeded by his young son Bâla Mûladeva,[2] under the regency of his mother, Nâyikîdevî, who resisted an invasion by Muḥammad Shahâb-al-dîn Ghorî; but his rule lasted only some two years.

In A.D. 1178, his brother, Bhîmadeva II, succeeded to the throne and ruled for the long period of sixty-three years. At the commencement of his reign Aṇahilawâḍa was invaded by Mu'izz-al-dîn of Ghazni, who was repelled. In 1197 Quṭb-al-dîn Î-bak advanced against the Mers, who were combined with Gujarât, and they forced him back on Ajmir and shut him up there till relieved by Mu'izz-al-dîn; but early next year Quṭb-al-dîn defeated Bhîmadeva and got temporary possession of Aṇahilawâḍa.[3] But about 1222 his ministers Lavaṇaprasâda and his son Vîradhavala, of the Vâghelâ or Vyâghrapallîya family, usurped the rights of their sovereign and set up as independent princes at Ḍholkâ, appointing as their ministers the wealthy Jaina brothers Vastupâla and Tejaḥpâla.[4] These constructed many temples at the principal Jaina tîrthas.

In the *Prabandhas* and in the inscriptions in the large temple at Girnâr known as Vastupâla-Tejaḥpâla's, most extravagant statements are given of the numbers of temples (*kîrtanâni*) built or restored by these brothers[5]; still the instances specified at different places are somewhat numerous, and Arisiṁha, a contemporary, ascribes forty-three such benefactions to Vastupâla.[6] Thus:—(1) In Aṇahillapurî he restored the temple of Pañchâsara-Pârśvanâtha which had been built by Vanarâja. This he is said to have done after a victory which he obtained, with the help of Dhârâvarsha of Chandrâvatî, over the Muhammadans at Âbû about 1226 A.D. (2) At Stambatîrtha or Khambay he placed a gilded flagstaff (*dhvajadaṇḍa*) on the Hindu temple of Bhîmeśa; set up an *uttânapaṭṭa* at the temple of Bhaṭṭâditya; excavated a well in the temple grounds (*pûjanavana*) of Bhaṭṭâraka; constructed a *raṅgamaṇḍapa* or hall before the temple of the sun-god Bakulasvâmi; restored the temple and maṇḍapa of Śiva-Vaidyanâtha; built a walled enclosure for the sale of sour milk (*takra*); erected two Upâśrayas or

[1] See *Ind. Ant.* vol. XVIII, pp. 80 ff. and 344 ff.

[2] *Asiat. Res.* vol. XVI, p. 288; *Ind. Ant.* vol. VI, pp. 186, 213.

[3] Elliot, *Hist. Ind.* vol. II, p. 229.

[4] *Ind. Ant.* vol. VI, pp. 190, 198, 213; vol. XI, p. 220.

[5] *Arch. Sur. Westn. India*, vol. II, pp. 169 f.

[6] *Sukṛitasaṁkîrtana*, Sarga XI, S. 2–34, in Bühler's Abh. S. 29–35.

Paushadhaśâlâs for Jaina monks; and a drinking-hall with round windows (or balconies—*gavâksha*) on two sides.

(3) At Ḍholkâ or Dhavalakkaka he built a temple of Âdinâtha called Śatruñjayâvatara; two Upâśrayas or monasteries; restored the Râṇaka temple called Bhaṭṭâraka's (Śiva's); and constructed a square covered reservoir or *Vâpi*, and a pump-room (*prapâ*).

(4) At Śatruñjaya he erected the Indramaṇḍapa before the temple of Âdinâtha; built a temple of the Jina Neminâtha of Ujjayanta and another of Pârśvanâtha; set up a statue of Sarasvatî; statues of his ancestors; and of himself, of Tejaḥpâla, and of Vîradhavala, mounted on elephants; made small temples on the four mountain summits consecrated to Avalokanâ, Ambâ, Sâmba, and Pradyumna[1]; placed a Toraṇa over the door of the temple of Jinapati (Âdinâtha); built small temples of Suvrata of Bhṛigupura and of Vîra of Satyapura to the right and left of the temple of Âdinâtha; placed a *pṛishṭhapaṭṭa* or tablet behind the image of the Jina, inlaid with gold and gems, which seemed to give the figure a halo (*bhâmaṇḍala*); and set up a golden Toraṇa.

(5) In the neighbourhood of Pâlitâṇâ (Pâdaliptapura) he excavated a large tank—the Lalitâsaras near Vâghbaṭapura; built an Upâśraya; and a pump-room (*prapâ*). (6) In the village of Arkapâlita or Aṅkavâliya,[2] he excavated a tank (*taḍâga*); built an almshouse (*sattra*), a temple of Śiva (*purabhido devasya*) and a rest-house for travellers.

(7) At Ujjayanta or Girnâr, he built two temples—of Pârśvanâtha of Stambhana and of Âdinâtha of Śatruñjaya (A.D. 1232).[3] (8) At Stambhana[4] he restored or contributed for the restoration of the temple of Pârśvanâtha, with images of Âdinâtha and Neminâtha; and established two pump-rooms (*prapâ*), near the temple.

(9) At Darbhâvatî or Dabhoi, he restored the gold capitals on the temple of Vaidyanâtha, which had been carried off by the king of Mâlava; and made a stone image of the sun-god. And, (10) at Âbû or Arbuda, he is said to have built a temple of Malladeva,—but this was perhaps at Śatruñjaya; Tejaḥpâla erected a temple of Neminâtha at Âbû.

From these pious deeds (*sukṛitas*) it would appear that Vastupâla was no very strict Śrâvaka, but ready to honour the gods of his sovereign, Vîradhavala, and to build or restore Brâhmaṇ shrines when it was to be to his credit or advantage.

In A.D. 1241-2, Tribhuvanapâla succeeded for a short time, but in 1243-4, Vîsaladeva the Vâghelâ ascended the throne,[5] and ruled for twenty years. He had wars with Mâlava, Mewâḍ, and Devagiri, and fortified Vîsalanagara in the north, and Dâbhoi or Darbhavatî in the south-east of Gujarât.

---

[1] Conf. Girnâr inscrip. *Arch. Sur. Wn. India*, vol. II, p. 172.

[2] Probably, as Dr. Bühler conjectured, Ankavâliya, on the river Lîlkâ, south-east from Bhîmnâth in 22° 14′ N. lat., 71° 59′ E. long.

[3] *Ind. Ant.* vol. XVII, p. 151 f.; *Arch. Sur. Wn. India*, vol. II, p. 170.

[4] Dr. Bühler thought this might perhaps be an old name of Ṭhâsrâ; but it was, almost certainly, the modern Thâmna, on the Śeḍhî river, in Ânand tâluka of the Khêḍâ district, lat 22° 43′ N., long. 73° 9′ E. Bühler, *Sukṛitasaṁkîrtana*, S. 34; Tawney's *Prabandha-chintâmaṇi*, p. 172.

[5] *Ind. Ant.* vol. VI, pp. 190 f., 210 ff.; vol. XVIII, p. 185; vol. XXI, p. 276; *Epig. Ind.* vol. I, p. 20.

Visaladeva dying in 1261, was succeeded by his nephew Arjunadeva, the son of Pratâpamalla, the younger brother of Visala, who reigned for thirteen years—till A.D. 1274.[1] He, in turn, was succeeded by his son Sârangadeva, who ruled for twenty-two years, and from his inscriptions it appears that the Gujarât kingdom still included Soraṭha or Kâṭhiâwâḍ, Chandrâvati and Mount Âbû.[2]

In A.D. 1296, Karṇadeva II ascended the throne of his father and ruled for eight years. He was a weak prince, known as Ghela, or "the insane." In 1298 Ulugh Khân, the brother of the Dehli emperor 'Alâ-ul Dîn Khiljî and Naṣrat Khân Jalesarî invaded Gujarât, occupied Aṇahilawâḍa, and Kambhâyat, sacked the temple of Somanâth and laid waste the country.[3] Karṇadeva fled to Râmadeva the chief of Devagiri, whilst all his wealth fell into the invader's hands. For some time afterwards the king led a fugitive life in the wilds of Bâglâna, where he probably died.

The imperial governor appointed by the Dehli emperor to administer the affairs of Gujarât, seizing as public property the Hindû and Jaina temples, destroyed them, as idol shrines, and with the materials constructed mosques in all the principal towns. Then was the great Śaiva fane at Siddhapur—the Rudramahâlaya, the largest and probably the most splendid temple in western India—wrecked and demolished.

The Mughal governors of Gujarât under the Dehli emperors were frequently changed and none of them seem to have had the interests of the country and its people in their minds: they were there to enrich their sovereigns at Dehli, and to mend their own fortunes.

Ulugh Khân alias Alp Khân held the government as *Nâzim* for about two years, and was succeeded by Alp Khân Malik Sanjar, who held the post for eighteen years. But after this there were six successive *Nâzims* in little more than three years—the sixth being Malik Khusrû Khân, a Hindu lad, who had gained the favour of the Sultân, then killed his patron and usurped the throne in 1320 as Nâsir-*al*-dîn Khusrû.

In 1321, Malik Wajîh-*al*-dîn Kuraishî, who had previously held the post, returned to Gujarât as governor, but was afterwards made imperial Wazîr with the title of Tâju-l-Mulk. He was followed in 1325 by Aḥmad Ayâz. About 1338, Muḥammad II ibn Tughlaq appointed Malik Maqbil, son of a musician, to be governor with the title of Khân Jahân Nâîb Bakhtaiâr: previously he had been the deputy of Aḥmad Ayâz, who afterwards received the title of Khwâjah Jahân. But insurrection having broken out in 1346, the emperor advanced in person into Gujarât, and in 1347 sacked Khambay and Surat, drove the Gohil chief Mokharâji out of Peram and captured Goghâ. A second revolt occurring soon after, Muḥammad Tughlaq returned to the relief of Bharoch, but his general Malik Yûsuf Baghra was defeated near Khambay and the governor Mu'izz-*al*-dîn was captured and put

---

[1] *Ind. Ant.* vol. VI, p. 191; vol. XI. pp. 241 ff.; vol. XVI, pp. 147 f.; vol. XXI, p. 276 f.; Bhandarkar's *Report*, 1883–84, p. 12; Tod's *West. India*, p. 506.

[2] *Ind. Ant.* vol. XVIII, p. 185; *Epig. Indica*, vol. I, p. 271; *As. Res.* vol. XVI, p. 311.

[3] Elliot, *Hist. Ind.* vol. III, pp. 43, 74, 163; *Ferishtah* (Briggs's transl.), vol. I, p. 327.

to death. Eventually, in a battle near Kaḍi, the imperial forces totally defeated the rebels. The emperor then marched on Junâgaḍh or Girnâr and spent two seasons in besieging the chief; at length he took the fort—probably the Uparkoṭ—the râja, Khaṅgâr, according to the *Mirât-i Ahmadi*, offering his submission; but it is more probable that Mokalasiṁha or Mugatsiṁha was at that time the chief of Soraṭh, and little except plunder was secured: he local chiefs continued to rule.[1]

Muḥammad Tughlaq appointed Nizâm-ul Mulk viceroy in 1350, and in 1361 Firuz Shâh III raised Ẕafar Khân to the government in his place. He died in 1371, according to the *Mirât-i-Ahmadi*, and was succeeded by his son Daryâ Khân, who had Shams-al-dîn Anwar Khân as his deputy.

Shams-al-dîn Dâmghânî now offered to the Sultân an advance of forty lâkhs of Tankahs on the revenues of Gujarât, a hundred elephants, forty Arab horses and four hundred slaves a year, if the province were handed over to him.[2] The Sulṭân proposed to leave Shams-al-dîn Anwar Khân in possession of the province on these terms, but as he declined, Dâmghânî was appointed in 1376. Soon finding himself unable to meet the stipulated amount, he turned rebel, and Sultân Fîrûz Tughlaq sent an army against him and was readily assisted by the chiefs and people whom Dâmghânî had oppressed. He was killed and Gujarât was then placed under Malik Mufarrah Sulṭânî afterwards known as Farhatu-l Mulk Râstî Khân, an oppressive governor who ignored the Dehli authority, and about 1388, when Sikandar Khân was sent to supercede him, he rebelled and defeated and slew him. During the troubles that followed the death of Sultân Fîrûz Shâh in 1388, Farhat-ul Mulk was undisturbed; but on the accession of Muḥammad Shâh III, the inhabitants of Khambâyat complained of the governor's tyranny and the Sulṭân appointed Muḥammad Ẕafar Khân son of Wajîhu-l Mulk to succeed him, 21st Feb. 1391. He met the forces of Farhatu-l Mulk at Jitpur, not far from Siddhapur, and defeated and slew him.

In 1407 Ẕafar Khân assumed independence as Muẕaffar Shâh, and founded the Aḥmad-Shâhi dynasty of the Gujarât Muhammadan kings, which held sway for a hundred and sixty-five years, till overthrown by Akbar in 1573, when the province was again annexed to the Dehli empire.

These Muhammadan Nâzims or governors, who ruled Gujarât throughout the fourteenth century, had their head-quarters at Aṇahilawâḍa, the old capital of the native sovereigns; and this was not changed till about 1411, when Aḥmad Shâh, who succeeded his grandfather, Muẕaffar Shâh, founded the new capital of his kingdom at Aḥmadâbâd. During that fourteenth century, the Hindûs whether Brahmanical or Jaina found little mercy at the hands of their conquerors, and their rich shrines were desecrated, plundered and demolished at the will or caprice of their masters. None of their great works were spared; and all we have left from which to judge of their style or magnificence are only a few ruined shrines and pitiful fragments, though some of these are still of great interest. Nor under such conditions

---

[1] *Târikh i-Sorath*, p. 130; Bayley, *Gujarât*, pp. 42, 54 f.

[2] Briggs's *Ferishtah*, vol. I, p. 456.

could new works of importance be attempted within the rule of the Muslim; and consequently from the end of the thirteenth till the close of the sixteenth century under the rule of the liberal Akbar, no Hindû or Jaina temple of any pretensions was raised in Gujarât.

For the later history of Gujarât, under the Aḥmad Shâhi dynasty and afterwards, the reader may be referred to the brief sketch prefixed to the *Architecture of Aḥmadâbâd*, or to the more general histories of the province.[1]

---

[1] *Arch. Sur. Westn. India*, vol. VII, pp. 1–10; and vol. VI, pp. 1–19; or Watson's *History of Gujarât*, pp. 31 ff.; Bayley's *Gujarât*; Briggs's *Ferishtah*, vol. IV, pp. 1–166; Grant Duff's *History of the Mahrattas*; and *Bombay Gazetteer*, vol. I, pt. 1, pp. 207–432; &c.

CHAPTER II.

ARCHITECTURE.

THE style of architecture that prevailed generally in Gujarât, in early times, and more especially in northern Gujarât and Râjputâna was that familiarised to Europeans by the name of the Jaina style, since it has been so largely used by the Jaina sect in both provinces. But, as has been said elsewhere,[1] the Jaina architecture, always singularly chaste and elegant, was essentially Hindû; it was that, probably, of the Brâhmaṇs first, or rather of the native race and age, but, in its evolution, it was bound to be modified in details by Jaina tastes and requirements. And the Hindûs, in turn, naturally accepted and copied the stylistic advances of their dissenting countrymen. Hence we might, with almost equal accuracy, designate it either as the Jaina or North-Western Hindû style of architecture. And of the old temples that have come down to us in Gujarât in even ruinous fragments, a large proportion are Brâhmanic,—such, for example, as the remains of the Rudra-Mahâlaya at Siddhapur, the large temple at Moḍherâ, and others at Kasarâ, Sûṇak, &c. to be described further on.

The *Salâṭs* or builders appear to have wrought always, as they still do, equally for all sects of Hindûs; but the Jainas, by their habits and occupations must, at all times, have held much of the wealth of the country in their hands; and from the special merit they believe to be connected with the building of a temple and the dedication of images of their Jinas, Tîrthakaras or Tîrthaṅkaras, they were much more given to temple-building than the Hindûs. With the Śaiva or Vaishṇava Hindû, one great shrine with its accessories for the *dii minores* of the sect was generally sufficient at one place, and the devout gratified their aspirations by gifts and legacies for its upkeep and that of its ritual. With the Jaina, the aim is to found a temple, large or small, at one or other of the great Tîrthas or holy places; or, if unable to do this, to dedicate an image or repair a shrine. Besides the Tîrthas at Śatruñjaya and Girnâr in Kâṭhiâwâḍ, at Pârśvanâtha or Sameta Sikhara in Bengal, at Sonâgarh or Sonâgir near Datiâ in Central India, at Mukhtagiri in the Betul district of the Central Provinces, Śrâvaṇa Belgola in Maisur, Âbû and Sâchor in Rajputâna,[2] &c., they have temples for worship in most of the towns where there are any considerable numbers of their sect.

Becoming the greatest temple builders in Western India, they had also, in their keeping at least, the old works on civil and religious architecture, such as the *Prâsâda-maṇḍala*, *Râja-vallabha*, &c., which they have preserved in their temple libraries, where they are jealously locked up in huge chests. The modern Salâṭs owe their knowledge indirectly to these, of which they possess rough Gujarâti

---

[1] *Arch. Sur. W. India*, vol. VII, p. 11; conf. Fergusson, *Hist. Ind. and Eastn. Archit.* p. 226.

[2] Mrs. Graham, *Journal*, p. 67, mentions also Kollâpur in Amarâvati district of Berâr; Dehli; Pennakonda (lat. 14° 5′ N., long. 77° 38′ N.) in Anantapur district, Madras; and Kânchipuram. Sirpur in Basim district of Berar is also a noted place of pilgrimage for Digambara Jainas.

abstracts, for their guidance; but they have also the teaching of certain Jaina professors and the traditions handed down from father to son. They are said to be, as a rule, however, somewhat jealous of the secrets of their guild.[1]

The architectural style of Gujarât is largely identical with that of the Hemâḍpanti temples of the Dekhan, and, as indicated long ago by Mr. Fergusson, has a close connection with that of the shrines erected by the Chalukyan kings in the Kanarese districts.[2] Gujarât is now the only district in Western India where the architecture of the past is still, to some extent, a living art, and where the early traditions of the craft have been handed down to the present day. In the Dekhan and Kanarese districts this is not so; there the art has died entirely out, and in its place has been substituted a style of work in brick and plaster—a mixture chiefly of Muhammadan and Hindû elements—perhaps not altogether wanting in the picturesque, but wholly deficient in that decision and refinement of design that characterises the older work.

But even in Gujarât, where the men have the *Silpa Śâstra* treatises, the style has become debased and compares unfavourably with the purer style of earlier and better days. How far this may be due to the fact that the Salâṭs are ignorant of Sanskrit, and possess only rough and untrustworthy abstracts or versions of the original works, would be difficult to estimate. Some of the Yati professors of the art may read and understand the original works, but they content themselves with instructing a few pupils in the technicalities and canons of the science; and, not being builders themselves, they take no more concern in the matter, whilst in practice their rules are apathetically set aside. A further cause for this is the loss of interest in the old mechanical and artificial rules, which are really at variance with the progress of a living and growing art. Like the analogous rules of the mediæval architects of Europe, they had their use in preventing ignorant builders from violating all ideals of proportion, whether in plan or profile, but the man of genius and taste did not trammel himself much with their conventional details.

In modern India, however, the old rules have not led up to development in art. Muslim oppression suppressed the building of fine temples among Hindûs, and induced a loss of architectural taste and a consequent degradation of the art, which now concerns itself little, if at all, with canons of relative proportions. The most paltry structures decked out with paint and tinsel satisfy the tastes of the people. Some recent structures are, however, to be met with, on which great labour and expense have been lavished, which, but for some glaring inconsistency or bad taste displayed somewhere, might bear comparison with the structures of early times.

Some may think that a return to the old lines might still be attainable in Gujarât by means of schools superintended by some of the best Yati professors, who should adhere to the rules and principles laid down in their treatises, insisting on their being carried out as far as possible in practice, exemplifying their use from the ancient monuments, and excluding all Western ideas. But, in attempting to resuscitate an antiquated style, if such were practicable, what would be the

---

[1] Personally I found them very ready to communicate their information and methods of design.—J. B.

[2] *On the Study of Indian Architecture*, 1867.

ultimate gain? To revive the dead past is not in the true line of progress any more than servilely to copy what is most recent. The old *Śilpa Sâstras* are well worth study in order that we may intelligently and correctly understand the old methods and the structural remains of ancient works.[1] They have a place in the history of Indian architecture, as Vitruvius has in Western art, but they would be poor guides for modern structures. Yet the intelligent study of these works would be of immense service to a Hindû builder who was able to assimilate improved methods and principles of design.

These architectural *Śâstras* are somewhat difficult to understand because the descriptions are couched in condensed metrical verses, and technical terms for parts of a structure carry meanings so different from their signification in usual parlance: thus *jaṅgh* (Sans., *jaṅghâ*, "the shank") usually means "the thigh," but is applied to a broad band of sculpture above the basement—*pîṭha* or *upastambha*.

These works commence with the directions for the selection and preparation of the ground and the foundation of the structure, and then pass on to the basement or *pîṭha*, the *mandovara* or walls, and finally to the spire or *śikhara*, giving the proportions or measurements for each part in succession. And as vernacular or Sanskrit terms[2] are used, for want of exactly synonymous English ones, in describing the details of temples, it may be necessary to define those in most frequent use.

The *gaj* or *hasta* is the standard of measurement employed, and is about 23¼ English inches (59 centimètres),[3] and is divided into 24 *aṅgula* or inches.

Prâsâda though generally meaning a four-sided building, such as a palace, mansion, temple, a tower or a terrace, is applied—at least in one sense—to the shrine of a temple when that is taken as a unit in the classification of temples by dimensions. Thus temples whose shrines measure outside from corner to corner, 3, 4, 10 *gaj*, &c. are styled three *gaj*, four *gaj*, ten *gaj* temples, &c. In plan, as may be seen in the plates of this volume, there are several varieties of these shrines or *prâsâdas*, the most elaborate being generally what are called *ashṭa-bhadra* or eight-faced. They approach very much to the star-shaped plans of the Chalukyan temples, formed by laying two squares over each other at angles of 45 degrees to form a plan with eight points, and four at half that angle to produce one of sixteen angles.[4]

The faces of the *vimâna* or shrine on the back and sides (Plate LXXXII) are each called a *bhadra* or ornament-panel. Between the *bhadra* at the back and each of those on the sides are one or more recessed angles; the central projecting angle is the *koṇa* or corner, the next on either side is called *uparatha*, and the next again

---

[1] It is a pity that Râm Râz's *Essay on the Architecture of the Hindus*, published by the Royal Asiatic Society in 1834, has never been followed up by versions of some of the northern *Śilpa Śâstras*. *Tenth Annual Report* of the *R. As. Soc.* p. xxix. The 53rd chapter of the *Bṛihat Saṅhitâ* is on Architecture, and the 56th on Temples; translated by Dr. H. Kern in *Jour. R. As. Soc.*, N.S., vol. VI, pp. 279-300, 316–21.

[2] Our Sanskṛit lexicons are singularly defective in architectural terms. The following definitions are from the notes supplied by Mr. Cousens.

[3] The *gaj* varies considerably in different districts.

[4] See *Arch. Sur. Westn. India*, vol. III, pp. 20, 21, and pl. xviii.

pratiratha. In the recesses between these corners are sometimes smaller projections, each of which is called a *nandi*, but in place of these we have often narrow slits or channels called *pâṇithara* (Guj.) or *jalanthara.* These appear in the plan of the Kasarâ temple (Plate LXXXVIII, 1). The presence of the extra corners—*pratiratha* and *uparatha*—depends on the size of the shrine and the elaborateness of its plan; but when employed they are to be constructed in strict accordance with the rules.

Generally the lesser shrines have only a small porch or *maṇḍapam* in front, whilst the larger ones have halls attached—either closed in or open at the sides. A hall that is closed in, connected with the shrine (*garbhagṛiha*), but standing out in front of it, is called a *Gûḍha-maṇḍapa.*[1] The porch, in the previous examples, then becomes a sort of antechamber to the shrine.[2]

In some of the largest temples, like that at Moḍherâ, there is a detached open hall variously called the *Sabhâ-maṇḍapa* or assembly hall, the *Raṅga-maṇḍapa,* painted hall or theatre, and *Nṛitya śâlâ* or dancing hall, wherein assemblies were held for discussion, shows, dancing, &c. which could not properly take place in the smaller *gûḍha-maṇḍapa.*

The roofs of the maṇḍapas are supported by the walls, and when larger by these and the pillars inside, which are usually so arranged as to uphold a central dome. The bays between the pillars are known as *chaukis*—a term applied also to the entrance porches of the *maṇḍapas.*

The parts of a column—*stambha* (or Guj., *tekaṇa*)—correspond with the mouldings of the outer walls of a temple. The upper mouldings of the shaft form the *bharaṇî* or supporting member, upon which rests the *śiras* or capital; and on this and its superimposed brackets rest the lintels supporting the roof. The base of a pillar is called *kumbhî*, and corresponds to the *kumbha* of the walls. In plan the *kumbhî* follows that of the shrine with its recessed corners, and above it are the mouldings styled *keval,*[3] surmounted by a *paṭṭikâ* or fillet carved with a row of faces, and known as *grasapaṭṭi* (see Plate XIII).

The shaft from the *kumbhî* to the *bharaṇî* is called the *stambha* or pillar, on the lower section of which—in highly sculptured temples—are carved niches on each face, often containing standing figures of the *dikpâlas* or demigods who are guardians of the points of the compass, whilst above them are figures of seated *devîs* of the class to which the temple is dedicated. The corbels over these are called *hîra-gṛihas* and are intended to hold the lower tenons of bracket figures—usually *gandharvas* or divine musicians—held in position above by the larger projecting brackets of the *śiras.* They also support the *toraṇas* as in Plate XLI.

When there is a sur-capital, the neck or section of the shaft supporting it is called the *uchchalâka,*[4] and is employed to meet the extra height of the roof of the central dome where the side bays are lower—that is, only reaching the level of the lower brackets. Over the upper brackets are placed the lintels or beams (*pâṭa*). In the case of the pillar, Plate XIII, fig. 1, being the forward one at the entrance

---

[1] Connected with *gadhita*, "enclosed," *gudhyati*, "to envelop," or *gûḍha* "hidden."

[2] This is the *antarâla.* Conf. Bühler's *Arisiṁha*, p. 30; Tawney's *Prabandha-chintâmaṇi*, p. 142.

[3] Query, *kevaṭa*, "hollowed," a sunk member?

[4] Or *virakaṇṭha.*

of the Râṇî's well at Pattan, it is probable that the upper brackets upheld the end of a *toraṇa*, whilst between it and the corbels below, bracket figures were inserted. In this pillar there are two capitals (*śiras*).

Pillars with a square base and octagonal shaft are styled *śridhara* pillars; those with the water-pot and foliage ornament such as the old pillars in the outlet sluice of the Khân Sarovar at Pattan (Plate XXXII) and of the temples at Sûṇak and Kasarâ (Plate XIII, figs. 2 and 3, and Plate LXXXVIII, fig. 3) are called *ghaṭapallava*; pillars upon which Kubera, the regent of the north, is represented, are called Kubera pillars, and so of others.

The width of the base of the pillar is derived from the size of the *prâsâda* or *vimána*, one tenth of its side being generally taken for the square of the pillar. The height is determined by the outside wall, the *páṭa* or lintel being on a level with the *chhâjâ*; and the whole height is divided into parts for the heights of the several sections of the pillar.[1]

The outer walls are divided vertically into the *pîṭha*, *upapîṭha* or basement, and the *maṇḍovara* or wall-face up to the entablature.

In building a temple, a paved platform (*kharaśilâ*) is first laid upon a well-rammed bedding of concrete, or, in older temples, upon a solid mass of brickwork. On this is raised the *piṭha*, a solid substructure the upper surface of which forms the floor of the building. The outer face of this basement is carved with a series of horizontal mouldings which follow the same order, though some of them may be omitted at will.

The *grasapaṭṭi* is a string-course or moulding sculptured with grinning faces; with horns—called also *kîrttimukha* and *kîrttivaktra*—which is a decorative form of great antiquity, being found in the cave-temples as well as in structural buildings.[2] Elephants are represented in line, with their heads and forelegs projecting from the basement as if supporting the building; and where such a member appears, the base is called *gajapîṭha*.[3] The *aśvathara* or row of horses, when employed, occupy a similar position; the *narathara* or band of men forms a sort of frieze on which to represent mythological scenes and incidents.[4]

To explain or account for the origin of the *kîrttimukha* or *grâsamukha* the following account is given in the *Padma-purâṇa*:—Jalandhara the Asura or demon, produced by the contact of a flash from Śiva's eye with the ocean, on hearing the praises of Pârvatî, sends to Śiva and demands her from him. Śiva enraged, produces a terrible being from his third eye whose mouth was like a lion's, whose tongue hung out, and whose eyes were like lightning, whose hair stood on end,

---

[1] For these proportions as laid down in the *Mânasâra*, see Râm Râz, *Architecture of the Hindus*, pp. 28-40.

[2] This ornament is very prominent on old temples in Java; conf. Ijzerman, *Beschrijving der Oudheden nabij de Soerakarta en Djodjakarta*, pl. i, and atlas, pl. ii, 2; Groneman, *Tjaṇḍi Parambanan*, pll. viii, ix; Leemans and Wilsen, *Bôrô Boedoer*, pll. v, vi, &c.

[3] The elephant in this position appears on the Dâgabas of Ceylon: conf. Smither, *Architectural Remains: Anuradhapura*, pll. 17–30, 34, 40, 44, 48, 50.

[4] For illustration compare the wall of the Halabîd temple represented in Fergusson's *Ind. and Eastn. Archit.* p. 402.

and whose body was white. He looked like another Narasiṁha, and as soon as created he rushed at Râhu (the demon with only a head and arms) who had brought Jalandhara's message; but Mahâdeva interposed, telling him that Râhu was only a servant—the messenger. Then the god tells him to devour himself; and this he does, leaving only his head. This so pleased Mahâdeva that he said he should be called henceforth Kirttimukha—"face of fame or renown," and should be represented at the doors of his shrines, to be first worshipped on entering.[1] Hence the face is always found on the front of the threshold of the shrine, and worshippers sprinkle it on entering and are careful not to step on, but over it.[2] The myth here has arisen from the representation. With its accompanying festoons of beads and flowing arabesque, it is an elaborate and as effective an ornament as is found in these old works. The Gujarâti salâṭs regard it as the face of some fabulous sea-monster, which they call *grâs*,[3] and account for it quite differently from the myth.

Bases or *pîṭhas* are divided by the *Śilpa Śâstras* into three classes:—(1) Those whose projection is half their height; (2) those in which it is one third; and (3) those in which it is only one fourth the height. A base of the first class, with the larger projection, is termed a *lâtina pîṭha,* and one of the third is called *savandhâra*.[4]

The walls of temples are broken up by vertical lines as well as by horizontal mouldings, and are thus divided into panels or facets. These lines run up from the lowest member of the base to the summit of the temple and often to that of the *śikhara* or spire.

The Śikhara is one of the most characteristic features of a Hindû temple, and when it exists, it indicates at once the order or style to which the building belongs. We may distinguish three distinct styles of spires:—the Dravidian, which prevails almost exclusively in southern India,[5] and which rises in horizontal storeys; the Aryan Hindû or northern type—employed in upper and central India, Râjputâna, and Orissa—which tapers upwards, with or without smaller forms of śikharas clustered against the central spire; and, thirdly, the Chalukyan style, a sort of hybrid evolved from the two previous and confined chiefly to the Kanarese-speaking districts. The temples of Gujarât belong to the northern type. In Plates XCIV, XCV, representing old temples at Sanderâ, the śikhara as well as the plan of the smaller shrine is practically identical with those of the older shrines of Orissa.

Though the origin of the form of the śikhara is obscure and a subject of archæological discussion,[6] its object over a shrine is obvious enough; like the towers

---

[1] Col. Vans Kennedy, in his *Researches into Ancient and Hindu Mythology* (pp. 456 ff.), gives the legend of Jalandhara at considerable length from the *Uttara-khaṇḍa* of the *Padmapurâṇa*, but there is no reference there to this legend. See also Wilkins, *Hindu Mythology*, pp. 367–72.

[2] Conf. 1 Samuel v. 5. The head having fallen on the threshold, it was fateful to step on the stone.

[3] This again may be connected with *grâsa* "a mouthful," or with *grahas* "one who seizes" and "a planet."

[4] Measurements obtained by rule may be varied in two ways; thus:—the dimension obtained by rule is termed *madhyama* or "mean"; but when one fifth is added to this it is termed *jyeshṭha* or *vṛiddha*, that is, "augmented" construction; and when the standard dimensions are diminished by a fifth it is *kanishṭha*, or "smallest" construction.

[5] Fergusson, *Hist. Ind. and East. Arch.* pp. 319, 340 ff.; *Architecture of Dharwar and Mysore*, p. 43.

[6] Fergusson, *Hist. Ind. and East. Arch.* pp. 221–225.

on western churches and the minârs of mosques, it is a landmark to guide the worshipper to the sacred centre; so also is the flagstaff, with its flag and bells added over it, which can only be planted in the finial or *kalaśa* when the image has been installed and the shrine consecrated for worship.

In the Gujarât works on architecture there are said to be no less than twenty-four varieties of *śikharas*, which are built either hollow or with brick cores. In the earlier examples the line of curve (*rekhâ*) of the spire rises at first almost vertically and curves more rapidly inwards as it approaches the summit.[1] On the top of the *śikhara* is the large round flat cushion-shaped stone with corrugated circumference, called the *âmalasara*, and which is often surmounted by a second and smaller one termed *âmalasarî*. On this stands the vase-like finial known as the *kalaśa*.[2] The corner lines of the *śikhara* should, when produced, meet at the vertex of the *kalaśa*.

In later temples the spire tapers about equally all the way up. The small half and quarter *śikharas* applied to the sides of the main or central spire are termed respectively *ûruśṛinga* and *śṛinga* (cusp or "turret"). The number and disposition of these depend chiefly on the number and arrangement of the divisions on the faces of the *prâsâda* (conf. Plate LXXXII). Above the sanctum rises the central spire, and over each *bhadra* or separate face are applied *ûruśṛingas*, one above another, lying close against the tower; and over the *koṇa*, *uparatha* and *pratiratha* corners are placed the *śṛingas*. The small niche in the lowest uruśṛinga, flanked by little pilasters and containing figures, is called a *gavâksha* (window—Guj., *gokhal*); and the square blocks between the *śṛingas* and *ûruśṛingas* are termed *kûṭas*.

The doorways are designed with much care:—The usual proportion of height to width of opening is as 2 to 1. The jambs are carved into antepagments or vertical mouldings, some projecting and others recessed. Each of the fasciæ thus formed is called a *śâkha*, and door frames may be of three, five, nine,[3] &c. *śâkhas*, according to the number of these fasciæ or corvæ. The inner one is usually decorated with a creeper and leaves, running round the door, or with a lozenge-shaped ornament, or a square and circle, and is called the *pattra*. The moulding decorated with dancing figures is styled *gandharva-śâkha;* one with a series of small niches is called *rûpa;* one with lions, a *siṁha-śâkha;* and the sharp knife-edge or wedge-shaped moulding the *kalva*.

The door threshold is called *udumbara*, from the front of which projects a semi-circular drum, and on each side of this is a projecting *kîrttimukha* face. The whole step is called *maṇḍâraka*, whilst the low semi-circular step—in the place of a door mat—and which is often very elaborately carved, is termed the half moon or *ardha-chandra*.[4] On the centre of the lintel is a small projecting

---

[1] Conf. Fergusson, *Ind. and East. Archit.* p. 222.

[2] This is the "sweet dew jar" or "vessel of immortality" (*amarakâraka*) of the Chinese; see Beal's *Si-yu-ki*, vol. II, pp. 118, 136 n., 205 n.; and conf. infra., p. 30; and *J. R. As. Soc.* vol. XXI, p. 690.

[3] "A door with three, five, seven, or nine-fold frames is much approved." Varâha Mihira, *Bṛihat Saṅhitâ*, lvi, 14.

[4] Roughly translated "moon stone." See Fergusson's *Ind. and East. Archit.* pp. 196, 197. Merutuṅga speaks of the lotus-slab (*padmaśilam*) of the antechamber or *maṇḍapa*; *Prabandha-ch.* p. 57.

block on which is carved the Deva to whom the temple is dedicated, his devi, vehicle, or other sectarial emblem—usually Gaṇeśa for a Śaiva temple.

The roofs of maṇḍapas are often very ornamental. They rest on lintels supported by the columns usually arranged as corners of an octagon From these the dome is raised in successive diminishing rings or courses, laid flat upon one another and corbelling inwards. Hindû domes are never constructed with radiating voussoirs: this form of dome appears, indeed, to have been unknown in India. The interiors were richly ornamented with carved mouldings upon each layer of the structure, which completely masked the joints of the masonry, and gave to the whole the appearance of one sculptured mass. The smaller bays in the side aisles were generally covered with flat slabs laid side by side and sometimes carved.

Attached to many of the more notable temples were *Kîrttistambhas* or ornamental arches.[1] These imposing structures are formed of two lofty pillars richly carved, upon which rests a highly decorated entablature, the arch being in the form of a beautiful *toraṇa* or garland arch supported at the ends by the lower capitals of the pillars and rising to the architrave. They usually stood out in front of the main entrance of the temple, as may be seen at Moḍherâ, where only the shafts of the pillars now remain. At Vaḍnagar there are two very fine ones, at the Rudramahâlaya at Siddhapur, there were probably three, and others are found at Kâpadvaṇj and elsewhere (see Plates VII, XLIV, LVII, LIX).

Connected with temples elsewhere there are also gateways or arches that appear to be analogous to these Kîrttistambhas; thus, in front of an old temple at Galiganâtha, close to Aiholê in the Bîjâpur district, is the remains of a gateway that seems to have been used for swinging the image in the temple on festival occasions; the "swinging gateway" at Rewâ, and the Kirttistambha at Orangal were, in all likelihood, for the same purpose; and at Baroli in Mewâr, one pillar and the base of another belonging to such an arch still remain;[2] at Pathari also there is (or was) the remains of a fine one of the same class. These may suggest that many of these arches were used for the same purpose. In the seventeenth century marble embankment at Râjanagar or Kâṅkrauli in Râjputâna are three (originally six) such arches, which may possibly have been employed for swinging on festive occasions.[3]

From what has already been said, it naturally follows that the oldest shrines in Gujarât are most in accord with the rules of the *Silpa Śâstras*, and these latter are consequently much better illustrated by such buildings than by temples of later date. In the earlier remains we find the style at its best. It is more than probable that the earliest masonry was of brick, for building stone is not found in the northern plain of Gujarât, and when used it has to be brought from

---

[1] *Kîrtti* and *kîrtana* means a "monument," temple, or any work calculated to make famous its constructor. Fleet, *Corp. Inscr.* vol. III, p. 212 n.; *Ind. Ant.* vol. IX, p. 36 n.

[2] See *Arch. Sur. W. Ind.* vol. I, p. 43; Sir L. Griffin's *Famous Monts. of Central India*, pl. lxxxvii; Tod's *Annals of Rajasthan*, vol. II, p. 712; Burgess, *Architecture and Scenery in Gujarât and Râjputânâ*, p. 36 and pl. xxii; Fergusson, *Ind. and East. Archit.* pp. 392, 451; and *Picturesque Illustrations*, p. 36.

[3] Burgess, *Archit. and Scen. in Gujarât*, &c. p. 26 and pl. xiii.

Dhrângadhrâ in Kâthiâwâḍ, Aḥmadnagar in Îdar, or from the Aravalli hills to the north. Large bricks, of the very old type, are frequently dug up round villages like Pañchâsar; and over a large area about the Moḍherâ temple the ground to a considerable depth is full of very old brickwork. The two old temples at Sarotrâ and Śaṅkheśvara also are partly of brickwork. The cores too of the massive embankments round old tanks such as the Sahasara-linga talâv at Pâṭaṇ, and the tank at Sûṇak are of solid brickwork, the outer facing only being of stone. The site of the ancient city of Chandrâvatî abounds in brick mounds—the remains of many temples that were destroyed by the Muhammadans in the fourteenth and fifteenth centuries and obliterated by railway contractors late in the nineteenth.

Except in the Rudramahâlaya at Siddhapur such huge blocks of stone as we meet with in the temples of the sixth and seventh centuries at Aihole in the Bijâpur district and elsewhere, are not found in the Gujarât temples; but, like them, they are constructed without mortar. The stones are carefully dressed and retain their positions by the mere weight of the superincumbent masses. Hence, whenever the foundation subsided or pillars gave way, the loosened stones slid off one another and the whole structure fell to pieces.

In the Kanarese districts and Dakhan, as evidenced by unfinished work, it seems to have been usual, in some cases if not generally, to carve the details upon the stones after the blocks were placed *in situ*; but in Gujarât and Râjputânâ it appears to have been the rule, and is so still, to finish the whole of the work and piece it together before placing the stone in its position.

The material chiefly used is the sandstone quarried in the north of Kâṭhiâwâḍ; but in the northern parts of the province many of the temples were built of white marble. Most of what once existed at Chaṇḍrâvatî, Bhilaḍi, Mudeṭha, and many at Aṇahilapattana appear to have been constructed of this material; and the remains at Sarotrâ and Roho are entirely of white marble. This was obtainable, and is still so, in the neighbourhood of Chandrâvatî.

But marble shrines have now almost disappeared, their material having been carried off to break up for lime: nor is this vandalism of remote date, but has been continued till the present time. The temples were desecrated or overthrown by the Muslim invaders, and in most cases they were left thenceforth to fall into ruin, and ultimately became a quarry for materials to the Muhammadans and builders of later date. Thus we find fragments built into all sorts of erections constructed during the last two centuries. Notable instances of this are seen in the walls of Pâṭaṇ and at the Khân Sarovar outside the walls (see Plates XIII, 4–6; XVIII, 2–7; XXVI, 4; XXXI, 4; XXXIII, and XXXV, 1–3). In the former, built by one of the Gaikwâḍs, are found very large quantities of material so applied, among which are pillars, door architraves, parts of ceiling slabs, figures, &c. built in anyhow; in fact, the greater part of the stone used in the walls is from old temples.

But the greatest destruction of these shrines took place when the Muhammadans first settled in Gujarât. They dismantled the temples wholesale and appropriated the material in constructing their first mosques. The Âdînah Masjid, said to have been formed by Ulugh Khân at Pâṭaṇ in 1297 A.D.,[1] was perhaps the largest in the province—if we may judge by the site showing its extent. And the blocks that remain of it, lying about on that site, are all fragments from Hindû temples. Many of the old mosques have, in turn, now disappeared, and the materials have again been utilised in other buildings.

On studying the plans of these Hindû temples it will be noticed that the walls are of very unequal thickness in different parts. This arises when the outer faces of the cella are practically at an angle of 45° with the inner—the sides of the outer square running past the corners of the cella.[2] This leaves the walls very thick at the back and sides, but thin at the corners of the shrine.[3] This is illustrated in the quarter plan of the shrine of the Sûṇak temple on Plate LXXXII, 2. But many temples, especially of later date, such as those at Delmâl (Plate LVI), have the walls of more uniform thickness, the offsets on their exteriors being shallow. The inner lines of the walls of the cella, when produced, should usually coincide with the faces of the *pratirathas* on each side of the *koṇa* or middle corner; or, conversely, the edges of the *pratirathas*, joined across the plan, give the inner faces of the shrine walls (see Plate LXXXII, 1).

The walls are generally built in two shells—the outer carrying all the mouldings and the inner dressed smooth on the face. These are seldom well bonded; and the outer, not unfrequently, has fallen completely away, whilst the inner may be still intact. The beds of the blocks are dressed in the usual way with the edges so carefully finished as to give a fine joint. Between the shells it hardly seems as if filling in was a general practice; often it was but imperfectly attended to. The roof of the *garbhagṛiha* or shrine was formed either by laying long slabs across, or, in the larger examples, by laying large slabs over the corners and so forming a smaller square which could again be contracted by slabs cutting off the corners until the central opening could be covered by a single stone.

The Śikhara or spire was carried up on the walls of the shrine, or of an outer wall, in cases where there was a *bhrama* or *pradakshiṇâ*—a circumambulatory passage round about the shrine.[4] The spire was often built hollow, the weight of the *âmalaśira* (or *âmolaśilâ*)[5] and *kalaśa* or finial serving to lock the heads of the walls together.

The most prominent characteristic of these temples is the profuse decoration with sculptures that covers them, and which is distributed on a definite plan. The sculptures were to a certain extent limited to certain sets of patterns which were used over and over again; and variety was produced by occasional omissions

---

[1] Bayley, *Gujarât*, p. 38; inf. p. 60. It was apparently still standing about 1760. Van Twist says it was a Hindû temple turned into a mosque; and this is quite probable.

[2] This is not necessarily often the case; conf. plan of Kâjarâṇi temple at Bhuvaneśvara, in Râjendralâl Mitra's *Antiquities of Orissa*, vol. II, pl. xlix; or Fergusson's *Archæology in India*, p. 48.

[3] For explanation see Fergusson, *Ind. and Eastn. Archit.* p. 412 f.

[4] This is the sense in which *bhrama* is to be understood in *Prabandha-chintâmaṇi*, Tawney's tr., p. 135.

[5] Conf. ante, p. 27, note 2.

or by rearrangements provided for in the *śâstras*. At first sight one is almost bewildered by the superabundance of detail on one of the finer temples; but closer inspection and comparison of different examples lead to the conclusion that the builders largely followed stereotyped plans and designs from which they all worked in common.

Whilst their florid and arabesque designs are executed with an amount of skill and invention that is simply astonishing, their figure sculpture is of very mediocre value. In the representations of the human form the head and trunk are often passable, but the legs and arms are generally weak and wanting in muscle. This defect has been commented on by different authors and variously ascribed to the physical characteristics of the race and to the overlaying of the limbs with richly carved ornaments. To them we may refer and need not here discuss the question at length[1]: art for itself was not a pursuit that attracted the mind of the Hindû, and his sculpture was too conventional[2] to be true to ideal types in nature.

In the representation of their superhuman beings, drapery is scarcely expected, and in the temple sculptures, where it is intended, it is usually indicated by a few lines drawn across the figure and a fold or two on the legs and in front of them. This was the convention in the earlier cave sculptures and paintings, where a single line indicated the edge of Buddha's robe across the breast from the left shoulder. The figure of the Tîrthakara on Plate XIX, at first glance, appears to be nude, but the lines of the loin-cloth appear just over the hands, and the ends of it are seen below the crossed ankles. On Plate LVI, figs. 5 and 6, we have figures of Sûrya, the sun-god—the favourite divinity of the early Kâṭhîs—who wears a jacket with richly embroidered neck and front, yet the breasts are carefully represented. Still his person is fully "clad in the dress of the Northerners so as to be covered from the feet upwards to the bosom."[3] In the figures on the pillar on Plate LIV, fig. 1, the drapery is distinctly shown in folds upon the legs only, which lose none of their outline by this skin-tight clothing. On Plate LVI, fig. 7, and LVIII, fig. 1, the *devis* have no sign of clothing; and in the cave temples, and later works in the Dekhan, we have the same treatment in the statuaries.

Indian sculpture is properly a *rilievo;* detached statues rarely occur—they are always meant to have a slab attached or wall behind them.[4] The pose in the earlier figures is calm and quiescent, but poor and inartistic in later times. Ornament is chiselled with the utmost care and minuteness of finish on necklaces, bracelets, and chains.

These details may help to afford some idea of the general features of the construction of Hindû shrines in Gujarât; further information will be found in the descriptions which follow.

---

[1] See Grünwedel, *Buddhist Art in India*, Eng. ed., p. 32 f.; Râjendralâl Mitra, *Indo-Aryans*, vol. I, p. 121.
[2] Conf. *Bṛihat Saṁhitâ*, in *J. R. As. S.*, N.S., vol. VI, pp. 322–30.
[3] *Arch. Sur. W. Ind.* vol II, p. 215, and p. lxv; *Bṛihat Saṁhitâ,* lviii, 46.
[4] Grünwedel, *Buddhist Art in India*, Eng. ed., p. 30.

This chapter may be appropriately closed by a quotation from Forbes's *Râs Mâlâ*[1]:—

"It is a curious fact, and one which strongly brings out to view the passive vitality of their institutions, that after each succeeding storm has swept over the land, while the clouds are as yet undispersed, and the reappearing sun discloses little but fissures that have been rent by tempestuous torrents, the Hindûs are observed at once, without an effort, and, as it were, instinctively, proceeding in the old ways, apparently as little sensible of sorrow for the past as they are for the future. Maḥmûd of Ghazni had hardly accomplished his disastrous homeward retreat, leaving behind him Aṇhilawâḍa despoiled, and Somanâth a heap of ruins, when the sound of the hammer and the chisel was heard upon Ârâsur and Âbû, and stately fanes began to arise at Kumbhâriyâ and Delwâḍâ, in which an elaboration almost incredible, and a finish worthy of the hand of a Cellini, seem to express the founder's steadfast refusal to believe in Mlechh invaders, or iconoclastic destroyers, as other than the horrid phantoms of a disturbing dream. And now, as the second Bhîma closes his troubled career—as the sun of Aṇhilawâḍa sinks with him, never again to rise in unclouded brightness, while the crescent,[2] perhaps, still waves over the capital, while the roar of battle has not well died away, and the cry of alarm and pain still resounds through the land—at Âbû and Śatruñjaya the work is again resumed, and shrines, surpassing even the magnificence of former days, arise as dwelling-places for those silent, ever-brooding, unmoved Tîrthaṅkaras."

---

[1] Vol. I, p. 262, 263; 2nd ed. p. 202.

[2] The accomplished author had forgotten that the crescent only became the symbol of the Saracens after the capture of Constantinople.

CHAPTER III.

AṆAHILAVÂḌA-PATTANA OR PÂṬAṆ: HINDÛ REMAINS.

PLATES III, IV, XIII.

AṆAHILAVÂḌA also known as Aṇahillapura, Aṇahilapâṭhaka, Aṇalavâṭa, Naharwâlah, and now as Pattana or Pâṭaṇ, lies on the left bank or south side of the Sarasvatî river, in the flat, sandy plain of northern Gujarât, in lat. 23° 51′ N., and long. 72° 11′ E., about 66 miles north by west from Aḥmadâbâd, and double that distance from Barodâ. Encircled by walls of the eighteenth century, the town is quite modern in appearance, and there is little left—certainly nothing striking—to suggest the antiquity and former splendour of the capital of the Châvaḍâ and Solaṅki dynasties and one of the oldest and most renowned cities of Gujarât. Though known in the Muhammadan histories under the name of Nahrwâra, Nahlwâra or Naharwâlah, its position or identity with Pâṭaṇ seems to have been almost forgotten in the eighteenth century. D'Anville sought to identify it, but could only conjecture that it must have stood on the site of Aḥmadâbâd[1]; and still later Rennell, in the first edition of his *Memoir of a Map of Hindustan*, published in 1788 (p. 149), failed to trace the name; though in a later edition (1793) he had identified it. Yet Father Tieffenthaler had long previously written of Pattan as "a very ancient city surrounded by walls, . . . whose old name was Nehrvâla."[2] Unaware of this, Colonel Tod regarded the position of this ancient capital as still amongst the desiderata of Indian geography until, in 1822, he discovered it in one of the suburbs of modern Pâṭaṇ.[3] Albiruni in the early half of the eleventh century describes its situation with accuracy, calling it by its native name of Anhalwârah[4]; and Idrisi, who compiled his work on the authority of Ma'sûdi—who visited India in A.D. 915—and other Arab travellers, says, "from Bharoch to Nahrawâra is reckoned eight marches through a flat country, where they travel in wheeled carriages. In all Nahrawâra and its environs, people never travel otherwise than in carriages drawn by bullocks which are directed at will. These vehicles are furnished with cords and straps and serve for the transport of merchandise."[5]

---

[1] *Eclaircissements*, p. 74.

[2] Tieffenthaler, tom. I, p. 385; and Walter Hamilton in his *Description of Hindustan* (1820), vol. I, p. 623, speaks of the ancient metropolis of Gujarât named Nehrwalla or Puttan, remarking that it was written Anhulvada. Lassen, *Ind. Alterth.* bd. I, S. 137. Van Twist (1648) says the city of Pattan was formerly 12 kos or six leagues in circumference, with houses of hard stone within its walls which three different times had been broken down, by which calamities the city had begun to decline in business and population. The inhabitants were mostly Banyans who were engaged in making silk stuffs for home use and coarse cloths, &c. —*General Beschrijvinge van Indien*, p. 16. In Wicquefort's French version of Mandelslo (vol. II. p. 193) this information is summarised.

[3] Tod, *Travels in Western India* (1839), p. 144; *Trans. R. As. Soc.* vol. I (1824), p. 208.

[4] *India*, Sachau's trans., vol. I, pp. 153, 205; vol. II, p. 7.

[5] *Géog. d'Édrisi*, trad. Jonbert, tom. I, p. 175, 176.

"As for the city of Nahrawâra," Idrisi adds, "it is governed by a great prince who takes the title of Balharâ. He has an army, elephants, worships the image of Budha, wears a crown of gold on his head, and is dressed in rich stuffs; he often rides on horseback, especially once a week, accompanied only by females to the number of a hundred, gorgeously dressed, wearing on their feet and hands circlets of gold and silver, and their hair braided. They give themselves to amusements and mock fights, whilst the king precedes them. The Vazîrs and officers of the troops never accompany the king, except when he goes to fight with rebels or to repel the attacks of neighbouring kings who may encroach upon his territory. He possesses many elephants, and in them consists the principal strength of his army. His power is hereditary as well as the title of Balharâ which signifies *king of kings*.[1] The city of Nahrawâra is frequented by great numbers of Musalman merchants who visit it on business. They are honourably received by the king and his ministers and enjoy protection and security."

He adds again, "the inhabitants of Nahrwâra live upon rice, pease, beans, haricots, lentils, maise, fish, and animals dying a natural death—for they do not kill either birds or other animals. They have a very great regard for oxen, and —by a privilege peculiar to that species—they bury them after death. When these are enfeebled by age and unfit for work, they are set free from all labour, attended to and fed, without committing charge of them to anyone.

"In every country in India and Sindh where Musalmans are found, they bury their dead secretly, by night and in their houses; but no more than the Indians are they addicted to long lamentations."[2]

Concurrent tradition, as already stated, assigns the foundation of Aṇahilavâḍa to Vanarâja the founder of the Châvaḍâ dynasty about 746, or according to some accounts in 765 A.D. It was probably a town of some size before, and was made his new capital. Under his successors it rose to importance, and under the Solaṅki dynasty, who ruled a larger territory, from the middle of the tenth till the end of the twelfth century, it greatly increased in population and importance. Colonel Tod dwells on this and gives the following version, or rather paraphrase, from the *Kumârapâla charitra* of Jinamaṇḍava (A.D. 1436) describing its glories as in the middle of the twelfth century, in which considerable allowance must be made for Oriental hyperbole[3]:—

Aṇahilapura, it says, "was twelve kos (or eighteen miles) in circuit, within which were many temples and colleges; eighty-four *chauks* or squares; eighty-four *bâzârs* or market-places, with mints for gold and silver coinage. Each class had its separate *mahalla* or quarter, as had each description of merchandise, *i.e.*, *hâthî-dânt* or elephants' tusks, silks, purples, diamonds, pearls, &c., &c., each had its separate *chauk*. There was one bâzâr for *śarrâfs* or money-changers; one for perfumes and unguents; one for physicians; one for artizans; one for goldsmiths, and one for silversmiths; there were distinct *mahallas* for navigators, for bards, and for genealogists. The eighteen *varṇa* or castes inhabited the city. All were happy together. The palace groaned with a multitude of separate buildings

[1] See ante, p. 9. [2] *Géog. d'Édrisi*, t. I, pp. 177, 178. [3] *Trav. in W. India*, pp. 1561.

—for the armoury, for elephants, horses and chariots, for the public accountants and officers of state. Each kind of goods had its separate *mâṇḍavî* or mart, where the duties of export, import, and sale were collected: as for spices, fruits, drugs, camphor, metals, and everything costly of home or foreign growth. It is a place of universal commerce! The daily amount of duties was a lakh of *ṭankas*.[1] If you ask for water they give you milk. There are many Jaina temples, and on the banks of a lake is a shrine to Sahasralinga Mahâdeva. The population delights to saunter amidst the groves of *champaka*, *punnâg*, *tâl* (palmyra), *jambu* (rose-apple), *chandan* (sandal), mango, &c., &c., with variegated *velâ* or creepers, and fountains whose waters are *amṛita*. Here discussions (*vâda*) take place on the *Vedas*, carrying instruction to the listener. There are plenty of Bohrâs,[2] and in Virgâm there are also many. There is no want of *birterans* (Yatis or Jaina priests), or of merchants true to their word and skilled in commerce; and many schools for the *Vyâkarna* (literally, grammar schools). Aṇahilawâḍa is a *nara-samudra* (sea of men). If you can measure the waters of the ocean, then may you attempt to count the number of souls. The army is numerous, nor is there any lack of bell-bearing elephants."

Much of this may be poetical exaggeration; still the Muhammadan writers agree that the city was large and splendid. It was, however, in the path of Maḥmûd the iconoclast of Ghazni, when he marched on Somanâtha in 1025 A.D. and Bhîma—unprepared to oppose the horde of fanatics—fell back on Kachh and left Aṇahilavâḍa an easy prey to the barbarous invader, who sacked it and carried off much spoil.[3] But no sooner had Maḥmûd retired towards the Indus than Bhîmadeva re-occupied his capital and began to restore it. Under this brave prince (A.D. 1022–1073), his son Karṇadeva, and grandson Siddharâja, Aṇahilavâḍa attained its greatest splendour and the Solaṅki dominion its widest extent and highest prosperity. Karṇadeva founded the town of Karṇâvati—near or on the site of the modern Aḥmadâbâd, and erected or restored several shrines in his capital, whilst Siddharâja and his successor Kumârapâla were famous for the number and magnitude of their buildings. Bhîmadeva II became king in 1178 and in that year defeated Mu'izzu-*l* Dîn of Ghazni who invaded his kingdom, but in 1195 he was attacked by Quṭbu-*l* Dîn, the general of Muḥammad Ghori, and the Gujarât army being defeated near Aṇahilavâḍa, the Moslems again sacked the city.[4] Bhîmadeva immediately after, assisted by his feudatories Prahlâdana and Dhârâvarsha of Chandrâvatî, with the Mers and Chief of Nagor, defeated Quṭbu-*l* Dîn and besieged him in Ajmer until he was relieved. Again in 1197 he invaded Gujarât to avenge his previous reverse, and won a victory over Bhîmadeva's forces, which again gave him temporary possession of Aṇahilavâḍa, after which he returned to Dehli.[5] A century later, 1297 1298, Ulugh Khân and

[1] About 5000 rupees.

[2] Perhaps from Sansk. *vyavahâri*, a trader, the Bohrâs seem to have originated in Gujarât.

[3] Elliot, *Hist. Ind.* vol. I, p. 98; vol. II, p. 468; vol. IV, p. 180; *Ind. Ant.* vol. VI, pp. 185 f.; Raverty's *Tabaqât-i Nâṣirî*, p. 86.

[4] Raverty's *Tabaqât-i Nâṣirî*, p. 519 n.; *Epig. Indica*, vol. I, p. 22.

[5] Duff, *Chronology of India*, p. 171; Bayley, *Hist. of Gujarât*, pp. 37–39.

Naṣrat Khân Jalesarî, the generals of Sulṭân 'Alâu-*l*-dîn invaded Gujarât, sacked the temple of Somanâtha, defeated the Râja Karṇa Vâghela—who fled and took refuge with Râmadeva of Devagiri—and captured Nahrwâlah (Aṇahilavâḍa). Then Gujarât became a province of the Mughal empire, and thenceforward the great architectural works of the Solaṅki and Vâghela kings were wilfully and maliciously dilapidated by Islâm bigotry. Ulugh Khân, known as Alp or Alaf Khân, one of the first governors of Nahrwâlah, we are told by 'Alî Muḥammad Khân, the author of the *Mirât-i Ahmadi*, "built the Âdînah masjid of white marble which remains at the present time (1756). . . . There is a fine masjid which it is said at that time stood in the centre of the city, but is now far away from the inhabited part. There are many remains of grand buildings which show what a great and splendid city Pattan was in olden times. For nearly three *kos* round the present city the ground is strewed with bricks and blocks, which attest the truth of this relation. Ruined bastions and walls found in the open country likewise prove this. In the lapse of ages, from the construction of new buildings and other changes in the city, many vestiges of old times have disappeared. During the times of the Râjas, so much marble was brought from Ajmîr for the construction of temples and other buildings that abundance of it is found at the present time on digging in the ground. All the marble used at Aḥmadâbâd and other places was brought from thence." Such is the testimony of a well-informed Muhammadan writer and revenue officer in Gujarât about a hundred and fifty years ago.[1]

What remains could exist of its former splendour when for five centuries its ruins have been despoiled of chiselled marble and carved stone, and continues to be dug over for such materials? Even that "magnificent relic" of which Tod spoke so admiringly—"the skeleton arch of a noble gateway" is now no more.[2] Every vestige of it has been carried away;—adding another to the many losses that are so frequently occurring to make us wish some efficient check could be put on such vandalism in the destruction of relics so valuable to the antiquarian, the architectural critic, and the historian.

The fragments of marble shrines that had not been carried off have latterly been dug out, sold and carted away to be burnt into lime; and all that is left are broken slabs, scattered throughout the town, built into the city walls, and into gateways, wells, mosques, dwelling-houses and cattle-sheds.

The present city of Pâṭaṇ has a population of about 33,000, of which about an eighth are Jainas or Śrâvaks[3] who count over a hundred temples, large and small, in the town.

---

[1] Bayley's *Gujarât*, p. 38; Bird's *Polit. and Stat. Hist. of Gujarât*, p. 163 f. It is much to be regretted that this most valuable work has never been translated and published in full. Bird's volume (1835) is a not very accurate rendering of only about a seventh part, and that the least valuable portion of the work. Sir Clive Bayley in the first chapter of his *History of Gujarât* (1886) gives only a fragment of what Bird had published. Colonel John W. Watson had made considerable progress with a full version when he was cut off by a sudden death. No work is of more value for the history of Gujarât under Muhammadan rule.

[2] Vide infra, p. 45.

[3] In the northern *prânt* they number about 32,000.

PLATE III

AṆAHILAPAṬṬANA: RUINS OF THE RÂṆÎ WÂV.

Colonel Tod gave what he calls an imperfect sketch of the area of the ancient city,[1] but the relative positions he lays down have to be reversed: the larger portions of the area of the old capital lay, not to the east of the modern town, but to the west of it, in which direction there are old foundations and mounds containing remains to a distance of four or five miles. In this direction is the village of Wadali--said to occupy the site of the Ghî-ka-Mândavi or Ghî market of the old city. On the east of the present town, to the distance of about a mile, as well as beyond the north and south boundaries of it, there are also traces of old Aṇahilavâḍa,—showing that the circumference of twelve *kos* or eighteen miles assigned to it by the *Charitra* was not much, if at all, exaggerated.

Modern Pâṭaṇ or Pattan has been so despoiled of almost every structure of antiquity that there now remain only a few fragmentary objects to be noted as belonging to the Hindû period. These are—part of the Râṇî Wâv or step-well ascribed to Udayamatî the consort of Bhîmadeva I; the Sahasraliṅga talâv, ascribed to Siddharâja Jayasiṁha; and old images, pillars, and fragments of sculptured slabs. The Jaina temples, at least in their present forms, are mostly—if not all—of later age than the fifteenth century. The Musalman remains date from the end of the thirteenth century downwards, and consist chiefly of the Gumaḍa, Ghazni, Shaikh Jodh, Shaikh Sarat, and other mosques, the Khân Sarovar tank, Bahâdursingh's well, and old wood carving.

The Râṇî Wâv.

In the fields a short distance to the north-west of Pâṭaṇ, and not far from the embankment of the Sahasraliṅga Talâv, are the remains of the Râṇî Wâv—once one of those beautiful step-wells so well known in Gujarât. It is said to have been constructed under the auspices of Udayamatî, the queen of Bhîmadeva I (A.D. 1022–63), and mother of Karṇadeva. At present nothing of this is left except a huge pit, 285 feet in length, with a portion of the masonry of the well shaft (Plate III) at one end and the fragments of a pillar at the other. The pit slopes down from the latter to the former, where there is still a pool of stagnant water.

Except these every stone of the walls and pillars has been dug out and carried off. Colonel Tod's account indicates that the materials had been used to construct a new well in the modern city; and current report, thirty years ago, related that the pillars and materials of this wâv were removed for the erection of Bahâdur Singh's wâv inside the town.[2]

Judging of its original size by the distance from the well-shaft to the solitary pillar, and considering the amount of sculpture that must have decorated the galleries, the Râṇî Wâv, when intact, must have been second to none in Gujarât. A part only of the west wall of the *bauḍi* or well-shaft now remains, from which we learn that the walls had been built of brick and faced with hewn stone. From this wall project the large vertical brackets in pairs which supported the different galleries of the well. This bracketing is arranged in

[1] *Trav. W. Ind.* p. 223.

[2] See p. 52 infra.

tiers and is richly carved, and constructed on the same principles as the gateways of Jhinjhuvâḍa and Dabhoi.

It is impossible now to say what the exact plan of this well may have been—whether it had a single stair like that at Vâyad (Plate CIV) or was cross shaped with three flights of steps as in the great well at Adâlaj. The approximate length only can be ascertained from the distance between the well-shaft and the remaining pillar at the east end of the pit (Plate XIII, fig. 1). And even this last mark is being demolished. As late as 1887 a short upper shaft with a fragment of a cornice surmounted the capital, but in 1890 this had been thrown down. As this column stands at about the level of the surrounding ground, it probably occupied a position very near the entrance to the well. Much of it has been filled in by the débris, and it is now quite uncared for, except that, on the high bank above the pool, a common masonry structure has been made for drawing up the water by the *môṭ* or leather bag to irrigate the adjoining field. Bushes and creepers festoon the crumbling masonry.

If the photograph (Plate III) be compared with the lithographed print from a drawing by Mr. Arthur Malet given in Tod's *Travels in Western India* (p. 224), it may be surmised that, beyond the further silting up of the pool at the bottom of the pit, there has been no great change in the condition of this ruin during the last seventy or eighty years--or, perhaps, since its spoliation in 1805. Malet described the sketch as of "the ruins of a *bauri* (a well with a flight of steps down to it) in the old fort at Pattan. The steps and the galleries have fallen in, and the only part remaining is one side of the well, finely sculptured."

As already mentioned, the construction of this well is ascribed to Udayamatî, the queen of Bhîmadeva I, and the style of the last pillar corresponds with that of the columns in the Jaina temple of Vimala Śâ on Mount Abu, which was erected in A.D. 1032, during the same reign—and there is nothing about the style of the fragment to prevent its being coupled in date with that shrine. In the absence of conflicting evidence, then, its traditional date may be accepted. The half obliterated sculptures that can still be traced are characteristic of Hindû rather than of any other mythology.

The Sahasraliṅga Talâv.

To the great Jayasiṁha Siddharâja (A.D. 1093–1143) are ascribed the construction of various artificial lakes or reservoirs in Gujarât. One of the largest of these was the Sahasraliṅga talâv, or tank of the thousand Śaiva shrines at Pattan, the remains of which are still pointed out to the north-west of the town. It must have been a reservoir of immense size, and derived its name from the numerous little temples, containing *liṅgas*, placed on the steps around it. In the centre was an island on which stood the temple of Rudreśvara —destroyed of course by the Muslims, who raised a large octagonal Rauzah on its ruins; but of this only the dilapidated remains now exist.

The basin of the lake is now converted into tilled fields. The great embankment surrounding it appears to be composed throughout of solid brickwork, and this was once faced with stone masonry forming flights of steps to the water's edge. On and above these steps stood the thousand shrines of which fragmentary remains are still found buried in the débris of the embankment. An inspection of the Mansur or (Minah-sarovar) at Viramgâm, which still remains fairly intact and is also ascribed to Siddharâja, gives a pretty good idea of what must have been the magnificence of this much larger one. This lake was round, or rather multilateral, whilst the Viramgâm tank is an irregular oblong about 500 feet wide by 1,500 long. Round the latter are the shrines—once over five hundred, of which three hundred and thirty-seven still remain—similar in size and construction to those that once graced the margin of the Sahasraliṅga Talâv.

This great tank is said to have been begun by Jayasiṁha Siddharâja shortly before he set out against Yaśovarman, the sovereign of Mâlava, and is the theme of legend and song. The best known of these is perhaps the ballad of Jasmâ the beautiful Odani. The story of it has been told by Forbes in his *Râs Mâlâ* (vol. I, pp. 111 f.); and the following is a pretty literal version of the principal portion of the original ballad or *rasado*, as collected in 1869[1]:—

At Pâṭaṇ rules Siddharâv Solaṅki,
Greatly the people praise him.
Thither a man came—a beggar,
In words he clearly set forth—
The policy of the state he applauds;
Then praised he the Padminî.[2]
"Where," asks the king, "is a maiden like this?"
Said the beggar "In Mâlawa land,"
From then by the arrow of love was he pierced;
How to see her the king was perplexed,—
At length king and queen retired to their rest;
Between midnight and dawn the queen dreamt dreams:—
"Rise up O king," she exclaimed, "get made a Talâv,
The birds, without water, are dying;
Beautiful is my Mâlawa land,
Where their thirst the Sarasas quench,
Call for Dudhmâl, your nephew,
That he may go; write and send a letter
To the Odan,[3] in the Mâlawa land;

[1] *Notes of a Visit to Gujarât*, pp. 94 f. *Rasado, Pavado, Jhagada, Garbu*, and *Kisso*, are terms used to designate these metrical stories, many of which are of considerable merit and great interest. They are well deserving of collection and publication ere they are forgotten and lost before the new learning of the West.

[2] Women are divided into four classes:—of these (1) the *Padmini* (having the smell of a lotus) is the first and most excellent, (2) the *Chitriṇi* (variegated, wonderful), *Hariṇi* or *Mṛigi* (doe), is the well educated, accomplished and beautiful; (3) the *Saṅkhini* is tall, neither stout nor thin, handsome, with long eyes and hair, marked on the neck with three lines, irascible, and with strong passions; and (4) lastly, the *Hastini*, short and stout, with broad hips, thick lips, curly hair, good natured, and amorous. Conf. Forbes, *Râs Mâlâ*. vol. I, p. 160 n., or 2nd ed. p. 123, n.

[3] The Ods are a low caste, whose occupation is that of excavating tanks.—K. Forbes, *Râs Mâlâ*, vol. I, p. 111, n.

Write a hundred thousand of Ods,
And of Odanis write half a lâkh;
Give to the hand of the Bhârat[1] the letter,—
Let him go and to Jasmâ deliver it."
The Bhârat arrived in Mâlawa land;
Women in line were drawing up water,—
"Where," asked he, "is Jasmâ's dwelling?"
"That I know not, O brother!
A little way onward enquire."
At the *Châwaḍî* play little children:
Of them he asked where was Jasmâ's house,—
"The lofty mansion towering up to the sky,
On the door hang festoons of pearls."
A silver seat for the Bhârat was brought:—
"How came you here?" he was asked.
"Our king to make a *talâv* has purposed,
And for you he has sent—therefore come."
"Rise maid! at the lamp-flame read the letter":—
"A hundred thousand Ods is here written,
Half a lâkh, is written, of Odanîs."
Then went there of Ods a *lâkh*,
And half a lâkh of Odanîs;
At the rendezvous (*kheḍa*) they dined at night;
Then they reached the land of the Râja;
To the Râja came the news of Jasmâ's arrival.

Râja: "For the Ods provide a place to live at the *ghandhâra;*
Give to Jasmâ an abode in our palace."
Jasmâ: "Fit place for your queens is the palace:
For us Odans *ghandhâros* are pleasant."
Râja: "To the Ods give *khichaḍi*[2] for food:
For Jasmâ to eat cook the *churmâ.*"
Jasmâ: "O king, to your princes give *churmâ*
For us Odans *khichaḍi* suits best."
Râja: "To the Ods give coarse cloths for beds,
But for Jasmâ prepare couches."
Jasmâ: "On couches, O King! sleep your queens:
For us Odans, *satharas* are pleasant."

Pradhân: "Jasmâ! show to us who is your *jeṭha*[3]
How may the king recognise him?"
Jasmâ: "He with the golden spade is my *jeṭha*
He with one of silver—my husband."

---

[1] Bard and herald; Sansk., *bhârata* and *bhâṭ;* in Gujarât he is often identified with the *chârana* and his personal security is sufficient for the payment of a debt.

[2] Dal and rice.

[3] Husband's elder brother.

Pradhân: "Which is your brother, and which your father?"
Jasmâ: "There! there stands my brother,
With his waist bound, near to my father."
Pradhân: "Which is your sister? Jasmâ, show us your mother."
Jasmâ: "Young is my sister, my mother is delicate."
Pradhân: "Which among these is your *naṇada*?[1]
Which call you mother-in-law?"
Jasmâ: "Dark is my mother-in-law, my *naṇada* brown."
Râja: "Jasmâ, lift little clay, that your waist do not bend."
Jasmâ: "O thoughtless king! do not foolishly talk!
Our business how can we neglect?"
Râjâ: "O Jasmâ! you are a Padminî;
Such labour for you is unfitting,
Come but to our dwelling,
As a queen, you shall have enjoyment,
I shall please you in all you desire."
Now the wind blew up the fringe of the dress of the fair
And her beautiful form was revealed,
The *chotlo* (chignon) of the beauty he saw;
Much wealth and five villages offered he,—
Still the request of the king was rejected.
Thereafter the king grew enraged,
And all the Ods put he to death.
A pile of sandal, Jasmâ got raised,
And all the Ods' bodies she burned.
Jasmâ "O king! why stare you aloft?
A golden sparrow flies there:
While burning myself, these words I pronounce—
'Eat, drink, but remain ever childless!'"

Jasmâ then cast herself on the pile,
And the king kept gazing upon it.

Another version relates that Jasmâ having left with her tribe, on the completion of the *talâv*, the râja pursued them to Moḍherâ, slaying some to get possession of Jasmâ who plunged a dagger into her bowels, cursing Siddharâja and saying the tank should hold no water. Returning he found it empty; and the Pradhân, on consulting the astrologers, informed him that if a man's life were sacrificed, the curse would be removed. This method of averting a curse is told in so many cases all over India that it was apparently resorted to not so very rarely. The Dheḍs or scavengers, from whom such victims were often claimed, then lived away from the towns, wore untwisted cotton round their heads and a stag's horn hung from the waist to distinguish them, so that they might be avoided. The king ordered that a Dheḍ named Mâyo should be beheaded in the tank, and as a reward the Dheḍ requested that his tribe should not

[1] Husband's sister; Sansk. *nanandâ*.

be compelled to live at a distance from the towns, nor wear a distinctive dress Those privileges were granted to the Dheḍs for the sake of Mâyo, and the tank then retained the water.[1]

About thirty-five years ago, the Ods—potters and brick-workers—built a small but neat temple to the memory of Jasmâ; it is not far from the Râṇî Wâv and is a Śaiva shrine.

When Bairâm Khân, the famous minister of Humâyûn, after rebelling against Akbar, was sent to Makkah, he came to Pâṭaṇ and was hospitably received here by Mûsâ Khân Fûlâdî, the governor. With his retinue, he encamped on the plain, and on Friday, 31st January 1561, when alighting from a boat, after a sail on the Sahasraliṅga tank, Bairâm was stabbed by Mubârik, a Lohânî Afghân, whose father had been killed in the battle of Mâchhiwârâ. His body was carried to the tomb of Shaikh Husâin-*al*-dîn, and seventeen years later it was interred in holy ground at Mashhad.[2]

As already mentioned, this great talâv no longer contains water; it has of course been largely silted up, but the porous nature of the sandy soil, and the erosion of the river which now skirts its north side, may have their share in it; whilst, like most other tanks of the kind, probably it was formerly filled from time to time through channels that are long since cut off.

Tomb of Shaikh Farîd, &c. (Plates XIV–XVII).

About a mile and a half north-west from Pâṭaṇ on the left bank of the Sarasvatî, and not far from the north side of the Sahasra-liṅga Talâv, stands the *dargâh* or shrine of Shaikh Farîd.[3] Though now the tomb of a Muhammadan saint, this was originally a Hindû or Jaina temple of considerable architectural merit (Plate XIV). The river on the north is now cutting round the back or south side of this group of buildings, and threatens ere long to insulate it entirely. The erosive action of the river has already undermined and brought down the east porch of one of the three structures. Of the group, two buildings are constructed in the usual Muhammadan style, namely, the mosque on the west of the tomb and another tomb behind that of Shaikh Farîd, seen in the view.

The latter seems to have been a large open *maṇḍapa* belonging to some fine temple that once occupied the spot. This structure had a small porch on both the east and west faces. That on the west has a very pretty carved roof in geometrical pattern, represented in Plate XV. That on the west, now fallen, had also a roof formed of three large slabs, which were recovered from the stream. Placed together they form one of the finest pieces of carved stonework, perhaps, in Western India, and is represented on Plate XVI, where it may be studied. The sculpture is bold and well cut, but owing to the friable nature of the stone and its

---

[1] *Râs Mâlâ*, vol. I, pp. 112, 113; or 2nd ed., p. 86.

[2] Blochmann's *Âîn-i-Akbarî*, p. 317.

[3] This individual is probably quite distinct from Shaikh Farîd i-Shakharaganj, whose tomb is at Ajhodhan near Pâk Pâṭaṇ in the Panjâb. Blochmann's *Âîn-i-Akbarî*, p. 325; *Ind. Ant.* vol. X, pp. 93, 154.

falling into the stream, it has sustained considerable damage. The design is that of a large scroll starting from a point in the circumference and flowing round and turning inwards in fine arabesque curls. The carving is raised nearly a foot from the surface of the slabs, and is so undercut that when in position it would appear pendent from the ceiling. This kind of florid scroll work was a favourite form of decoration with the Hindû workmen,[1] and we find the same sort of ornamentation in the cave temples,[2] the shrines in the Kanarese districts, and in old temples all over India. In the Bhulavaṇi temple at Śatruñjaya, which is partly one of the oldest temples now there, is a roof slab with the same design upon it, only on a smaller scale, but with proportional depth of cutting; and in Vimala Śâ's temple at Abû is another in marble, beautifully carved, about half the dimensions of this one at Pâṭaṇ.

Across the river from Shaikh Farîd's dargâh is another Muhammadan shrine—that of Báwa Qâzi or Bâwa Hâji, in which are some well carved ceilings. They have evidently belonged to a Hindû temple, and are represented on Plate XVII. The building is otherwise of no particular interest.

---

[1] This slab was represented on plate V of the *Technical Art Series of Illustrations of Indian Architectural Decorative Work*, Calcutta, 1888. See two fine specimens of similar work, from some Hindû temple, now in the Jâmi' Masjid at Aḥmadâbâd, in *Muham. Archit. of Aḥmadâbâd* (*Arch. Sur. W. Ind.* vol. VII) p. 33 and pl. xxxiv.

[2] *Cave Temples*, xlii, 2; xlix; lviii; lxvi, 3; lxxxiv; &c.; *Buddh. Cave Temples* (*Arch. Sur. W. Ind.* vol. IV), p. 57; *Elura Cave Temples* (*Id.* vol. V), pll. ix; xiii, 3; xxi, 1, 2; xxxi, 1, 2; xxxiii; *Id.* vol. I, p. 30 and pl. xl.

CHAPTER IV.

JAINA REMAINS—IMAGES, TEMPLES, &c.

Plates IV, XVIII–XXII.

FOREMOST among the few old images left at Pattana, and perhaps the best known, is the white marble figure of Vanarâja, to which reference has already been made. Its claim to be the original image of the traditions, we have seen, is not authenticated; and the much worn state of the two inscriptions below it and the adjacent statue of the *Divân*, prevent our learning much about its history. The figure of Vanarâja, bearded and with the *chhattra* or royal umbrella over his head, stands 3 feet 1½ inches high, and the awkwardness of the pose and want of art in the whole composition need not be described, as it is sufficiently manifest in the illustration No. 1. The figures of the king and of his *mantri* or minister Jamba, who stands against the returning wall on his right, are accompanied by several attendants, who are represented, as usual with subordinates, on a much smaller scale. The figures are all characteristically Jaina in detail and have no artistic merit. They are in one of the numerous cells that line the *bhrama* or circumambulatory passage round the back of the shrine in the temple of Pañchâsara-Pârśvanâtha.

1. Statue of Vanarâja at Pâtaṇ.

The temple stands in the middle of a block of houses and has no architectural features of any note about it. The maṇḍapa is open in the centre and, like most Jaina temples of the present day, is of gaily painted woodwork, and the shrine is cut off by a screen, through which is seen the row of white marble images. That of Pârśvanâtha, in the centre, is rather larger than life size, and is alleged to be the same that was brought to Aṇahilawâḍa by Vana-râja when he first established his capital here in Saṁ. 802. But it would be hard to believe that such an image could have escaped destruction at the hands of the Muslim conquerors for so many centuries, and that it was not merely a later *uddhâra* or restoration, as is the temple itself. But on the seat of the image is an inscription stating that in "Saṁvat 1652 (A.D. 1596) on Monday Vaiśâkha-śuddha 15th, Parika Sahasvira, an inhabitant of Pattan, caused the throne of Śrî Pârśvanâtha to be made: the ornament of the seat of Bhaṭṭâraka Śrî Hîravijaya Sûri,[1] Śrî Vijayasena Sûri of the Tapâgachha performed the installation."

There are also in the Gandharawâḍâ ward, in a small ruinous cell, a couple of old images:—of Umâ-maheśvara and Gaṇeśa. Under the former is a short inscription stating that in "Saṁ. 802 (A.D. 745) Chaitra sudi 2, Friday, Vanarâja installed Umâmaheśvara at Aṇahilapattana: prosperity." Under the other is a similar epigraph with the same date, and there is another of Gaṇeśa in a small temple outside the west gate—also dated Saṁ. 802. But the characters of all these inscriptions are of a date very much later than the ninth century, and, like the Jaina figures, they must be restorations or inventions of a later age.

The magniloquent Colonel Tod[2] went into ecstasies over "the skeleton arch of a noble gateway," that eighty years ago stood about a hundred and fifty yards from the Kâlikoṭ. "How," he asks, "has this arch escaped the general ruin? We can find no motive, but its intrinsic beauty, to account for its solitary towers, with the pure Hindû *Kaṅgaras* and embattled parapets, being untouched by Hindû and Tûrk. . . . There remain only the skeleton ribs from the spring to the apex, without a particle of loading; the pilasters supporting these ribs have lost nothing of their perpendicularity, and they are as firmly riveted to the masonry which supports them as on the day of erection. They are chaste and well-proportioned to the arch, and the capitals are purely Hindû, being ornamented with chain festoons, having the *vîra-ghaṇṭâ* or war-bell, the most ancient and general decoration of the columnar architecture of the Jainas, suspended by a chain between each festoon, like the columns at Baroli.[3] On each side, and about half-way up the segment of the arch, is the lotus." However we may discount the Colonel's theories, we cannot help regretting that this fine arch no longer exists: its very site is now forgotten. A few fragments of a *toraṇa* that may have belonged to such an arch lie uncared for near the market place.

In the Vahivâṭdâr's Kacheri enclosure are a few fragments of pillars and sculptures, saved from the general spoliation; but great quantities have been built into houses and walls, particularly into the *dharmaśâla* of Girdhar-râi Vaikuṇṭharâi and the temple of Nîlakaṇṭha Mahâdeva near the Gaṅgadi gate, where there are some richly carved and damaged old pillars; and the modern walls of the town are largely built of old materials. See Plates XIII, figs. 4–6, XVIII, figs. 2–7, for specimens of these fragments.

---

[1] This Hîravijaya, the pontiff of the Tapâ-Gachha, was born Saṁ. 1583, Mârgaśîrsha sudi, at Prahlâdanpura (Pâhlanpur); obtained *dîkshâ* in 1596, Kârtika vadi 2, at Pâṭaṇ; *vâchakapada* in 1608, Mâgha sudi 5, at Nâradapuri; *Sûripada* in 1610 at Sîrohî; and died 1652, Bhâdrapada sudi 11, at Umnânagara. The Jainas of the Tapâgachha division claim that he converted the emperor Akbar to their religion; but those of the Kharataragachha ascribe this to their contemporary pontiff, Jinachandra (Sam. 1612-1670). Hîravijaya was succeeded by Vijayasena, born S. 1604 at Nâradapurî; obtained *dîkshâ* 1613; and received from the emperor Akbar the *biruda* of Kâlîsarasvatâ; he died S. 1671, Jyeshṭha vadi 11, at Stambhatîrtha or Kambhâyat. *Ind. Antiquary*, vol. XI, p. 250, 256.

[2] *Travels in West. Ind.* pp. 224–27.

[3] Tod, *Annals of Rajasthan*, vol. II, p. 710; conf. Fergusson, *Picturesque Illust. of Hindu Archit.* pp. 35, 36; *Ind. and East. Archit.* p. 451; Burgess, *Archit. and Scenery in Gujarât and Râjputâna*, pp. 36, 37.

OLD JAINA TEMPLES, &c.

The temples of the Jainas in Pattana are said to number a hundred and eight or ten, among which that just mentioned of Pañchâsar Pârśvanâtha is one of the largest, while those of Nimeśvara or Naminâtha, Śântinâtha and Gautamasvâmi rank next, but none of them are of much architectural or archæological importance.[1] Still, in some of the older ones are found a few objects of interest. The temple of Sâmla Pârśvanâtha in Dhaṅgarwâḍâ has a beautifully tesselated marble floor; the pillars of the *maṇḍapa* are of wood; and the image is a large one, of black marble, without date.

Ṛishabhanâtha or Adîśvara, whose image in his temple in the Khaḍâkotri street in Pattana is represented on Plate XIX, was the first of the Tîrthakaras of the Jainas in the present æon, and is said to have lived more than a hundred billions of oceans of years ago—for the Jainas regard the world as eternal, and in their legends they revel in inconceivable periods of past ages.

The twenty-four Tîrthakaras, or Tîrthaṅkaras, are represented so identically alike that, without their special cognizances, it is almost impossible to distinguish the image of one from another. Generally they are carved in white marble, but the twentieth—Munisuvrata, and the twenty-second—Neminâtha—are said to have had black skins, and are, therefore, often carved in black marble; Mallinâtha, the nineteenth, and Pârśvanâtha, the twenty-third, are also said to have been dark blue (*nîla*), and their images also are often of black stone.[2] But the figures themselves are all exactly of one pattern, conventionally stiff, without art or grace, and, in Śvetâmbara temples, often with the eyes covered by lenses of rock-crystal, which give them a strange, unnatural appearance. The hair is carved in small round knobs or curls, as in statues of Buddha, and with the centre, or top-knot, raised like the *ushṇîsha* of the Buddha; but in place of his *ûrṇâ* between the eyebrows the Jina has a jewel. The bust is bare, with a breast-jewel (*kaustubha*) in the centre and small plates or shields on the two breasts. In the worship, certain points of the body are marked with *vâsa* paste—made from sandal or camphor, musk, amber and saffron[3]; the points marked are—the crown of the head, the forehead, the neck, the breast, the shoulders, the navel, the wrists, the knees, and the toes.

The images in the temples of the Śvetâmbara sect are represented with a cloth round the loins, the end of which comes out in front under the feet, which are crossed before the body, after the Bauddha fashion. The images of the Digambara sect of Jains are quite nude.

---

[1] The more notable places or shrines of the Jainas in Gujarât, as enumerated by Colonel Miles (1832), are,—(1) Śatruñjaya; (2) Girnâr; (3) Gaurî Pârśvanâtha in Thar and Pârkar, to the west of the Râṇ, but the image was brought, on occasions of pilgrimage, to Morwâḍa—18 miles N.W. of Râdhanpur; (4) Śaṅkha Pârśvanâtha in the village of Śaṅkheśvara; (5) Târiṇga; (6) Âbû; (7) Kumbhâriyâ near Ambâ in Dântâ; (8) Kâvi in Jambusar tâlukâ; (9) Narwâḍa, 5 miles north-west from Aḥmadâbâd; (10) Nawânagar; and (11) Aḥmadâbâd. *Tr. R. As. Soc.* vol. III, p. 348; conf. *ante*, p. 21.

[2] Of the first eighteen Tîrthakaras, fourteen are described as of golden complexion, two white and two red; and of the last six, two were yellow, two blue, and two black.

[3] *Ind. Ant.* vol. XII, p. 191, where a full account of the Jaina ritual is given. For some account of the Jaina sect, see Bühler, *Ueber die Indische Secte der Jaina* (Wien, 1887); and E. Washburn Hopkins, *Religions of India*, pp. 280-97.

The legends represent the earlier Tîrthakaras as of immense size and living for ages, but each in succession as smaller and of shorter life; thus Ṛishabha is said to have been 500 rods in height and to have lived 8,400,000 former (*pûrva*) or great years[1]; but Vardhamâna, the last Jina, was of ordinary human stature, and lived only seventy-two common years, dying, perhaps, in 527 B.C.

The Jaina mythology arranges the details respecting each of these beings in statistical form, giving the names, rank, and caste of each, names of their parents, dates and places of birth, consecration and death, stature, age, chief disciples, converts —male and female, ascetic and laic; sacred tree, guardian Yaksha and Yakshaṇî or *Sâsanadevî*, cognizance, &c. Among the twenty-four, five seem to be special favourites,—Ṛishabha, the first; Śânti, the sixteenth; and Nemi, Pârśva and Mahâvîra, the last three.

Ṛishabha they represent as having descended from a heavenly palace called *Sarvârthasiddha*,[2] where he had lived for thirty-three oceans of great years, and was born of Marudevî the wife of the *kulakara* or patriarch Nâbhi, in the city of Vinîtâ in the district of Kośala, whence he was called Kauśalika.[3] He belonged to the Kâśyapa gotra, and was born on the 8th day of the dark half of the month Chaitra. He had five epithets—Ṛishabha, Prathama-Râja or first king, Prathama-Bhikshâkara or first mendicant, Prathama Jina—first Jina, and Prathama Tîrthakara or first Arhat; he is also called Vṛishabhasena, Âdinâtha, Adîśvara, Âdibuddha and Śrî Yugâdijina or Yugâdîśa—lord of the Yuga or age.

He lived as a prince two millions of former or great years, and six million three hundred thousand as a king. He had several wives and a hundred sons; one wife, Sumaṅgalâ, bore to him as twins Bharata and his sister Brahmî or Bambhî, and another wife—Sunandâ—bore the twins Bâhubali and Sundarî. He gave kingdoms to all his sons, Kośala to Bharata, and Takshaśilâ to Bâhubali, and then took consecration (*dîkshâ*) as an ascetic. Bharata soon overcame his ninety-eight other brothers and seized their dominions; with Bâhubali he is said to have had a severe contest and on being defeated the latter betook himself to a religious life.

When he retired from public life, we are told that Ṛishabha—being incited by a Laukântika god, after fasting two and a half days in the dark half of Chaitra, when the moon was in the nakshatra Âshâḍhâ—he put on "a divine robe" and with four thousand nobles and Kshatriyas, who became Sâdhus with him, he left the town of Vinîtâ, followed by a train of gods, men, Asuras, &c., and became a houseless mendicant. For a thousand years he neglected his body, meditating on himself. Then on the 11th of the dark half of Phâlguna, when the moon was again in the Âshâḍhâ asterism, under a Vaṭa or Nyagrodha tree (the Indian fig or banyan)

---

[1] A *pûrva* year is 7,560 thousands of millions of common years—that is, a *pûrvânga* is 8,400,000 years, and a *pûrva* is 8,400,000 *pûrvângas*. Jacobi, *Jaina Sûtras*, part II, p. 29 n.

[2] Meaning "by whom all objects are effected"; this is also an epithet of Śâkyasiṁha or Buddha; Sarvârthasiddhi is a heaven or divine abode.

[3] See *Ratnasâra*, bhâg II, p. 708; Tawney's *Kathâkośa*, p. 192 f.; Jacobi's *Kalpa Sûtra*, p. 283. Colebrooke (*Essays*, vol. II, p. 208) gives Ayodhyâ as his birthplace; but though Ayodhyâ was, in later times, the capital of Kośala, the Jaina accounts may not accept this name as belonging to so very early an age.

outside the town of Purimatâla,[1] after having fasted three and a half days, he attained the highest knowledge or *kevala:* he was now a Jina, an Arhat and a Kevalin—an omniscient being. In this state he lived for ninety-nine thousand years. And, lastly, after a strict fast of six and a half days in the company of ten thousand monks, on the summit of mount Ashṭâpada, he died—became a Siddha, a Buddha, a Mukta, finally liberated. This Ashṭâpada seems to be understood by the Jainas as Śatruñjaya in Kâṭhiâwâḍ, which, among many other aliases, is called by that name and is specially sacred to Ṛishabha, as Girnâr is to Neminâtha.

Ṛishabha, we learn, had eighty-four Gaṇas or assemblies of followers each under a *gaṇadhara* or leader. His community consisted of eighty-four thousand Sâdhus or Śramaṇas; 300,000 nuns or Sâdhvîs, with Brahmî-Sundarî over them; 20,600 sages able to transform themselves; 12,650 professors (*vâdinî*); 9,000 Avadhijñâni--sages possessed of *avadhi* knowledge; 20,000 Kevalins; 12,750 sages of vast intellect[2]; 4,750 (*chaüdapûrvî*) sages who knew the fourteen *Pûrvaś*[3]; 350,000 Śrâvakas or male laics with Sreyâṁsa at their head; 554,000 Śrâvîkâs or female lay followers, with Subhadrâ at their head; and to these are sometimes added 20,000 male and 40,000 female disciples who had reached perfection, and 22,900 sages in their last birth.[4]

Ṛishabha's colour was golden; his Yaksha or familiar spirit was Gaumukha, who is represented on the front of the throne at his right hand with the head of an ox; and his Yakshiṇî was Chakreśvarî, placed at the other end of the throne or *âsana.* She has generally a shrine beside the temple of Ṛishabha.[5] His *chihna* or cognizance is the bull (*vṛisha*), which is carved on the front of the cushion on which he is seated. The Muni Puṇḍarîka was the first—*Prathama gaṇadhara*—or chief of his followers, and has usually a shrine beside, or in front of that of Ṛishabha; and as he finally became a Siddha on the 15th of the month of Chaitra, that day is a holiday with the Jains.

These and other similar details, with alterations only in the numbers, names, and dates, are repeated for each of the twenty-four Tîrthakaras.

It is interesting to note the close resemblances of the details in a shrine such as this with Bauddha images and their adjuncts. The wheel and deer under the seat are parallel with the symbol for Buddha's first sermon at Banâras[6]; the umbrella over the head, above which are dancing figures named *Yugalâya;* the standing attendants by the sides of the principal figures, &c. have all their counterparts in the decorations of the shrines of both sects. The upright figures represent the Arhat in his immobile position of penance in abandonment of bodily feeling, and are styled Kâyotsarga (Guj., *kausagiya*). On each side the outer pair of attendants are six small figures of Tîrthakaras, making up the twenty-four in all. Other small figures

---

[1] Jacobi, *Jaina Sûtras* (*Sac. Bks. E.* vols. XXII. and XLV.), pt. I, p. 283; pt. II, p. 57.

[2] In the state of mental perception which precedes the attainment of perfect knowledge. The *Ratnasâra* gives 12,750 as the number; the *Kalpa Sûtra*, apparently, 12,650.

[3] The whole body of original Jaina scriptures.

[4] Jacobi, *Kalpa Sûtra*, p. 284; and *Ratnasâra*, bh. II, pp. 708, 709.

[5] Gaumukha has also the cognizance or *chihna* of a bull, and Chakreśvarî that of a Garuḍa.

[6] Conf. *Cave Temples of India*, Plates xiv, fig. 1, and xxxv, fig. 1.

ANAHILAWÂḌÂ: INNER BALCONY IN VÂḌI PÂRŚVANÂTHA TEMPLE.

appear at the feet of the Kâyotsargas and at their ears, &c. The figure in front of the throne is probably the goddess Sarasvatî, and below her is the *dharmachakra* or wheel of the law, with a couchant deer on each side of it. The corners of the throne are supported by *siṁhas* or lions, giving this seat the name of *siṁhâsana*. Below are nine small figures representing the *navagrahâs* or nine planets.[1]

Turning now to the temple of Vâḍîpura-Pârśvanâtha in Jhaveri street, built in 1594, we find it covered by an elaborate and well carved roof (Plates IV, XX, XXI). It is in the form of a dome rising to the height of 11¼ feet, and 11 feet in diameter. Round it above, and completely enclosing the dome against bats and swallows, is a wire grating or cage. The roof is decorated in concentric circles with figures and bands of ornament, and has a lotus-shaped pendant hanging from the apex. Eight large bracket figures are placed at equal intervals round the inside. These are female musicians and dancers; and between each pair of these is a seated male figure with two attendants. These are the ashṭadikpâlas or eight regents of the points of the compass and are arranged in the ceiling according to their proper quarters,[2] and each with his *vâhana* or conveyance carved below his seat. Some fine carving, now much injured, has filled up the corners or spandrels of the octagonal roof, between the lowest circle of the dome and the lintels (Plates XX, XXI). Under the dome and helping to support it are four balcony windows, projecting inwards from each side of the apartment, which are very delicately worked. Lower still is a dado running round the four walls, and carved with musicians and dancers in niches, with rows of geese and other ornamental carving below. The rosettes in the spaces between the brackets below the window-sills are rich and effective (Plates IV and XX). All the carving, designs and figures, in this woodwork are precisely the same as are found in stone. With the Hindû workman, whatever was practicable in stone seems to have been regarded as equally so in wood, and *vice versâ*. In the group of figures on the ledge of the window-sill is Gaja-Lakshmî in the centre, with musicians playing and a couple of girls—hands joined and feet together—whirling round in true school-girl style.

Built into the wall of the principal maṇḍapa of this temple is a marble slab measuring 16½ inches across and 28 inches high, on which is a lengthy inscription in fifty-two lines, in almost perfect preservation. It opens with—

"Hail! may the glorious Jina Pârśva of Vâḍîpura, who resides in Pattana, ever grant wealth, prosperity, and eternal happiness to the builder of the temple (*chaitya*) of the community (*saṁgha*). In the temple of the glorious Pârśvanâtha of Vâḍîpura is this eulogy written, preceded by a genealogy of the venerable pontiffs (*gurus*) of the Bṛihat Kharatara (*gachchha*). Bowing to Arhat! In the reign of the Pâdishâh, the illustrious Akabbara, in the year 1651 after the era of the illustrious king Vikrama, on the 9th of the bright half of Mârgaśîrsha, on the civil

[1] The planets are styled *grahâs*, because they are supposed to "seize" or influence the destinies of men in a supernatural manner. The nine include sun, moon, five planets, and the ascending and descending nodes—Râhu and Ketu. They are sometimes represented over the door lintels of Hindu shrines, as at Anjar in Kachh. *Arch. Sur. Westn. Ind.* vol. II, p. 210.

[2] They are—Indra of the east, Agni or Vahni of the south-east, Yama of the south, Nairṛiti of the south-west, Varuṇa of the west, Marut or Vayu of the north-west, Kuvera of the north, and Îśa or Śiva of the north-east. Including Dharṇidhara of the nadir, and Soma of the zenith, they form the *Ûrdhvalokanivâsi*.

[3] *Notes of a Visit to Gujarât*, pp. 101, 115-20; *Epig. Indica*, vol. I. pp. 319-24.

day Monday (11th Nov. 1594) under the lunar asterism Pûrvabhadra, in a propitious hour, it (*the temple*) was first begun."

Then follows a list of the Yugapradhânas or pontiffs of the Kharatara-gachchha or school, to whom the temple belongs. It begins, about the end of the tenth century A.D. with—"(1) Uddyotanasûri, who, descending in an unbroken line from the ruler of the faith, the glorious lord Mahâvîra, made vihâras resplendent.[1] (2) Vardhamânasûri, who consecrated the temple built on mount Arbuda (Âbû) by the *daṇḍanâyaka* Vimala and worshipped the *sûrimantra* that had been corrected by the glorious lord Sîmandhara.[2]

"(3) Jineśvarasûri,[3] who in Saṁ. 1080 obtained the title (*biruda*) of Kharatara after overthrowing the Chaityavâsins in the Darbâr or court of Durlabharâja king of Aṇahillapattana. (4) Jinachandrasûri. (5) Abhayadevasûri, who, in consequence of a revelation from the guardian deity (*Śâsanadeva*) of the faith made known the image of Pârśvanâtha of Stambhanâ,[4] and thereby was freed from his loathsome leprosy, who obtained fame by composing the *Navângî* and other works.[5]

"(6) Jinavallabhasûri who awakened 10,000 Śrâvakas of the Vâgaḍa country,[6] by sending a letter consisting of ten *kulakas*, and exalted the Jaina doctrine by composing excellently written good poems and various *śâstras*, such as the *Piṇḍaviśuddhi*.[7] (7) Jinadattasûri, who by his power subdued the company of 64 Yoginis 55 Vîras (and ?) Pîras of Siṁdh,[8] who obtained the rank of Yugapradhâna by reading the golden letters written by Ambaḍa's hand, and by magic walked across the five rivers of the Panjâb.[9] (8) Jinachandrasûri, who awakened the illustrious Mahatiyâṇa chief (*pradhâna*) of the Usvâtas and other clans in Śrimâla, and had the *naramaṇi* (jewel) in his forehead."[10] Then follow these names of Sûris, mostly without any important remark:—(9) Jinapatti (S. 1223–1277), (10) Jineśvarasûri II. (11) Jinaprabodhasûri (1331–1341), (12) Jinachandrasûri III

---

[1] With Uddyotana's pupils originated the 84 gachchas of the Jainas. He died on a pilgrimage from Mâlava to Śatruñjaya—*Ind. Ant.* vol. XI, p. 248.

[2] Vardhamâna had been a pupil of the Chaityavâsin Jinachandra, but passed over to Uddyotana, and is the first Sûri peculiar to the Kharataragachchha. Sumatiganin (died A.D. 1221) represents that he went from Marudeśa to the court of Durlabha, and in a *râjasabhâ* held a debate with the Chaityavâsins who advocated the propriety of residing in temples. His opponent was Sûrâchârya, to whom he opposed his pupil Jineśvara. The Chaityavâsins were defeated and left the town, and Jineśvara received the title of Kharatara ("very keen"), and when he succeeded to the chief seat, this became the name of his sect. He wrote a *kathâ*, or story, in 1036 A.D.—R. G. Bhandarkar, *Report on Sansk. MSS.* 1882–83, p. 45 f. He consecrated Vimala Śâ's temple at Âbû in Saṁ. 1088.

[3] He was originally called Śiveśvara, the son of Soma, a Brâhman, and with his brother Buddhisâgara and sister Kalyâṇavatî, was converted by Vardhamâna—receiving his *dîkshâ* name of Jineśvara.

[4] Now Thâmna, on the Śeḍhi river, in the Ânanda tâluka of Kheḍi district.

[5] He was the son of Dhana, a *śreshṭhin* of Dhârâ, and Dhanadevi, and was originally called Abhayakumâra. He died at Kappaḍavaṇija in Gujarât. He wrote commentaries on *Samavâya* and *Bhagavatî* in Saṁ. 1128.—Klatt, *Ind. Ant.* vol. XI, *ut sup.*

[6] Kachh or Duṅgarpur.

[7] Jinavallabha was first a pupil of Jineśvarasûri, a Chaityavâsin of the Kûrchapuragachchha, and afterwards became a pupil of Abhayadeva. He was consecrated sûri in Saṁ. 1167 and died six months afterwards. R. G. Bhandarkar, *ibid*, p. 47, 48.

[8] *Chakradvipaṁchâśadvîra siṁdhudeśîya pîra.*

[9] He obtained the *Sûrimantra*, or was appointed Sûri, at Chitrakûṭa, Saṁ. 1169, and died at Ajmer 1211 (A.D. 1155).

[10] He was made âchârya in Saṁ. 1211, and died at Dehli Saṁ. 1223.

(S. 1341–1376), (13) Jinakuśalasûri (1377–1389), (14) Jinapadmasûri (S. 1400), (15) Jinalabdhisûri (1406), (16) Jinachandrasûri IV (1415), (17) Jinodayasûri (1415–1432), (18) Jinarâjasûri (1432–1461), (19) Jinabhadrasûri[1] (1475–1514), (20) Jinachandrasûri V (S. 1514–1530), (21) Jinasamudrasûri (1530–1555). And lastly we have:—(22) "Jinahaṁsasûri (Saṁ. 1555–1582) whom the illustrious Pâdishâh Sikandar (Bahlol, A.D. 1489–1510)—astonished at his austerities and meditation—honoured by releasing 500 prisoners. (23) Jinamanikyasûri (Saṁ. 1582–1612) who by magic crossed the five rivers of the Panjâb[2] and prevented (*or* warded off) through the power of his exceeding meditation a violent attack of the Yavanas (Muhammadans). (24) Jinachandrasûri VI, the ruling spiritual head, who conquered many opponents in disputations. He was called by the lord Jalâluddîna, the glorious Pâdishâh Akabbara, who was desirous of seeing him, having heard of his immeasurable greatness that unfolded itself in consequence of his stay at Stambhatîrtha (Kambhay) during the rains of Saṁvat 1648. He met the emperor, pleased him by the multitude of his virtues,[3] and obtained one edict (*phuramâṇa*) forbidding the slaughter of animals during eight days in Âshâḍha, and a second protecting the fish in the sea at Stambhatîrtha, as well as the title 'the most virtuous, glorious pontiff of the age' (*sattamaśrîyugapradhâna*). Further, at the command of the emperor, he crossed by magic the five rivers of the Panjâb[4] on the 12th lunar day of the bright half of Mâgha, Saṁvat 1652, and made five Pîras appear, by which feats he obtained the distinction of *paramavara*, &c., and exalted the Saṁgha. He was attended by Âchârya Jinasiṁha, on whom he had conferred the dignity of *âchârya* in the presence of the emperor Akabbara. By his advice the temple of Vâḍipura-Pârśvanâtha was built."

Then follows the genealogy of the founder of the temple, who belonged to the Osvâl clan and the line of the Mantrin Bhîma. Five predecessors and their wives are named, then Ratnakuṁyarajî, married to Sobhâgade. A sister, probably, of Ratnakuṁyarajî, named Bâî Vâchhî, and a daughter, Bâî Jîvaṇî, are also mentioned as co-founders of the temple. The image was consecrated in V. Saṁvat 1652, in the Allâî (Ilâhî) year 41, on the 12th lunar day of Vaiśâkha-vad, a Thursday, under the asterism Revatî, i.e., 13th May 1596.[5]

There are manuscript copies of this list of Jaina chiefs, but this epigraphic record is not without its historical interest.

Hindû Temples.

Among the Hindû temples are those of Kâlika Mâtâ and Sindhvâî Mâtâ. The first is just outside the Kansâro gate of the city on the north-west, in a grove of trees, where are also two towers, which are perhaps of considerable age. In front of them is the shrine, which has been restored in comparatively modern

[1] Jinavardhana had been appointed in 1461, but was deposed for misbehaviour and is not reckoned in the Paṭṭâvalî.

[2] Conf. No. 6 above.

[3] Conf. Elliot's *Hist. of India*, vol. V, p. 528.

[4] Conf. Nos. 6 and 23 above.

[5] *Epig. Indica*, vol. I, pp. 319–23; *Ind. Ant.* vol. XX, p. 141.

times, but with old materials—indeed nothing here seems to be built with aught else. In approaching the temple we come to a square, open canopy, over a figure of Hanumân, the monkey-god—as usual filthy with oil and red lead. This stands upon a bridge, across what was probably the old fosse. It consists of three arches —not exactly pointed, but with very sharp curvature at the apex, and having the voussoirs radiating. This leads to a gateway giving entrance to a court of no great age, which, with a smaller one to the left, forms a sort of dharmaśâla. In an enclosure to the right is the shrine—a small, low, temple containing Kâlikâ and Bhadrakâlâ in white marble; and in a recess is a small, dirty, marble figure of Ambâ Mâtâ. There is also a *jaladhara* with the representation of a human head in it, which the Brâhmans show as the head of Jagadeva Parmâr, which, legend says, the Mâtâ demanded and Jagadeva gallantly offered, in order that Siddharâja's life might be spared by the Fates. The story is of considerable interest, and is well told in Forbes's *Râs Mâlâ*.[1] This court is strewn with carved stones and into the walls are built some sculptured marble slabs.

To the left of these enclosures, and between the old towers, are the remains of another court, probably belonging to the old shrine—with loose blocks of stone lying about, of which some have been well carved.[2]

At the temple of Sindhvâî Mâtâ is a *pujâri* who possesses the copper-plate grant pretending to be from Vanarâja, to which reference has already been made as a comparatively recent forgery for the purpose of diverting certain octroi duties to the use of the shrine and its custodians.

The Bahâdur Singh Wâv, already mentioned, is an ordinary step well, within the city, built of materials carried off from the old Râṇi Wâv. It is plain, and of no particular merit, having five openings above besides the *bauḍi* or shaft for lifting water by means of a leather bag. Two storeys of the masonry are above the water, and on each side of the entrance is an inscription recounting the virtues of "Bhârot Śrî Bahâdur Singhji Jaskaran, a servant of Śrî Lâlaji" (i.e., of Vishṇu), who in Saṁvat 1862 (A.D. 1805), in the time of Gaikwâḍ Śrîmantrâv Śrî Ânandarâv Mahârâja Śrîmant Faṭhsingha, commenced the construction of this Wâv, which was completed by his son, Hematsinghabâi Trikamdâs, in Saṁ. 1868 (A.D. 1811) costing Rupees 14,925.[3]

Wood Carving.

Plates XXII and XXXVI.

Wood carving, as applied to the decoration of house façades, has long been, and still is prevalent in Gujarât. At Pâṭaṇ many beautiful specimens of this work may still be found, particularly in the houses of the late Bhârot Kahânji Umaḍsinghji in Khaḍa Khotaḍi's Mahallâ, and of a Vâṇiyâ in another quarter of the town (see Plates XXII and XXXVI). On these house fronts the decoration is generally confined to the upper storeys, the ground floor being left comparatively plain, and in many cases altogether out of keeping with the work so lavishly devoted to the upper portions of the façade.

[1] Vol. I, pp. 118–53. [2] *Notes of a Visit to Gujarât*, 1869, pp. 89–90. [3] *Ibid.* p. 97.

CHAPTER V.

MUHAMMADAN BUILDINGS AT PÂṬAṆ.

PLATES XXIII–XXXV.

THE earliest Muhammadan building of which we find mention is the Adinah or Jâmi' Masjid, built of white marble in A. Hij. 705 or A.D. 1305 by Alaf Khân, one of the first governors of Nahrwâlah—as the Muhammadans called Aṇahilavâḍa—and is spoken of as still existing in the middle of the eighteenth century.[1] Wicquefort in his translation of Mandelslo's travels[2] has added, apparently from Van Twist,[3] the statement that there was "in the midst of the city a Muhammadan mosque that had been built in former times by the heathen, being a beautiful and costly work supported on 1050 pillars of marble and other stone." And Thevenot in 1666[4] refers to the same building, and perhaps on the same authority, for he had not seen it, and seems to have confounded the old capital with Prabhâsa Pattan. He says "it is a great town" and "hath a fort and a very beautiful Temple wherein are many Marble pillars. Idoles were worshipped there, but at present it serves as a mosque." This building no longer exists, but the site, still pointed out, is outside the present walls of Pâṭaṇ, not far from the west gateway, and therefore within the limits of the old city, which extended still farther westwards. It is about a hundred yards behind or west of the rauza or dargah of Makhtûm Khân or Makhtûmji Sâheb—a *Pîr* or saint. At present there is a great trench or moat, forty feet wide and fifteen to twenty feet deep, running quite round and enclosing a rectangular platform, well raised, and measuring 400 feet from north to south by 330 feet from east to west. Across the west side of this area was the mosque, which, if we may judge from the trench out of which the foundation stones of the building seem to have been dug, was about 90 feet deep and extended the whole width of the platform. This would, then, have been the largest mosque in northern Gujarât, and—as the *Mirât-i Ahmadî* puts it—"the pillars of the same, as known to common people, are so numerous that one often makes a mistake in counting them. They also relate that it was once an idol temple, converted into a mosque; but it is, in short, a wonderful and noble building, which was then in the centre of the city, though now distant from the part inhabited."[5]

[1] *Ante*, p. 36.

[2] Wicquefort, *Relat. du Voy. d'A. Orlearius*, &c. (Paris, 1659), tom. II, p. 103 f. Davies's *Mandelslo* (1662), p. 62; Harris, *Collection of Voyages and Travels* (Lond. 1774), vol. I, p. 765.

[3] *General Beschrijvinge van Indien*, door Jan van Twist (Amsterdam 1648), p. 16. Van Twist was head of the Dutch factories in Gujarât. Ogilby, in his *Asia*: the first part (1673), p. 214, has copied from the same source or from Davies's translation of Wicquefort, but he has 150 instead of 1,050 pillars. I owe the above information and extracts to Mr. Wm. Foster of the India Office.

[4] Not 1606, as the *Baroda Gazeteer* has it, p. 604. *Travels of M de. Thevenot* (fol. Lond. 1687), pt. iii p. 32.

[5] Bird's *Mirât-i Ahmadî*, p. 163 f.; *Notes of a Visit to Gujarât*, p. 85.

These accounts show that this once famous structure had been a Hindû or Jaina temple, but simply altered to convert it into a mosque,[1] a work of no great difficulty. Its immense size, as indicated by the number of pillars, is in favour of this idea. A Muhammadan Vazîr would hardly have undertaken to construct a masjid requiring a thousand columns, even though he could count on getting so many from the temples of the subjugated people. And at a later date we find one of the Aḥmad Shâhî kings turning the temple of Somanâth into a mosque, while destroying only the back wall and *śikhara*. And the pity is that this building, which survived apparently till the middle of the eighteenth century, should have been so recklessly destroyed by the Marâṭhas, and made a quarry for material with which to build the modern town walls.

The numerous stones that still lie, half buried in the site, are all fragments from old Jaina or Hindû work. Toward the north side of the courtyard, in front of where the mosque stood, was an underground cistern or tank, some of the vaulted chambers of which still remain. The whole area occupies the highest spot of ground on this side of the city; and if surrounded by a moat it might on an emergency have sheltered a large number of troops.

The Gumaḍa Masjid is a very simple building, in the usual form of Gujarât mosques, built in the trabiate style with pillars and lintels only (Plates XXIII to XXVI). It is not constructed, as the earlier mosques generally are, of Hindû columns, but of pillars and beams dressed expressly for the building. (See Plate XXV, 1, for the pattern of the pillars.) The lower sections of the minârs are of carved work (Plate XXIII, 2, XXIV, and XXV, 3, 4) after the style of several at Aḥmadâbâd belonging to the fifteenth century, but the upper portions, above the roof, are of brick and plaster. The cornice and *kângaras* are in the usual style.

In the sandstone of which the walls are built are hard or flinty nodules, about two inches in diameter; and when these occurred on the surface of a stone they have been left by the masons as small protuberances—rather than spoil their tools in dressing them down. These from their supposed resemblance to boils or ulcers (*gumaḍuṅ*) have given the name "Gumaḍa" to the masjid. People afflicted with boils come and anoint these stone "boils" with *guṛ* (molasses) in expectation that by this charm their sores will be cured.

The mosque is quite open in front, measuring 65 feet in length inside and 26 feet deep, inclusive of the front pillars. These six pillars with the pilasters in antis, divide the façade into seven bays, and, with two other rows and the pilasters along the back wall, give three aisles in the length of the mosque (Plate XXIII). In the back wall are three *mihrâbs* or *qiblas*, with oblong interiors, neatly and not too elaborately carved. Over the central *miḥrâb* (Plate XXV, figs. 2, 3) is a Persian inscription in four lines, recording the erection of the mosque.

Behind the *miḥrâbs* on the back wall are buttresses, on which, as usual, much pains have been bestowed in carving them with numerous horizontal

[1] Mr. Fergusson has indicated how this might readily have been done. *Ind. and East. Archit.* p. 264. And in the case of the Sûryakuṇḍa, an interesting structure at Verâwal, we have a mosque formed from an old Hindû temple, which, including the cloisters, has about 260 pillars. *Notes of a Visit to Somnâth, &c.*, p. 22 f.

PLATE V.

ANAHILAVĀDĀ-PAṬṬANA: NORTH SIDE OF KHĀN SAROVAR TANK

mouldings and stepped off in vertical lines to add to their effect (Plate XXIII, 3, 4). In the back wall are three windows, each about 2 ft. 5 in. wide, filled with stone lattice work in square compartments, of which two are represented on Plate XXVI, figs. 1, 2, presenting patterns of perforated work similar to what we find so abundantly at Aḥmadâbâd. In the north wall is the stair leading up to the roof and two windows; and in the south end are three—of which the central one is about 3 ft. 8 in. wide; but these have no lattices in them now —if ever they had.

The masjid known as the Ghazni mosque is quite a modern building and has nothing of interest about it. The masjid of Shaikh Jodh, now partly in ruins, is near the wall in the south quarter of the town (Plates XXVII and XXIX). It is a large, lofty, and well-proportioned building, measuring 122 feet in length and is constructed chiefly of pillars from old Hindû temples—stilted to give them height and surmounted by a wood and concrete roof. The back and end walls are of brick faced with plaster. There being eleven bays in the front of three aisles deep, there are five miḥrâbs in the back wall, and these (excepting the old Hindû pillars) are the only decorated parts of the building, and are but sparingly ornamented (Plate XXVIII). They are of the usual type, and the central one has a recess above for an inscription slab that has disappeared. There is one window only in each end, and the stair up to the roof is outside the north wall—an arrangement unusual in the mosques of Gujarât, though we find it in the case of the great Jâmi' Masjid at Jaunpur of the middle of the 15th century. The façade is arched, but as shown in the section (Plate XXVII, 2) the pillars inside are carried up to the roof. They are widely spaced and are connected above by wooden beams on which rest rafters and boarding which support a thick concrete roof. The pulpit has disappeared, eleven of the pillars in the south end have come down and the greater part of the roof. In the front court, towards its north end is a dargah, 21 feet square, covered by a dome, and containing three graves.

Outside the walls, to the south of the town, are several Musalman tombs, known as the Rauzas of Muhammad Tahir, of a Qâzi, of Shaikh Sarab, &c. (Plate XXX). The domes of these are supported on old sculptured Hindû pillars of white marble. On the capital of one of these (Plate XIII, figs. 2, 3) is a short inscription in Devanâgari recording the setting up of the column by the wife of Âjâyad in Saṁvat 1256.

THE KHÂN SAROVAR.

PLATES V, XXXI–XXXIV.

The Khân Sarovar is the largest tank still in use at Pâṭaṇ and is a really noble sheet of water, situated just outside the somewhat imposing south gate of the town on the road to Chânsama. It is nearly square, measuring 1228 feet from north to south by 1273 feet from east to west. Stone steps descend to the water and the masonry is still in a fair condition. On its margin are some Hindû and Muhammadan buildings, such as a temple of Becharâji, a temple built by Damâji Gaikwâḍ, the ruins of a large and fine Îdgah, and some others.

Originally this reservoir may have been the work of some of the Solaṅki kings, but if not originated, it was completely renovated by Khân i 'Azam Mîrzâ 'Azîz Kokah, the foster brother of Akbar, who, on the conquest of the country, made him governor of Gujarât as far as the Mahindrâ river, a post which he held at that time for two or three years. And he was re-appointed towards the end of the 34th year of Akbar (A.D. 1589) in succession to Mirza 'Abdurrahim Khân Khânân and held the position for five years till 1594.[1] It was during this second period that the reservoir was constructed. It is placed in the course of the stream and the supply waters pass first under a small bridge into a large, circular, tank, and then through the columns of a second bridge and along a well-built channel to another basin of sixteen sides, whence a short masonry-lined channel, nearly 21 feet wide, leads to the sluice discharging into the *sarovar* or lake (Plates XXXI and XXXIV). A platform about 21 feet wide covers the lower end of the channel and is supported by the front wall of the sluice, 9 feet thick, and by four pillars. The inlets are three circular openings through the front wall, each 5½ feet in diameter. Over the front is a stone rail connecting two small pavilions that stand on the ends of the massive wall. On the south-west is the outflow or waste-weir (Plate XXXII), with three openings, separated only by pillars of Hindû workmanship and certainly of older date than the end of the sixteenth century. By this arrangement the water is prevented from rising above a certain height during the rains, when the river flows.

The four sides of the talâv are lined with stone steps, leading down from the broad platform that surrounds the reservoir to the water's edge, and at intervals on each side are broad flagged slopes for cattle (Plate V).

Near the east end of the north side is the modern substantial Śaiva temple (Plate V) built by Damâji Gaikwâḍ in 1766–67.

In the construction of this Talâv, abundance of material from old temples has been used, especially in the inlet and overflow sluices. In the former, in the covered chamber behind the three inlets, are built into the wall some very old and boldly carved pilasters. They are short and heavy looking but the work has been executed with freedom and decision of outline (Plate XXXIII, 4). The execution and style are akin to what we meet with in cave architecture, and might belong to the eighth or ninth century. Similar, and of the same class of work, are the pillars, already referred to in the outlet sluice on the other side of the tank (Plate XXXIII, 1, 2, 5, and 6): the columns and architraves have evidently been taken from some temple of considerable age and importance.

A mile from the Khân Sarovar s the curious maze or labyrinth called Padmanâth—said to have been bestowed on the potters of Nahrwâlah also by Khân 'Azîz Kokah,[2] in gratitude for the cure of an ulcer from which he was suffering, effected by a Kumbhâr or potter. As a reward the man asked this

---

[1] Blochmann, *Âîn-i Akbari*, pp. 325 f.

[2] So the compiler of the Baroda volume of the *Bombay Gazetteer*, p. 604; but my informants in 1869 ascribed it to Khân Mîrza 'Abdurrahim Khân Khânân, who was Subahdâr (1576-1589).—*Notes of Visit to Gujarât*, p. 90 f.

piece of ground on which to form *tulasi kyâras*—beds for sacred basil. It is of considerable extent, and the walks are eight feet wide or more, and are cut to some four or five feet below the level of the plots which are covered by a dense growth of trees as well as of tulasi plants. This Padmanâth Kumbhâr is now looked upon as an incarnation of Vishṇu,[1] and has many followers, who worship him under the symbol of the tulasi plant. The potters still ply their trade at this place.

[1] Padmanâbha is a name of Vishṇu, but in an old inscription at Gwâlior he is also called Padmanâtha; see below, pp. 63, 64.

CHAPTER VI.

SIDDHAPUR.

PLATES VI, XXXVII-XLVI.

THE town of Siddhapur lies seventeen miles farther up the Sarasvatî river than Aṇahilavâḍa-pattana, being slightly to the north of east from it, and sixty-four miles north of Aḥmadâbâd. It is prettily situated on a rising ground on the west or north-west bank of the river which, after a slight turn to the north-west here, flows south past the town, and then resumes its south-westerly course through the sandy plain of northern Gujarât.[1] The Sarasvatî river, of which the name was perhaps transplanted from northern India,[2] is sacred to the goddess of eloquence and wisdom; and wife of Brahmâ[3]; and at Siddhapura, where the stream is supposed to turn to the eastwards (as much as southwards) or towards the rising sun, it is considered particularly holy. As the *pitṛiyajña* or *pitṛimedha*—the obsequial offerings to the paternal Manes must be made at Gayâ or at Prayâga, so the corresponding offerings to the maternal ancestors have to be performed at Siddhapur. This makes it, to a large extent, a Brâhmaṇ town; and hence on the level banks of the stream to the south-east is a striking foreground of convents used by Śaiva devotees and Gujarâti Brâhmaṇs—the Tîrthâdhikâris or priests for the *Śrâddha* ceremonies.[4] Among these buildings the handsomest is that constructed by Ahalyâbâi (1795), the widow of Khaṇḍerâv Holkar.[5]

The ancient name of the place appears to have been Śrîsthala or Śrîsthalaka (place of fortune or holy place), and possibly it may have been the Brâhmaṇs whom Mûlarâja brought from northern India, that applied to it the name of Siddhapura[6]—"city of the perfected." Legend ascribes the change of name to the twelfth century, when Jayasiṁha Siddharâja completed the great temple of Rudra Mahâdeva, and the name of Siddhapur was then given in honour of him. The Brâhmaṇs affirm that, "of all places of pilgrimage the greatest is Śrîsthala—so great sages of old have declared. It is the giver of all wealth[7]; he who but

---

[1] For a description of Siddhapur as it was forty or fifty years ago, see Kinloch Forbes's *Râs Mâlâ*, vol. I, p. 62 f. An edition of this admirable work, revised and corrected by recent discoveries and well illustrated, deserves to be published.

[2] The Sarasvatî of the Purâṇas is a tributary of the Gharghara or Gaggar, on which are the towns of Thâneśvar and Pehnvâ.

[3] Unlike most other Hindu Devatâs, she is usually represented with only two arms.

[4] These priests are not much respected by other Brâhmaṇs, and, like the Gayâwats of Behâr, they subsist on what they can squeeze out of the pilgrims. Conf. *Statistical Account of Bengal*, vol. XII, pp. 35, 49, 77; Montgomery Martin, *Eastn. India*, vol I, pp. 52 ff.

[5] Conf. Sir J. Malcolm, *Memoir of Cent Ind.* vol. I, pp. 14, 186; *Ind. Ant.* vol. IV, pp. 346 f; *Arch. Sur. Wn. Ind.* vol. III, p. 82.

[6] See grant of Mûlarâja, A.D. 986, *Ind. Antiq.* vol. VI, p. 192. Siddhapura in the astronomical works is the name of a fabulous city the antipode of Laṅkâ.—Albiruni's *Indica*, Sachau's tr., vol. I, pp. 267, 268, 303, 304.

[7] See *Ṛigveda*, i, 89, 3; i, 164, 19.

beholds it attains liberation. At Gayâ, heaven is three leagues distant; at Prayâga, a league and a half; at Srîsthala, a cubic only—there where Sarasvatî travels eastwards." And they have a song about it which runs:—

Tirath bhûmipâvan Siddhakshetra subhasâr,
Nirmal nir vahe Sarasvatî sada moksh-ko dwâr, &c.

"A Tîrtha, a place to make clean is the good Siddhakshetra,
Where flows Sarasvati's pure stream—ever beatitude's door.
A city three worlds to purify, by Siddhs ever adored.
Gods, Rishis and men have desire to live there.
And there dwell Devas unnumbered, as a *tîrtha* regarding it.
Of Kâsi, Gayâ, Godâvarî, and all other tîrthas, the best,—
Where Kardam and Dehuti lived, and Kapila[1] was born.
Here is Bindusarovar's pure fount and Mâtṛigayâ;
Applied to the bodies of men defiled and fallen,—it washes their myriads of sins.
Here is Prâchi Mahâdeva, whose renown by Veda and Purâṇa is sung:
Of all Tîrthas, the essence—is that named Kapilâśram."

The *mâtṛiyajña* is performed at the hermitage of Kapila or Kapilâśrama—about two miles west of the town, where are three sacred waters—the well called Jñânavâpikâ, and the tanks Alpasarovara and Bindusarovara or Vindusaras. By bathing in the last and using its water in *śrâddha* ceremonies, the Brâhmaṇs say that Paraśurâma, who had cut off the head of his mother Reṇukâ, was purified from his guilt; and from then it became a fixed rule that every Hindû should perform such ceremonies to satisfy his mother's spirit.[2]

In the tenth century Mûlarâja began to embellish Śrîsthala by the erection of the famous Śaiva temple known as the Rudramahâlaya, of which the gigantic fragments that still remain impress the beholder with admiration at the scale and grandeur of the conception. In his youth Mûladeva had slain his maternal uncle Sâmantasiṁha, usurped his throne, and put to death his mother's kindred; and in his old age his crimes hung heavily on his mind. He made pilgrimages and sought the ghostly advice of Brâhmaṇs from far and near. To a band of them he gave Srîsthala, and handing over the government to his son Châmuṇḍa, he retired thither to end his days in their company (A.D. 996).[3]

Early in his reign, about A.D. 944, Mûlarâja had founded the Rudramahâlaya, but it had been interrupted by invasions and other causes, and though used, it remained incomplete, and during the following two centuries it probably fell into ruin. But the work was taken up by the great Siddharâja Jayasiṁha, who probably reconstructed the whole on a scale vastly surpassing that originally

---

[1] A Ṛishi and incarnation of Vishṇu.

[2] For an account of the ceremonies, see *Ind. Antiq.* vol. XIII, pp. 282 ff., conf. *Râs Mâlâ*, vol. II, pp. 375 ff.

[3] *Notes of a Visit to Gujarât*, pp. 62, 63. If not the same as the temple built by Mûladeva, there was here a notable shrine called Svayaṁbhu-Mahâkâladeva, that was wrecked by some invader styled Kshapâtâdhipa in Siddharâja's time. Hemachandra, *Dvyâśraya*, s. xii, in *Ind. Ant.* vol. IV, p. 235.

contemplated, and the great work was scarcely finished at the time of his death in 1143 A.D. So far as can now be made out, it covered an oblong of about 230 feet by 300, in the centre of which stood the temple—two or three storeys in height, with a maṇḍapa 50 feet square inside, having porches on the east, north and south sides and the shrine on the west. In or round the court were eleven other shrines to the Rudras.[1] The court was perhaps surrounded by small cells after the manner of some of the Jaina temples,[2] with the principal entrance on the east and a ghâṭ or flight of steps down to the Sarasvatî river on that side. Of this splendid temple—ruthlessly demolished by the Muhammadans—first under Ulugh Khân in 1297 or 1298, and further by Aḥmad Shâh in July 1415—only a few magnificent fragments remain, the four pillars of the north porch, and five of the east porch to the *maṇḍapa*—one being an engaged pillar inside the door, four pillars in the back of the maṇḍapa, a beautiful *Toraṇa* or *Kîrttistambh*—and one cell at the back of the court; also a number of pillars and the doors of three other cells—possibly all *in situ*—which have been turned into a mosque about 57 feet in length.

Colonel Tod[3] says he found two inscriptions—one mentioning the founding of the temple in Saṁ. 998, and the other its completion by Siddharâja in Saṁ. 1202, 4th of Mâgha, krishṇa paksha. These are no longer to be found, but a *Kavita* or Gujarâti ballad to which he refers is still repeated among the people. It says:—

"Mûladeva, of the Châvaḍa race reached the rank of a king:
The beneficent, subject-protector, ever liberal of mind;
Houses, land, and wealth he gave; ever to others doing good.

. . . . . .

So prospered Mûladeva Mahârâja, having over his head the umbrella:
His lustre shone like the sun, and cooler than even the moon,
Than Indra more powerful, and bestowing more pleasure than Magha,[4]
Gifts like Karṇa's gave he, and greater than Vikrama was he,
To remove the sorrows of others than Sâgara more generous;
Than Kubera more wealth he amassed in his dwelling;
Truth, Harischandra-like, he observed; and forgave as the Earth,
Greatly admired was the fame of Mûladeva Mahârâja.

. . . . . .

Beholding the land of the gods,[6]—to the Mahârâja it was pleasant;—
Calling Brâhmaṇs from far, a glorious work he began,

---

[1] The modern title of Rudramâlâ is derived from *Rudra-Mahâlaya*--the great Rudra temple, or Rudra-prâsâda, as it is styled by the Jaina chroniclers. That there were eleven shrines is stated in the *Kavita* quoted below.

[2] This arrangement is not usual in modern Hindu temples; but in some of the larger ones in eastern and southern India it still exists, and the remains of such an arrangement is found at the old temple of Virupâksha at Paṭṭadkal.

[3] *Travels in W. Ind.* p. 142. In 1869 I found three or more less obliterated inscriptions at the east entrance; *Notes of a Visit to Gujarat*, pp. 66, 67.

[4] *i.e.*, Varuṇa, supplicated to show his wide and deep benevolence. Muir, *Sansk. Texts*, vol. V, p. 64.

[5] Pṛithivî.

[6] Devadeśa—the holy land—an epithet of Gujarât: *Râs Mâlâ*, vol. I, p. 9.

Wealth untold, land and clothing he gave, and there took up his happy abode.
Then summoning all Vipras,[1] villages and garâs[2] he bestowed;
To eat and drink made them welcome, and to high offices raised them:
Honour increased to the Brâhmaṇs; — His name through four ages endures.
Well was Rudra-mâlâ begun by Mûladeva Mahârâja.
Years many passed, but unfinished still was the work.

. . . .

But then, in the line of Solanka, came Siddharo-râja,
Rudra-mâlâ who finished,—the *pratishṭha*[3] performing.
By the birth of Siddha, Siva an *avatâra* became;
At Pattanpur ruled he—the god-like, the generous.

. . . .

Like Lankâ, his city was beauteous with youth in their bloom;
There lived the eighteen varied castes, all prosperous and happy—
The Brâhmaṇ reciting his Vedas, the Kshattriya—brave in the battle.
The Vaiśya devoted to trading, to service the Śûdra.
One the other excelled, enjoying wealth and prosperity.
Thieves and backbiters—how could they live there,
Where the orders of Siddharâja were proclaimed?
In Saṁvat ten hundred, begun by Mahârâja Mûladeva,
In Saṁvat twelve hundred and two, Siddharâja completed the work;
In Saṁvat twelve hundred two, Mâgh month, kṛishṇa paksh,
On Monday the fourteenth, in the Nakshatra Śrâvaṇa and Variyas yoga,
Siddharâja in the Rudra-mâla, Sivaśankara established.

. . . .

"Columns sixteen hundred adorned it.
Eighteen thousand images set with rubies and pearls,
Gold brocade flags floated and pennons thirty thousand
Kalaśas of gold, to deck it out seventeen hundred,
Fifty six lâkhs of horses, and elephants formed a line.
Carved screens a lâkh and a quarter were there,
And of resting places seven thousand two hundred;
Siddharâja Jayasiṁha, for the Rudra-mâla Prâsâda,
Fourteen *Karors* of Mohars, for the cost, put on paper.[4]

. . . .

---

[1] Praisers, Brâhmaṇs.

[2] An assignment of land for maintenance; in early times a religious endowment. See *Râs Mâlâ*, vol. I, pp. 63-65.

[3] Installation or inauguration.

[4] Colonel Tod, in 1822, had this metrical account "spouted" to him by "Śankla the chronologist"; and in 1869, this man—Śankla Jivasukrâm Pâdhya,—was still alive as a very old man. It was from his nephew that I obtained the Gujarâti ballad here partly translated. Tod speaks of "1600 columns: 121 statues of Rudra, each in its separate cella: 121 golden pinnacles (kalaśa): 1800 smaller statues of other divinities: 7212 resting places in and about the temple: 125,000 carved screens: and of other *putlis* or images, viz. of heralds bearing flags, heroes, demigods, mortals, or animals, thousands and tens of thousands." *Travels in W. India*, p. 142. The differences may readily be accounted for, as there are often variations in the versions of such ballads.

"Rudra-mâlâ shone like the Kailâsa of Śiva
Gems, rubies, and diamonds, set in it, sparkled like lamp-flames,
Covered with gold, like the mountain of Meru;
Inlaid with gems were the doors of it,
Festoons filled with pearls were there;
Studded with screens and with lattices,
The Maṇḍaps on its four sides were rendered attractive.

. . . . . .

"Four doors on four sides and Maṇḍaps three, I describe;
Other shrines all around it, numberless shine;
The varied works appear to the eye most enchanting.
In the midst, to great Rudra, eleven shrines he erected.
Siddhasiṁha, with the Brâhmaṇs there meeting together,
For its name 'Rudra-mahâla' established,—
Gananané, in the midst, sounds the naubat, the cymbal *gananané*,
Gananané, re-echoes the bell, till the ear is stunned by the sound."

The Jaina chronicles can hardly be expected to devote much attention to the Hindû shrines, but Merutuṅga[1] has this notice:—"Then, once on a time, Siddharâja, being desirous of building the temple of Rudramahâkâla in Siddhapura, established a certain architect in his entourage," and as already stated[2] the temple was completed, and decorated with statues, among which was one of himself with his hands joined in an attitude of supplication.[2] And the orders which he is said to have given respecting the lowering of the flags on all Jaina temples seem to indicate that the temple was dedicated in Siddharâja's lifetime, perhaps in Saṁ. 1198, and not in 1202 as the *Kavita* says, for he died in Saṁ. 1199 or A.D. 1143.

The shrine was sacred to Mahâkâla or Mahâdeva called Rudra "the howler, the terrible," who is spoken of in the Vedas under many names and attributes. He is the god of storms, the father of the Maruts or Rudras. Besides Rudra he has the seven other names of Bhava, Îśâna, Bhîma, Paśupati, Śarva, Ugra, and Mahâdeva; and these names are sometimes used for Śiva himself and at others for the seven manifestations of him, which are called his sons.[3] He was worshipped under the form of the Liṅga.[4] In the Trimurti or triad, Rudra occupies the third place with Brahmâ and Vishṇu, and in the five-faced Śiva he has the same position,—Maheśvara and Sadâśiva being added to the triad.

The eleven Rudras of later mythology are sometimes represented as sons of Kaśyapa and Surabhî, or of Rudra and Pṛiśni, but their names vary considerably in different *Purâṇas*, being selected apparently at will, from the numerous epithets

---

[1] *Prabandhach.* Tawney's transl. p. 90; conf. Bird, *Mirât i Ahmadi*, p. 157; *Râs Mâlâ*, vol. I, p. 116.

[2] *Ante*, p. 14, Merutuṅga says:—*Trayoviṁśatihasta pramâṇa paripûrṇa prâsâde 'śvapatigajapatipati-narapatiprabhṛitinâm uttamabhûpatinâm mûrtiḥ kârayitvâ tatpuro yojitañjaliṁ svâṁ mûrtiṁ nirmâpya deśabhange 'pi prâsâdasyâbhaṅgam yâchitavân.*

[3] *Ṛigveda*, viii, 28, 5; Muir, *Sansk. Texts*, vol. IV, p. 305.

[4] Muir, *ib.* pp. 404 ff.

of Śiva: the *Vâyu* gives them as,—Ajaikapâd, Ahirvradhna, Hara, Nirṛita, Îśvara, Bhuvana, Aṅgaraka, Ardhaketu, Mṛityu, Sarpa, and Kapâlin.[1]

If the central shrine then were dedicated to Mahâkâla or *the* Rudra, there may have been eleven other surrounding chapels appropriated to these manifestations. In the *Purâṇas*, the Rudras are spoken of as very numerous, and the statement reported by Colonel Tod of eleven times eleven statues of these divinities is not otherwise improbable; but it is apparently an exaggeration, for though the court were surrounded by cells, it is difficult to see how there could be room for more than half this number—unless there was a double *bhamti* or cloister.

What remains of this great shrine is indicated on Plate XXXVIII, which is Mr. Cousens's restoration of the plan. The portions in black at A, B, C, E, G and H are what remain of the original; the parts hatched are restorations, and the tinted areas are occupied by modern houses. The four pillars, at C, have a lintel lying upon them 27 feet long on the west face, but bevelled on the east as if forming the side of an octagon (Plates VI and XXIX). This lintel is 3 feet 8 inches thick, and over a sculptured string-course that has lain upon it stand other two pillars supporting a second lintel, the upper edge of which is 42 feet from the ground. From the arrangement of the other fragments, this could only have formed the inner side of the great maṇḍapa in front of the antechamber to the shrine. Mr. Kinloch Forbes made this antechamber of small size—about 23 feet by 11—which is perhaps too little; Mr. Cousens would make it about 42 feet by 17, with eight pillars on the floor, which is larger than might be expected; and it is so unusual to place columns in this situation that probably there were none—the front of the shrine forming the back wall of the antechamber or *antarâla*. Mr. Cousens's arrangement of the shrine, D, is more satisfactory, however, than Mr. Forbes's, for the *bhrama* or circumambulatory passage, in so large a temple, was likely to be of some width and lighted from outside. In the restoration of such a shrine we must necessarily be influenced by the remains of others of similar age. But the Muhammadan invasions of Gujarât and Râjputana were particularly destructive of all the finer Hindû works, and the remains of the Vaishṇava temple of Padmanâtha at Gwâliar, erected in A.D. 1093, or at the commencement of Siddharâja's reign, is almost the only one of a like type to which we can refer. Its maṇḍapa, as may be seen in the illustration No. 2,[2] is of three storeys—the porticoes being of two,—and it is not improbable that this temple was similarly

[1] Another list names the last eight as—Virupâksha, Sureśvara, Jayanta, Bahurûpa, Trayambaka. Aparâjita Vaivasvata and Sâvitra. The *Mâtsya* agrees with the *Vâyu* in the first four and last names, but has Pingala, Dahana, Aparâjita, Mṛigavyâdha, Senânî and Sajja for the others. Elsewhere we find the names of Manyu, Manu, Mahinasa, Mahat, Śiva, Ritadhvaja or Kratudhvaja, Ugraretas, Bhava, Kâla, Vâma, Dhṛitavrata, Vṛishâkapi, Śambu, Kapardin, Raivata, Śarva, Bhîma, &c. Conf. on Rudra, Macdonell's *Vedic Mythology*, pp. 74 ff.

[2] By kind permission of Mr. Murray: See Fergusson's *Ind. and Eastn. Archt.* pp. 243, 244 (conf. Cunningham, *Arch. Sur. Rep.* vol. II, pp. 357–61; and Sir L. Griffin's *Famous Monuments of Cent. India*, pp. 71-82, and Plates xlii, xliii, and xlv). Whilst much has been done for the "restoration" of this and other temples in the Gwâliar fort (1880 82), no drawings have been made to show, in any detail, the plan and mode of construction of so important a monument. A full delineation of the Gwâliar temples, illustrating the structural methods employed in them, might throw important light on Hindû architecture. We know but little more about them now than forty years ago. The Govinda-deva temple at Brindaban is similar in style but belongs to the 16th century.

constructed. Colonel Tod, indeed, states that the Rudraprâsâda was said to have been five storeys in height, and one portion, then remaining, was "a mass of two

2. PADMANÂTHA TEMPLE AT GWÂLIAR.

storeys, each supported by four columns, and the columns of a third storey, preserving without any entablature, their perfect perpendicularity"; and further that the earthquake of 1819 had thrown down two of the loftiest columns.[1] If no mistake has been made by the author, then, there were originally at least three pillared storeys on the east front of the *śikhara*.

The distance of the pillars at C from the front porch at A, and from the central line of the north porch, B, determines the size of the maṇḍapa, and makes the diameter of the octagon just 50 feet,—an unusually large one. Then, since the end pillars at C are 25 feet, between centres, the corners cut off the square could have been only about 17 feet 8 inches in length between the centres of the angle pillars: a rather unusual proportion. But, dividing the side of the square into four and giving the two central spaces to the side of the octagon; and again dividing this side into four and giving two for the middle division, or the same as between the angle of the octagon and the corner of the square, we have the precise arrangement on Plate XXXIX,—and one that would naturally occur.

It will be observed on Plate VI, that the pillars of the second storey are not central over those below but stand on the west face of the architrave; and on Plates XXXVII and XL, where the east side of it is shown, fragments of a curved course about 14 inches deep remain over the lintel; and over this are

[1] *Trav. W. India*, p. 141 f. He adds that the pencil of the Hon. Lincoln Stanhope enabled him "to give this singular remnant to the public"; but there is no such illustration in the work.

SIDDHAPUR: RUDRAMAHÂLAYA—PORTION OF THE RUINS.

the remains of two more courses projecting forwards, as indications of a roofing or dome that sprang from this level. The way in which the bracket capitals on the four pillars at C (Plate XXXVIII) radiate is shown in the side diagram C′, and seems to point to an inner octagon of pillars enclosing an area of not less than half the outer one. As we know of no Hindû temple roofed by a dome of 45 feet inside diameter, whilst in the Gwâliar and other temples we find the lower frustum of a dome roofing the outer circle of the maṇḍapa, and supported on the upper and inner circumference by columns in the middle of the area—so here we may suppose there was either an inner circle of eight pillars supporting a dome of half the diameter—25 feet between the centres of opposite pillars—as in the restoration proposed by the Salâṭ consulted by Mr. Cousens (Fig. 3); or, if instead of the great L-shaped piers of the Gwâliar temple, three pillars were substituted,[1] we should have a central area within this second octagon, of about 10 feet square within the columns. On these twelve pillars the weight of the roof would rest, and the thrusts would be counteracted. A comparison with the plans and dimensions of the Somanâtha,[2] Moḍherâ and Târiṅga temples (Plates XLVIII and CIX) and of the larger temples at Khajurâho and Mahobâ, will help to make the construction of such a roof intelligible.

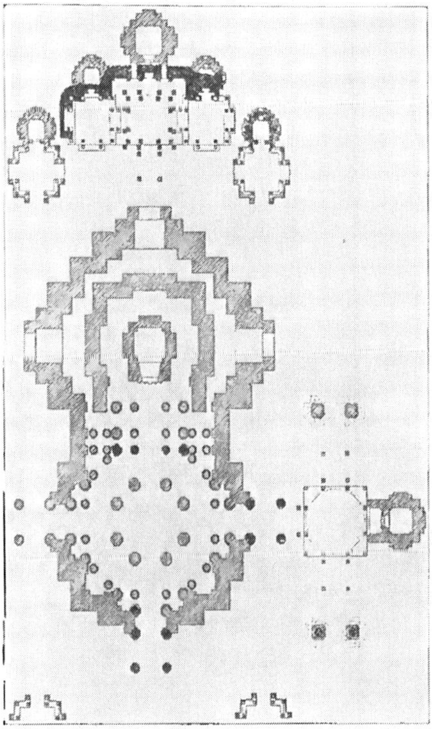

3. Part of the Plan of the Rudramâlâ, as restored by a Salâṭ.—Scale, 1 : 500.

[1] The dome in the Sâs Bâhu or Padmanâtha temple is about 30 feet in diameter and is supported inside by four piers whose inner corners are 8 feet 4 inches apart.

[2] The arrangement of the temple at Somanâtha, which probably belongs to the reign of Kumârapâla (A.D. 1168), is perhaps as good a general pattern as we have. The shrine is 18 feet 9 inches square and the square of pillars, enclosing the central octagon, measures 45 feet across between centres, whilst the dome is 34 feet across.—See Fergusson, *Ind. and Eastn. Arch.* p. 232, ill. 128; *Notes of a Visit to Somnath*, &c., pp. 18 f.

A Pâṭaṇ salâṭ—following the instructions of the *Prâsâda-maṇḍala*, and under Mr. Cousens's supervision—has attempted to reconstruct the plan. Among the data the fragment already mentioned of a curved course, over the architrave on the four pillars in line, gave the radius of the base of the dome. The bevelled ends of the architrave and the supporting brackets projecting below give indications as to the arrangement of other pillars within the area; and from these the plan (fig. 3) was derived. It offers a much smaller *garbhagṛiha* or cell than that proposed above—only 12 feet square—and surrounds it with a double *bhrama* or circumambulatory passage, which is quite unusual even in the largest temples, and this in turn disproportionately enlarges the plan of the *śikhara.* The pillars on the west of the maṇḍapa also are too much huddled together in it.

The salâṭ, noting the position of the four (once five) small shrines behind, concluded that it was necessary to plot one more in the north-east and south-east corners and one opposite each of the three porches—making ten in all, with the central temple as the eleventh.[1] He would also insert an additional Kîrttistambha to the west of the north and south porches. Mr. Cousens's restoration (Plate XXXVIII) has eleven small shrines, and in this respect is preferable; it makes room also at the front entrance for the Nandi pavilion (K).

Mr. Kinloch Forbes, in his restoration,[2] placed three more shrines in line to the north of H. and as many to the south of H′, and thus had eleven along the west side of the court. To the north of the porch, on that side and about 50 feet from it, he placed a great open propylæum extending about 75 feet from east to west, and the like on the south side; whilst a row of small cells extending east and west from these entrances enclosed the whole court. And, except that the propylons of Hindû temples are rarely if ever open pillared porticoes, there is no objection to such an arrangement.

To reconstruct the elevation with any probable approach to truth would be impossible without more data. The *maṇḍapa* was probably of three storeys and the *śikhara* could hardly have been less than a hundred and twenty feet in height, while from its sides, above the shrine, would project beautiful balconies, such as we find on the temple of Kâlikâ Mâtâ at Dabhoi[3] and elsewhere.

Plates VI and XXXIX show the west face of the pillars at C, or the side toward the antechamber; but how that apartment was roofed is not clear. The great architrave over the lower columns on this side is plain. Above it are two narrow string-courses carved in scroll pattern.

Plate XL presents on a larger scale the side of the richly carved architrave facing the maṇḍapa with the capitals of the two central pillars. This is only partially seen in the photograph, Plate XXXVII.

The amount of carving with which the four pillars on the floor of this great maṇḍapa were ornamented may best be understood by a study of Plates VI and

---

[1] In the cut, No. 3, parts of two only of the three shrines in front are included, the fourth is placed further from the central temple and in line with its axis.

[2] Plate III, fig. 3, in *Râs Mâlâ*, vol. I, at p. 253.

[3] See *Antiquities of Dabhoi*, Plates I, II, V–IX, and XI.

XXXIX. The size of the stones too is quite exceptional in Gujarât temples, for the shafts of these pillars are of single blocks 12 feet in height, and the outer pair which form the main supports are much more massive than the intermediate ones: exclusive of the brackets they are 4 feet in diameter, while the smaller are 3½ feet and have not the heavy attached brackets of the first.

In the large decorated columns, Mr. Cousens remarks that the divisions and mouldings are the same, and arranged in the same order and relative height, as the mouldings and horizontal divisions of the walls of the temples to which they belong. The base or *kumbhi* is octagonal and is surrounded by eight niched facets, each of which is invariably occupied by a small figure of a seated *devi*. Above the *kumbhi* and separated by a narrow neck, is the section corresponding to the *jaṅghâ* of the walls, containing the standing figures. These are usually reliefs of the gods in their various forms. Above these are two bands of devis —eight in each; then small projecting corbels to support the bracket figures that generally adorn the capitals of these pillars. Over these again rise the *bharani* and *śiras* or bracket capital (see also Plate XIII, 1). The columns are elaborately worked from top to bottom, and the outer ones have deep brackets thrown out from their sides to add to the support of the lintel above. The brackets of the sur-capitals, that carried the ends of the cross beams, by the directions in which they project, give us a clue to the arrangement of the other columns.

The pillars that remain of the north and east porches are surmounted by deep architraves supporting low parapets, and over those on the north stand two short pillars and two pilasters supporting the upper lintels of a second storey. The columns of these porches are of the same pattern as those already described; and those in the upper storey correspond pretty nearly in their mouldings to the upper portions of the lower ones. Of the north porch, B, the east side is represented in the photograph, Plate XXXVII, and more completely in the drawing, Plate XLI.

The porches have beautiful and delicately carved *toraṇas* or cusped arches between the pillars on the three outer sides. The inner sides of the architraves are also sculptured with scenes of revelry, hunting, and war. Four of these carved architraves are figured in detail on Plate XLII.

The remaining *Kîrttistambha* or *Toraṇa* stands to the north of the east or front porch (at E on Plate XXXVIII), and is the only one of which there is now any trace, but, if symmetrical arrangements were studied, there ought to have been one (at E) on the south side and, perhaps, a third either between the Nandi pavilion at K and the east porch, A, or at F on the top of the steps leading down to the river. Fifty years ago, when Mr. Kinloch Forbes wrote his *Râs Mâlâ*, the one on the north seems to have been almost intact, and his drawing of it is reproduced on Plate XLIV, 2. In 1869, it had been denuded of the principal sculptures in the pediment and of the beautiful garland-like arch that sprung from the capitals of the columns and touched the lintel above,—this lintel itself resting on the heads of dwarf columns that rise from the capitals of the main pillars. From the ground to the architrave is about 24 feet; the pediment rises about 8 feet above this; and the whole was finished in the most ornate style of Hindû art. It is now much defaced, particularly about the bases of the pillars, but still strikes the spectator as a fine piece of masonry.

The only other fragments of this great temple are a row of four small shrines on the west at G, H (Plate XXXVIII). Three of these have been connected together by the Muhammadans to form a mosque (G), and are considerably masked by additions; but the remains of the spires protrude above the general roof and mark their positions (Plate XLV). These four shrines, with a corresponding fifth on the south, were arranged so as to form a right-angle behind the temple. Each shrine has been complete in itself, and the outer walls and part of the *maṇḍapa* of that on the north (H), together with an almost perfect *śikhara*, all elaborately and richly sculptured, give us some idea of what the style of the main building must have been (see Plate XLIII). The *śikhara* which is nearly entire --wanting only the *kalaśa* or finial—is probably of the same form as the great spire that must have risen over the shrine to a very considerable height (fig. 4).

4. BACK OF A SMALL SHRINE IN THE RUDRAMÂLÂ COURT.

The Jâmi' Masjid, constructed out of these three shrines (Plate XLV), is formed by rearranging the original Hindû pillars to suit the convenience of the Musalman mosque; but though the imagery upon them has been hewn out, their style and variety of carving may still be seen in the examples represented on Plate XLIII. The roof of the central part of the mosque, about 28 feet in length, is higher than the two wings and is 21 feet deep, while the sides are each about 15 feet square. The *mimbâr* and central *miḥrâb* are behind the middle dome, and each wing contains a *miḥrâb* occupying the position of the doors of the two old shrines at the sides. The three domes of the mosque, as seen from the outside, differ little from low cones.

On a marble slab, at the entrance to the masjid there is an inscription in Persian and Devanâgarî characters[1] recording that "in Hijri 1055, Samvat 1702 (A.D. 1645) in the reign of the emperor Aurangzeb Sâheb Âlami Âdil,—knowing that the Lord (*Sâheb*) will in all works give success (*siddha*) at Siddhapur, 'Ali 'Askarî 'Adalî Sâheb built the 'Adil Ganj, to provide facilities for those buying and selling."

Another inscription was found, at a ruined wâv or well outside the town, beautifully engrossed in Persian characters on a marble slab. It runs thus:—

"God is Great!

"The building of this Bâi (*well*) was successfully completed in the time when the town of Sîtpur was the jâgîr of the scion of nobility Mîrzâ Muḥammad Anwar, son of the excellent Nawâb 'Azam Khân, under the superintendence of Hâjî Ismâ'îl al-Sharîf, son of Hâjî Bakhtyâr, in the blessed month of Ramazân 1010 (April 1601 A.D.). And with God rests the guidance to the right road, although there are that deviate from it.[2]

"Yamlîkhâ, Maksalmînâ, Kashfûṭaṭ, Tabyûnus, Azarfaṭyûnus, Yuwânisbûs, and the name of their dog is Qiṭmîr.[3]

"The writer is Luṭfullah."

'Azam Khân is best known as Khân-i-'Azam Mîrzâ 'Azîz Kokah, who was appointed by Akbar as governor of Gujarât as far as the Mahindra river in 1571, and held the appointment till 1575, and returned again in 1588, when he reduced Kachh and Somnâth with Junâgaḍh and captured Sulṭân Muzaffar, but was recalled in 1592–3. He died at Aḥmadâbâd in A.H. 1033 (A.D. 1624), and is the reputed excavator of the Khân Sarovar at Pâṭaṇ.

Plate XLIV, fig. 1, represents a sculptured base from the Rudramâlâ, 1½ feet square and nearly 2 feet in height.

Wood Carving.

Plate XLVI.

Gujarât, as already remarked, is full of examples of artistic wood-carving applied to the decoration of house fronts; and in a bye street, behind the mosque and not far from the Rudra-mahâlaya, there projects from a very dilapidated wall, a beautiful specimen of this kind, in the form of a balcony window (Plate XLVI).

---

1 *Notes of a Visit to Gujarât*, p. 72.

2 *Qoran*, xvi, 9.

3 These are the names of the *Aṣhâb-i Kahf* or "Lords of the Cave" as the "Seven Sleepers" are styled (*Qorân*, xviii). Their dog Qiṭmîr is much respected by the Muhammadans. Conf. *Ind. Ant.* vol. IV, p. 7 f.

Such work is of course of very varied ages—within the last two hundred years, though of late, perhaps, there has not been so much of it made as formerly. It is still, however, executed to a small extent. But though the old specimens hanging on dilapidated buildings are so rich in design, they are little appreciated and when taken down are mostly thrown aside or burnt as firewood: and much that remains is so bedaubed with brilliant colours as to obscure entirely the fine work of the carver's chisel.

CHAPTER VII.

MOḌHERÂ.

PLATES I, VII, XLVII–LVI.

THE village of Moḍherâ stands on a knoll rising out of the otherwise level country, eighteen miles south of Pâṭaṇ, and on the left bank of the Pushmâvati river,—a small stream that winds its way south-westwards aud joins the Rupên or Rupan. The place seems at one time to have been of cousiderable note, though the present village is little more than a collection of huts. To the west and down the river bank the surface is strewn with brick remains and occasional fragments of sculptured stones—images, pillars, &c. Indeed the ground is largely artificial, especially near the river and round the great Sun-temple, being mostly composed of solid brick-work,—the bricks being of the very early type and of uuusual size.

Moḍherâ or Moḍherâpura, sometimes called Munderâ, is said to have been the original settlement of the Moḍha Brâhmaṇs, and is fabled to have been given them "as a *kṛishnârpana* on the occasion of the marriage of Râma and Sitâ." The Moḍha Brâhmaṇs act as *gurus* to the Moḍha Vâṇiyâs, and are found largely in the Aḥmadâbâd and Kheḍa zillas. The great Jaina âchârya, Hemachandra, was of Śrîmoḍha parentage.[1]

On the west side of the village is a large tank or *talâv*, that has, at one time, been surrounded by steps, and perhaps also with shrines; but the stones have been carried off long since. On a rising ground to the north-east of this is a small deserted masjid of Hindû construction, supported by eighteen pillars equally interspaced.

Farther to the west, and near the river, is the old temple, beautifully situated, with a fine oblong kuṇḍa or tank in front of it. The shrine was dedicated to Sûrya or Âditya—the sun-god, and even now in its ruin and decay it is still an imposing structure, with a majestic beauty rarely met with in such remains. No finer or more interesting structure remains in northern Gujarât. The Sejakpur temple, near Thân in Jhâlawâḍ, is perhaps the only one in Western India that may fairly be compared with it.

Except Colonel Monier Williams, about 1809, and probably Capt. R. M. Grindlay some fifteen years afterwards, no European—not even the zealous Tod—seems to have visited Moḍherâ, and its interesting temple appears, for more than forty years, to have been almost unknown and quite unnoticed. Colonel Monier Williams,

---

[1] *Bomb. Gaz.* vol VII, p. 609; vol. IX, pt. i, pp. 11, 72; conf. Tawney's *Prabandha-chintâmaṇi*, p. 127, n. 5. Wilson, *Indian Caste*, vol. II, p. 111, says they derive their name from Modhâṇâ near Siddhapur,—and there is a small village, Mundhâṇâ, 3 miles E.N.E. of Siddhapur,—but Moḍherâ was probably meant by Dr. Wilson.

as Surveyor-General had visited the place, and in his Journal, as quoted by Capt. Grindlay,[1] he thus remarks:—

"There is one of the finest specimens of ancient Hindû architecture at Mundera I ever saw. It is a pagoda very similar in structure to those of the present day; but ornamented so profusely that it is very evident the founder was determined to make it the most finished piece of work that it was possible for the compass of human art to effect. . . . All the upper part of it is supported on pillars, which are of an order the most elegant, and enriched with carved work of exquisite beauty, and which would be considered in this refined age as the conception of a correct taste, and the execution of a masterly hand.

"Innumerable figures cover most of the bases of the pillars, and a considerable portion of the exterior surface of the building. They consist of gods and goddesses, and groups of males and females, . . .

"The domes were blown off, they say, by means of gunpowder, . . . by a Musalman prince. The lower circles remain, and are ornamented in a style of elegance that is uncommonly striking.

"In front of the pagoda there is a square reservoir of water, built of stone, perhaps sixty or seventy yards each way. Many beautiful little temples stand in recesses formed for them in the flight of steps to the water. This tank is overgrown with shrubs and grass. There is plenty of water in it, but of a brackish taste, and green and dirty appearance.

"I do not recollect observing in any building that I have seen in India such marks of the sheer effects of time as many of the stones about this pagoda and tank display. We spent some time every day in inspecting the place; but such is the variety of its beauties that it would have taken a much longer time than we had to spare to have discerned them all, or have gained a faint idea of the general design. Much of the sculpture represents the recorded actions of the gods or heroes. One course of figures, including men, women, horses, and other animals, variously engaged, form a belt of almost eighteen inches wide all round the exterior of the building, and represent some part of their sacred history; below this belt, and very near the ground, there is a range of elephants also completely encompassing the building; their heads and fore-feet are exhibited, and their bodies must be supposed to be the supporters of the fabric."

From the date of this record no further mention, so far as I know, of Moḍherâ appears till the publication in 1856, by Mr. Kinloch Forbes, of his most valuable work—so often referred to—the *Râs Mâlâ*.

In the old Vedic mythology of the Hindûs there were three chief Devatâs which form a sort of triad: Agni (fire) who resides on the earth, Indra or Vâyu who resides in the atmosphere, and Sûrya or Mitra whose abode is in the heaven. There can be little doubt that the third is identical with the Mithra of early Persian worship, and his dress "like that of the northerners," covering his person from the feet upwards, with the girdle—*viyaṅga*—round his waist, are confirmatory of this.[2]

[1] *Scenery, Costumes and Architecture in Western India*, pt. vi, pl. 36.

[2] The priests of the sun are styled Magn.—*Bṛihat Saṅhita*, lx, 19. The word *viyaṅga* is from the Baktrian *auvyâoṅha*.—Böhtlingk and Roth's *Sansk. Lexicon*.

PLATE VII.

MODHERÂ: THE MAṆḌAPA IN FRONT OF THE GREAT TEMPLE.

Temples to Sûrya were at one time spread over most of Western India.[1] In A.D. 437 a colony of silk-weavers that had emigrated from Lâṭa or southern Gujarât to Daśapura—now Dasôr or Mandasôr in Mâlava—built there a temple of the Sun, and in A.D. 473 the same guild restored it.[2] Lalitâditya-Muktâpîḍa of Kaśmîr, who ruled in the first half of the eighth century, built a temple of Âditya at Latapur and the famous shrine of Mârtâṇḍa, or the sun-god in Kaśmîr, of which the remains are still well known.[3] In the seventh century Hiuen Thsang mentions a famous shrine of Âditya or Sûrya at Multân, which four centuries later is spoken of by Al-Berunî.[4] The Chinese pilgrim also mentions another sun-temple at Kanauj.[5] At Kaṇṭhakoṭ in Kachh is an old Sûrya temple, and at Bhîmanâth near Prâchi Kuṇḍa in the south of Soraṭh is the ruin of another, much on the same plan as this and measuring 56 feet by 21 inside, with projecting windows both from the maṇḍapa and the *pradakshiṇâ* passage (figs. 5 and 6).[6] Figures of the sun-god are also met with in the Elura, Bhâja and Khandagiri Caves, at Gayâ,[7] and elsewhere,[8] all indicating that Saurapâtas or sun-worshippers must have been numerous in India in early times.

5. Bhîmanâth Temple, Section across the Maṇḍapa.

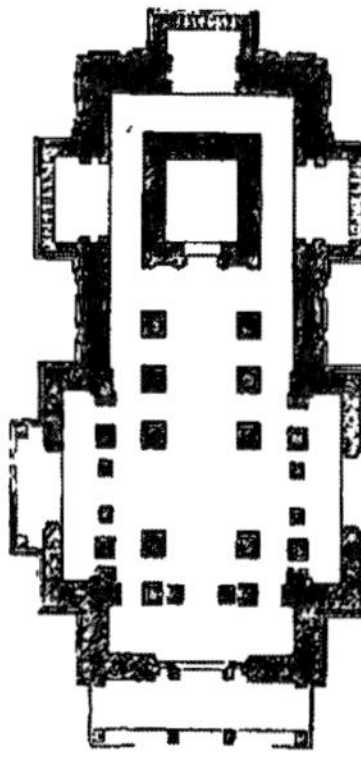

6. Sûrya Temple at Bhîmanâth.

Varâha Mihira, in the sixth century, describing the image of Sûrya, says[9] it "ought to be made with elevated nose, forehead, lower leg, thigh, cheek and breast, and clad in the dress of the Northerners, so as to be covered from the feet upwards to the bosom. He holds two lotuses growing out of his hands, wears a diadem and a necklace hanging down, has his face adorned with ear-rings, and a girdle (*viyaṅga*) round his waist. The Sun, when made with a body protected by a corslet, a complexion

[1] Solar worship, even at an early date, was wide-spread in Greece and the West, and Pausanius (*c.* 170 A.D.) mentions many places sacred to the Sun. Aurelian founded a splendid temple at Rome dedicated to him, and was very anxious to restore the great temple to the same divinity at Palmyra destroyed by his soldiery in 273 A.D.

[2] Mandasor inscrip. in *Ind. Ant.* vol. XV, p. 196

[3] Fergusson, *Ind. and Eastern Archit.* pp. 285–291; Stein, *Anc. Geog. of Kaśmîr*, p. 177 f., and *Râjataraṅgiṇî*, vol. I, pp. 139, 141, vol. II, p. 466.

[4] Beal, *Si-yu-ki*, vol. II, p. 274; Reinaud, *Mém. sur l'Inde*, p 98 f. Hiuen Thsang says the image was cast in gold; Al-Beruni says it was of wood and covered with leather. Al-Beruni's *India*, transl. by Sachau, vol. I, pp. 116, 121. He adds that it was worshipped or served by the Maga (p. 298), and a festival was held at Multân in honour of the sun, called *Sambapurayâtra*. *Ib.* vol. II, p. 184.

[5] Beal, *Si-yu-ki*, vol. I, p. 223.

[6] From unpublished drawings made by me in 1869.—J. B.

[7] *Arch. Sur. W. Ind.* vol. II, p. 215; conf. vol. IV, p. 6; Fergusson, *Archæol. in India*, p. 34.

[8] In a small shrine in one of the bastions of the fort at Hûli, in the Belgaum district, is an old image of Sûrya, apparently in good preservation. The horses are represented upon the *Vedi*, on a diminutive scale; two females with bows and clubs stand by his knees; and five small seated figures with clubs are carved on each side of his head and shoulders. Even in Java he was represented with the seven horses, but dressed in the same style as Vishṇu and other gods.—Ijzerman, *Beschrijv. d. Oudheden nabij de grens d. residentie's Soerakarta en Djogdjakarta*, p. 56, and atl. pl. xxi, fig. 86.

[9] *Bṛihat Saṅhita*, transl. by H. Kern, in *J. R. A. S.*, N.S., vol. VI, p. 328.

fair, like the interior of the white water-lily, a smiling and placid face, and a light crown brilliant through the gems, bestows bliss upon the maker."

Sûrya is known by such names as Âditya, Savitṛī, Mârtâṇḍa, Mitra, Bhânu, &c., but these names again are applied as if to different gods. He moves in a car drawn by one, several, or seven fleet horses or mares; his charioteer is Aruṇa or Vivasvat.[1] In early Vedic times the Âdityas were six, as there were six Ṛitus or seasons, and occasionally seven. The six were Mitra, Aryaman, Bhaga, Varuṇa, Daksha and Anśa; in other lists Daksha is omitted and Indra, Savitṛī and Dhâtṛī added. But the Âdityas were afterwards increased to twelve—the number of the months, viz.:—in the order of the months from Chaitra to Phâlguna—Dhâtṛī, Aryaman, Mitra, Varuṇa, Indra, Vivasvat, Pûshan, Parjanya, Aṁśu, Bhaga, Twashṭṛī, and Vishṇu the chief.[2]

To the sun as Sâvitṛī, is addressed the *Gâyatrî*—the most sacred verse of the *Ṛig-Veda* (iii, 62, 10),—which it is the duty of every Brâhmaṇ to repeat mentally in his morning and evening devotions. It consists of three short lines—

Tat Savitur vareṇyaṁ
bhargo devasya dhîmahi
dhiyo yo naḥ prachodayât.

It has been rendered:—"Of Savitar, the heavenly, that longed for glory may we win, and may himself inspire our prayers."[3]

Vishṇu's bow, starting asunder, is said to have cut off his head and it became the sun; in still earlier times he is associated with Agni, Sûrya, Ushas; and is represented as setting in motion, like a revolving wheel, his 90 steeds (= days) with their four names (= seasons), referring, doubtless, to the Solar year of 360 days. And through such associations, perhaps, it came about that, in later mythology, Sûrya becomes identified with Vishṇu under the name of Sûrya-Nârâyaṇa,[4] and to him an old temple near Devapattan-Somanâth is dedicated.[5]

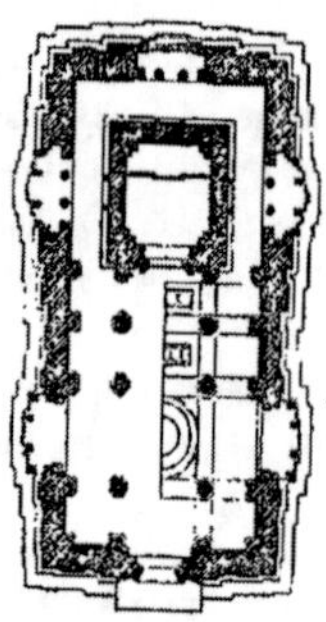

7. TEMPLE OF SÛRYA NÂRÂYANA, NEAR DEVAPATTANA.
Scale, 25 ft. to 1 inch.

The Muhammadans, not content with defacing the figure sculptures of this Moḍherâ temple, are said to have placed bags of gunpowder in the underground shrine, and blew it up with the upper cell, destroying the *Śikhara* or tower.

The whole temple consists of the *garbhagṛiha* or shrine, and *gudha-maṇḍapa* or hall, a *subhâ-maṇḍapa* or *ranga-maṇḍapa* or outer hall, locally known as *Sitâ's châvaḍi*, and the *Kuṇḍa* or sacred pool, now called the Râma-kuṇḍa. There were also some small subsidiary shrines which have

[1] *J. R. A. S.*, N.S., vol. I, p. 113 f.; Macdonell, *Vedic Mythology*, pp. 30-34; and see E. Washburn Hopkins, *Religions of India*, pp. 40-46.

[2] Elsewhere their names are given as Vishṇu, Śakra, Aryaman, Dhâtṛī, Twashṭṛī, Pûshan, Vivasvat, Savitṛī, Mitra, Varuṇa, Aṁśa, and Bhaga. Conf. Wilson, *Vishṇu Purâṇa*, vol. II, pp. 27, 285: Vans Kennedy, *Hindu Mythology*, p. 349.

[3] Different scholars have translated it variously; see Dowson, *Cl. Dict. of Hindu Mythol.* s.v.; Colebrooke's *Essays*, Whitney's ed. vol. I, pp. 111, 112.

[4] The Sauras might thus, probably, become merged into the Vaishṇavas.

[5] *Visit to Somnâth*, p. 24. This temple is of the same general plan as Bhîmanâtha, but smaller, being 45 ft. 4 in. by 21 ft. 8 in. inside: fig. 7 is from a private survey made in 1869.

been demolished. It had originally all the parts of a first-class temple, built as the *śilpa-śâstras* direct, in good proportions and richly decorated. The general lines of the main body of the temple enclosing the *maṇḍapa* and shrine, like the temples at Bhîmanâtha and Devapattana figured above, is rectangular—its length inside the walls being 51 feet 9 inches, or almost exactly double its width of 25 feet 8 inches. This area is divided into two nearly equal portions, the inner one occupied by the shrine and the front one by the hall or *maṇḍapa*. The cella or *garbhagṛiha*, which is 11 feet square inside, is enclosed by its own walls, between which and the outer walls of the temple is the circumambulatory passage—*pradakshiṇâ* or *bhrama*. This passage was roofed with flat slabs laid across and carved with rosettes on the undersides; and above this rose the *śikhara* or spire.

The hall roof is supported by eight principal columns, 13 feet 6 inches in height, arranged in an octagon, with four others in front of the shrine,—and by the walls which are broken on each side by the entrance and by two large windows. In the recesses of each of these windows are two columns 11 feet 6 inches high (Plate LIII, 3). The central area was covered by a splendidly carved dome, nearly the whole of which has fallen It rose in concentric tiers of mouldings one over another, each richly wrought, and from the apex there fell a beautiful pendant. The smaller bays of the roof, in the corners between this and the walls, are domed, but elsewhere they are flat-roofed. The walls inside are comparatively bare but broken by niches in each bay containing figures of Sûrya. All of these images have long Hessian boots, in some cases marked with lines crossing each other diagonally as if intended to represent impressed leather. In some cases the seven horses are represented below him; in others they are not (Plate LVI, 5, 6).

The columns are most lavishly carved from base to capital. In plan they are octagonal, changing to round near the top (Plate LIV, 1). The architraves over the pillars, which are 3 feet 4 inches deep, are also covered with carving.

The shrine is now a wreck: nothing but the bare walls remaining. The old Śaiva temple at Amaranâtha had a sunken cell; but this must rather have been of two storeys, the sunk cell being about 11½ feet below the level of that above. The floor separating them, with part of the roof, had fallen into the pit. On clearing out the débris, the seat of the image of Sûrya was found in the middle of the floor, with other blocks connecting it with the side walls. On the front of the seat are carved the seven horses (the *saptâśva-vâhana*) of the god, their fore-quarters projecting and prancing forward. How this cell was entered is not quite clear.[1] There does not appear to have been any entrance from the sides, and we can only conjecture that it was reached by a trap door and ladder from the floor above. That floor has fallen through—only a few projecting slabs round the edges still remaining. Possibly this chamber was properly a treasury mainly for jewels, &c. belonging to the temple.

---

[1] At Amaranâtha there was a stair down to the bottom; but there the descent was only about 7 feet, and there was no floor above. At Râjûr, to the north of Buldâna, is another old Śaiva temple, the shrine of which is still deeper, and to which a stair leads down from the door on the level of the maṇḍapa. At Châṇdol, in the same district, is another quite similar. At Aundh the principal liṅga is in a chamber below, and in the upper one is another; the steps lead down from an opening in the floor of the upper shrine. See *Ind. Ant.* vol. III. p. 316, pl. ii, for Amaranâtha.

The walls of the upper storey in the shrine are devoid of ornament; but, as appears from portions of some of the lower rings of mouldings still left, it was roofed by a carefully carved dome.

The doorway of the shrine is richly decorated and the figure of Sûrya is repeated over and over again, but the central block on the lintel—where the dedicatory image, or some closely associated figure, is always represented—has been destroyed. On the outsides of the shrine walls, in the *pradakshiṇâ*, are deep niches in each of the three faces[1]; but the figures that once occupied them have been removed.

In the windows on each side of the hall were inserted perforated stone screens, but that on the north side is much damaged, whilst that on the south has entirely disappeared, as have also the three that admitted light to the *pradakshiṇâ* passage.

The exterior of the temple walls has been profusely covered with sculpture. And in this case it may be observed that the mouldings and sculptures on the walls of the maṇḍapa are arranged in horizontal bands, whilst on the śikhara they follow vertical lines. The monotony of a simply horizontal arrangement, too, is avoided by the vertical lines of projecting and recessed faces. This feature is particularly marked in the case of temples with *ashṭabhadra* or star-shaped plans, such as the Galteśvara temple on the Mahî near Ṭhâsrâ in the Kheḍa district. The horizontal lines, under the play of light and shade on the vertical faces of varying prominence, give the whole a crisp and sparkling effect, difficult of attainment by other arrangements.

The whole building stands on a paved platform (*kharaśilâ*). The first group of mouldings, from the ground to the top of the *khara* (A to G on Plate XLIX, 1), forms the *piṭha* or plinth.[2] The lowest square member of this group (A) is called the *bhaṭa* (S. *upânâh*), and this member may be repeated twice or thrice, as in the Sûṇak temple (Plate LXXXII, 3). The inverted cimarecta moulding (B, and Plate LXXXV) is called *jâḍamba* (S. *padma*), and is usually decorated with broad leaves having deeply indented centre lines. On this lies the *kaṇî* (C), an astragal with a sharp edge between two deep recesses (*antarânti*, S. *antarita*). Above is the *grahapaṭi* or *grasapaṭi*—a band of *Kîrttimukha* faces (E), with a thin *chhâjalî* moulding (D) along its lower edge. A narrow neck (*âlinga*) separates this from another *chhâjalî*, over which is the *gajathara* (F)—a broad member carved with a row of elephants. Another neck (*âlinga*) intervenes between this and the uppermost member of the *piṭha*, known as the *khara* (S. *pattika*) carved with small figures of men in varied attitudes. To raise the height of the base in larger temples—another moulding—the *aśvathara* or line of horses, is introduced here; the plinth also is repeated twice or thrice for the like purpose.

Over the *pîṭha* is the *mandovara* or wall reaching from above the basement to the cornice inclusive (H to P). The lowest member is the *kumbha*, and the

[1] Similarly at the Sûryanârâyana temple, near Pattan-Somanâtha (fig. 7), there were figures in niches in the *bhrama*, on the outsides of the walls of the inner cells. The same was the case elsewhere.

[2] Plinths are divided into three classes, according to the relation of projection to height. When the lowest member projects half the height, it is called a *latîna-piṭha*; in the second class, this member projects one third of the height; and in the third, or *sâvandhâra pîṭha*, the projection is one fourth the height.—H. C.

torus above it is termed *kalaśa* (I) which is often carved with bands and beads. Above this again is a broad recessed fascia (*gala* or *kandhara*) supporting the *kevâla* (K), decorated with representations of chaitya windows. Another cincture intervenes between this and the *mâñchî* (L), which is similarly ornamented; a very thin astragal surmounts it, and then we come to the *jaṅghâ* (M) or panelled face of the wall, sculptured with figures of the gods. These are so arranged that the most prominent panels hold the images of the divinity to which the temple is dedicated, on each side of which the niches are reserved for female figures, dancers and musicians, while the more recessed or least prominent are filled by *ṛishis*, or ascetics. Were there no windows in the shrine walls here, their places would be occupied by the chief images; but in this instance the large niches on each side of the three windows contain the standing figures of Sûrya, each with his seven horses carved under his feet, and, perhaps his wives, beside him.[1]

Figures of Sûrya or the Âdityas occur everywhere on the architraves of the door jambs, both of the hall and shrine, in six large niches round the walls of the *pradakshiṇâ* and in other six on the inner walls of the maṇḍapa,—making the twelve Adityas; and also twelve images on the exterior of the shrine walls. Usually he is represented with only two arms[2] (Plate LVI, 5, 6), but as they projected forwards, they have been mostly broken off. The other superhuman figures on the walls are generally distinguished by four arms each.

To the north of the entrance, among the larger reliefs on the wall, is one which the villagers anoint weekly, calling it Kâla-Bhairava. It is a standing male figure, that appears to have three faces and three arms—one left and two right; there seems to be also three legs—two left (one behind the other) and one right. Kâla is one of the eight Bhairavas or monstrous forms of Śiva, and is much worshipped by the common people; but Agni[3]—the fire god—is perhaps the only one who is sometimes represented with three legs, and even with four right and three left hands. But the figure here is so encrusted with oil and red paint that it is doubtful what the real form of it is. In his upper right hand is a curved dagger, and the other hands are broken off. Down to the right of this figure a *makara*[4] seems to be represented.

---

[1] His conjugal relations are not very clear: Sañjnâ (conscience) is stated to have been his spouse and Chhâyyâ (shadow) his concubine; again Ushas (dawn) or the two Dawns are spoken of as his wives; and elsewhere, Savarnâ, Swâtî, and Mahâvîryâ are called his wives. The *Vishṇu Purâṇa* says the Sun's car is presided over by seven divine being—Âdityas, Ṛishis, Gandharvas, Apsarases Grâmaṇîs (Yakshas), Sarpas (Nâgas), and Râkshasas (Yâtudhânas),—one of each being placed in it every month. Thus the Âditya Dhâtṛi, the sage Pulastya, the Gandharva Tumburu, the nymph Kratusthalâ, the Yaksha Rathakṛît, the serpent Vâsuki, and the Râkshasa Heti, always reside in the sun's car in the month of Madhu or Chaitra, as its seven guardians; and so for the other months. Wilson's *Vishṇu puraṇa*, vol. II, pp. 284-86, 291-93.

[2] See Martin's *Eastn. India*, vol. I, p. 86, pl. xii, 2; p. 99, pl. xvi, 3; *Arch. Sur. Wn. India*, pl. lxv, 1, 2; Cunningham, *Arch. Sur. Rep.* vol. III, pl. xxvii, 1; Râjendralâl Mitra's *Buddha Gayâ*, pl. 1; and Fergusson, *Archæology in India*, p. 34.

[3] Agni in Vedic times was said to have seven tongues of flame for devouring the offerings of butter. Of these Kâlî was the black or terrific tongue. This application of the word seems to have led to the conception of the dread goddess of wrath.

[4] The Makara is one of the nine treasures of Kubera; also the banner of Kâma. Wilson's *Essays on Sansk. Liter.* vol. II, p. 380.; conf. Grünwedel, *Buddh. Art in India*, Eng. ed. p. 57.

Round the corner from this figure is Śiva standing with Nandi beside him. Under the window on the north side of the maṇḍapa are three smaller figures in line; that towards the east is a female holding a three-hooded snake in her upper left hand—the other hands are destroyed. Beneath her appears to have been a bullock, but its head is gone. The middle figure is also a female with four arms—now broken off; and she is canopied by a five-hooded snake. The third is a male deva—the arms broken off and his head also overshadowed by a five-hooded snake. These three have been selected for *pûjâ* by the villagers, and are smeared with red paint.

Under the window at the back are two *nâga*-hooded male figures (Plate LVI, 8). And as the Sun's car has a different Nâga or Sarpa among its occupants each month, we may suppose that Vâsuki, Kachauira, &c. are intended by these male Nâga figures, for the twelve are male divinities, and the only female attendants are the series of Apsarases—Kratusthalâ, Puñjikasthalâ, Menakâ, Sahajanyâ, Pramlochâ, Anumlochâ, Ghṛitâchî, Viśvâchî, Urvaśî, Pûrvachitti, Tilottamâ, and Rambhâ.

Returning to the face of the walls: above the figures is the *chhâjali* or little cornice, surmounted by a triangular pediment called *udgam*, above which is the *dhodia* (N); and over it again the projecting drip or *mâlakvâl* (O), similar in form to the *kevâla*. This is surmounted by the uppermost member of the *mandovara*—the chief cornice or *chhâju* (P). Above this rose the principal śikhara or spire with the subsidiary ones against it. These were probably built with a brick core and a stone facing. Only a few stones of the roof remain: one or two *amalasaras* and some fragments of the pyramidal roofing of the main hall and of the shrine.

But perhaps the most elegant and ornamental feature of this temple is the beautiful and richly decorated *sabhâ-maṇḍapa* or *châvaḍî* which stands in front of the temple proper, and separated from it by a narrow passage.

The *piṭha* or basement of this is formed of the same mouldings as that of the temple, but its height is slightly less and the proportions differ. Here the *jâdamba* (or *padma*) is much more elaborately carved with fretted leaf ornament and scroll decoration; and the members above this are quite different from those of the main building. The upper band is the *râjasena* (Q), which is filled with small figures in compartments. Over this is the *vedi* (R), corresponding to the *jaṅghâ* on the *mandovara* of the maṇḍapa, carved with representations of gods, goddesses and *dikpâlas*, placed in projecting niches. Above this the cornice mouldings are termed *âsinot* (S) and support the *kakshâsana* (T) which slopes outwards and, on the inner side, forms a back to the high bench or seat (*âsana*) running round the interior (*kaksha*) of the hall: on the outer side the compartments of this rail are carved with erotic groups. On the high bench formed by the *vedika*, stand the outer line of columns that support the roof. Inside the hall the pillars all rise from the floor.

The columns support the lintels (*pâṭa*) upon which the roof rests. It will be observed that above the lintels (Plates XLIX, L) there is a double cornice or *chhâju*. The roof rose as a stepped pyramid, decorated by countless little finials, whilst above each entrance was probably a group of sculpture.

The octagonal central area of the roof inside is considerably raised by stilting the supporting columns (Plate L). Above the capital a short shaft is added, crowned by a sur-capital to support the lintels; and this arrangement gives the opportunity to introduce ornamental *toraṇas* or decorative cuspid arches, resting on the lower brackets of the columns and touching the undersides of the lintels. The *toraṇas* are beautiful additions, and their introduction between the pillars contributes to the charm of the whole; but hardly one of them is now complete, and much of their beauty is lost by the destruction of the little scrolls that filled the spaces between the cusps and of the hanging tips of the cusps. The faces of the architraves are very richly carved; and over them rise the concentric rings of the decorated mouldings of the dome. Unfortunately nearly the whole of the dome has fallen in.

The columns are tall and graceful (Plates LIII–LV), and their mouldings, which are numerous and richly carved, are governed in their proportions by those on the exterior walls—the principal figure band corresponding to the *vedi*. The floor-level is that of the top of the *pîṭha*, and the mouldings between the floor and the larger figures on the shafts correspond to the *râjasena*, whilst the next zone, of smaller figures over a prettily carved torus, agrees to the *kakshâsana*.

The capitals are simple, composed of three tiers of flat members or annulets —two with wedge-shaped edges, and the uppermost with a "drop" projection. On this rests the brackets which are, as a rule, of one block. The side brackets of the eight central shafts are shaped as *makara* heads and from them spring the *toraṇas*; but the others represent fat dwarfs supporting the beams. These figures are styled *kîchaka*—said to be after the Kîchaka,[1] crushed to death by Bhîmasena and rolled into a ball.

In front of the east entrance to the Sabhâ maṇḍapa, and at the head of the flight of steps leading down to the Sûrya-kuṇḍa, stand two columns—all that now remain of a fine toraṇa or kîrttistambha arch, similar in style to those at Vaḍnagar, Siddhapur, and Kâpadvanj. The entablature, pediment, and *toraṇa* or garland now lie in a heap of fragments on the steps below. Each of these pillars, standing free as it does from the hall, has its own basement with mouldings complete.

The Sûrya-kuṇḍa, now known as the Râma-kuṇḍa, is under the east face of the Sabhâ-maṇḍapa, from which a broad stair leads down to the water's edge. The tank is rectangular and measures 176 feet from north to south, by 120 feet from east to west.

This tank or kuṇḍa, though much damaged, has been a very complete one of its class. The upper and outermost margin is surrounded by a low wall on the ground level. A small rectangular recessed bay projects outwards from the middle of each of the sides, and in the middle of three of these, on the first

[1] But the name is also that of a Râkshasa and of a Daitya.

terrace below the ground-level, small detached shrines stand, each facing the tank. These are at A, B, and C, on the plan, Plate XLVIII. From the fourth platform, D, on the west side, the stair leads up from the kuṇḍa to the temple; and this is the only proper approach to the tank. Slightly in advance of the east and west shrines A and C, and on each side of them, are two smaller ones facing one another; and again at the four corners of the kuṇḍa are other small detached shrines, the two on the west side, F, G, facing each other, as also the two E, H, on the east corners.

The sides of the tank descend to the water in terraces, of which the drop from one to another is somewhat considerable, and steps running parallel to them would give no resting-places; hence, from small landings above, a few cross steps at right angles to the sides descend at both ends to the next terrace below. Access is thus secured from terrace to terrace by these numerous little stairs. And attached to the front of the terrace wall, between each set of steps and on the front of the terrace, is a niche containing an image. On the small landings at the top of each of these flights of steps is a very low semicircular step (*ardhachandra*).[1]

On the side of the tank nearest the temple are the remains of a broad terrace which, at one time, probably ran round the temple, but excepting the indications of it on this side, it has quite disappeared.

The majority of the images now in the small temples at the tank are Vaishṇava,—that in the shrine on the east side and facing the temple is of Vishṇu reposing on Śesha (Plate LVI, 3). Another sculpture (fig. 1) represents the well-known Trivikrama legend, which is connected with the solar myths. Fig. 7 represents a sculpture locally known as Śîtalâ—the dreaded goddess of small-pox—who is described in popular mythology as naked, seated on a donkey, wearing a broken winnowing fan on her head, with a water jar (*kalaśa*) in the left hand and a besom in the right.[2] This figure hardly corresponds in its details with such a description; but Śîtalâ is one of seven sister goddesses of disease,[3] and the popular mythology varies with age and locality.

Śîtalâ is the same as Mâriamman of the Tamils, also called Mâttâṅgi and Vadugantâî, who is four-handed and one of the Grâmadevatas. She is worshipped in Gujarât on the 7th of Śrâvaṇa sudi; elsewhere *Śîtalâ-pûjâ* is celebrated on the 8th day of Phâlgun sudi. She is worshipped by women only.

On Plate LVIII, fig. 1, is represented a loose sculpture of a goddess on a slab measuring 3 feet by 5 feet 3 inches in height. Her four arms are broken off; she is seated on a lotus with two lions below, and is probably a form of Lakshmî.

The masonry of the tank, like that of the temple is without mortar, consisting entirely of blocks of stone fitted together in the way of all the older Hindû temples.

---

[1] Or perhaps *padmaśilâ*.—Tawney's *Prabandha-chintâmaṇi*, p. 67, n. 3; and conf. ante, p. 27, note 4.

[2] *Râs Mâlâ*, vol. II, p. 327; Wilkins's *Hindu Mythology*, p. 394; conf. H. H. Wilson's *Works*, vol. II, pp. 21, 192 f.

[3] Sherring's *Benares*, p. 65: The seven are said to be Śîtalâ, Masânî, Vasantî, Mahâmâî, Polamdê, Laṁkariyâ and Agvânî.—Ibbetson, *Panjâb Ethnography*, p. 114. European works on Hindû mythology are very defective in information respecting the popular objects of Hindû worship.

The water in the kuṇḍa is brackish and unfit for use, but Hindû visitors coming to the temple affect to receive virtue from bathing in it. Legend ascribes the formation of it to the pawing of Sûrya's horses.

The position of the temple on a mound facing due east is such that the rising sun at the equinoxes would shine straight through the Sabhâ Maṇḍapa doors into the shrine.

The age of the temple may be inferred from its style to belong to about the eleventh century or the reign of Bhîmadeva I (A.D. 1022–1063).[1] And comparing it with the style of the Jaina temple of Ṛishabhadeva at Mount Âbû, erected by Vimala Sâ in 1032,[2] it appears evident that the two shrines must belong to very nearly the same date. Now Mr. Cousens found on one of the blocks forming the back wall in the shrine, a date inscribed, but upside down, and reading "*Vikrama Saṁvat 1083*," that is, A.D. 1026–27.[3] The style of the alphabet, as shown in the accompanying facsimile, may be regarded as supporting this date, and affording important evidence that the temple was begun within two years after Maḥmûd of Ghazni's savage raid upon Gujarât and the temple of Somanâtha. It is thus contemporary with Vimala Sâ's temple at Âbû and the Râṇî Wâv at Pattana. Mr. Kinloch Forbes[4] has remarked that of the funeral temple of Rânîkadevî—the queen of Râv Khangâr at Wadhwân—built by Siddharâja, the spire alone remains, "which is much ornamented and nearly resembles in its style" this temple at Moḍherâ: it is quite probable, indeed, that the latter was the model for the cenotaph.

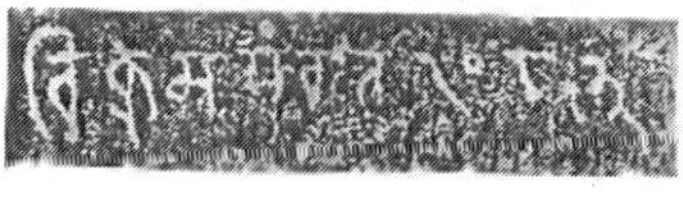

8. Date in the Shrine of Moḍherâ Temple.

[1] It has been suggested that this might be either the Karṇeśvara or Karṇameru prasâda, erected by Karṇa, *c.* 1070 A.D. *Prabandha-chintâmaṇi*, p. 80; *Baroda Gazetteer*, p. 609,—but Karṇameru was in Pattana.

[2] Fergusson, *Pict. Ill. Arch. of Hindostan*, pl. ix.; *Ind. and Eastn. Archit.* p. 236; or Burgess, *Scenery and Arch. in Gujarât and Râjputana*, pl. viii, pp. 13–15.

[3] We have a copperplate grant of Bhîmadeva, dated "Vikrama Saṁvat 1086"; *Ind. Ant.* vol. VI, p. 193; *Bhaunagar Inscripts.* p. 194; conf. *Ind. Ant.* vol. XIX, p. 253.

[4] *Râs Mâlâ*, vol. I, pp. 169, 170.

CHAPTER VIII.

VAḌNAGAR.

Plates LVII–LXIV.

VAḌNAGARA or Baḍanagara is a very old town, lying 19 miles in a direct line south-east by east from Siddhapura, and 8 miles north-east of Vîsalnagar or Visnagar, in latitude 23° 47′ N. and longitude 72° 42′ E. Vaḍnagara (Sansk. Vṛiddhanagara) is in the Kharâlu division of the Kaḍi district, and is the original home of the Nâgara Brâhmaṇs, whose influence with the princes of Gujarât is matter of history. In early times the place was known as Ânandapura.[1]

Dalpatrâma Dayâ states, on the authority of the *Nâgara Pravarâdhyâya*, that many Nâgara Brâhmaṇs of different gotras inhabited Ânandapura in Saṁvat 283.[2]

Under the name of Ânandapura we meet with it in Hiuen Thsang's Memoirs, as giving name to a state or province "having a circuit," he says, "of 2,000 *li* (about 330 miles) and the capital a circumference of about 20 *li* (3½ miles). The population is numerous and the people well to do. There is no chief (*or native*) ruler, but the country is a dependency of Mâlava, which it resembles in its productions, climate, literature, and laws. There are some ten *saṅgharamas* (convents) counting somewhat under a thousand devotees, who study the teaching of the Sammatîya school, belonging to the lesser vehicle (*Hînayâna*). There are many dozens of Deva temples, and sectaries of various sorts frequent them."[3]

The introduction to the *Kalpa Sûtra* of Bhadrabâhu mentions Ânandapura as one of the early centres of Jaina learning, and where that work was composed in the year 980 of their era (A.D. 454 ?) and publicly read before the king Dhruvasena to console him on the death of his son Senâgaja.[4] Mention is also made in the grants of the Valabhî kings of endowments given to Châturvedî Brâhmaṇs of "famous Anandapura" or Ânartapura,[5] and as these grants relate to places in the Kheḍa district, south of Aḥmadâbâd, it has been supposed that they refer to the modern Ânanda. This district between the Mahî and Sâbharmatî certainly belonged to the

---

[1] There is also a town called Ânandapura in the Deva-panchâla district of Kâthiâwâḍ (lat. 22° 13′ N., long. 70° 15′ E.), but it was founded by Ânanda Chuḍâsamâ in V. Saṁ. 1124. *Ind. Ant.* vol. VII, p. 8. Ânand in the Kheḍa district may possibly have been called Ânandapura also. Fleet, *Corp. Inscr. Indic.* vol. III, p. 173.

[2] *Jnâti-nibandha*, pp. 48 f. The use of the Gupta Saṁvat era (epoch 319 A.D.) was so common in Gujarât that this may refer to A.D. 602. Conf. *Baroda Gaz.* p. 624; *Ind. Ant.* vol. XXX, p. 249; *Râs Mâlâ*, vol. II. p. 233. For some account of the Nâgara Brâhmaṇs see *Bom. Gaz.* vol. IX, pt. i, pp. 13, 73; J. Wilson, *Indian Caste*, vol. II, pp. 96-99.

[3] Beal, *Si-yu-ki*, vol. II, p. 268, or Stan. Julien, *Mém. sur les Cont. Occid.* tom. II, p. 164; *Ar. Sur. W. Ind.* vol. II, p. 83.

[4] Stevenson's *Kalpa Sûtra*, pp. 2, 15; Jacobi, *Jaina Sûtras*, pt. i (*S.B.E.* vol. XXII), p. 270, and introd. p. xxxvii. The date of the *Kalpa-Sûtra* is not supported; Dhruvasena I ruled *cir.* 526–540 A.D. and Dhruvasena II, 629–641 A.D.

[5] *Ind. Ant.* vol. VII, pp. 71, 73, 76, 80, 81; Fleet, *Corp. Inscr. Indic.* vol. III, pp. 180, 190.

Valabhî kingdom in the seventh century, and at least till well into the eighth; but if we admit this second Ânandapura, not a hundred miles south of the first, we cannot distinguish the references. If the Valabhi kingdom, however, at that time extended into northern Gujarât, then "the victorious camp at the famous town of Anandapura" from which Śîlâditya VII, in A.D. 766, issued his grant of a village in the Kheṭaka district, must have been this same Vaḍnagara.

"This famous old town now presents but a poor appearance though in some ways it is picturesque. To the north-east is the large Sarmishṭa tank, of a circular shape, with an island on the middle of it, on which at midday large numbers of alligators are seen basking in the sun. The water is flanked with stone walls and steps, trees fringe it, and here and there a small temple has been erected. At the west end stands the town on a rising ground; the houses are perched above the lofty walls; steep stone stairs, one numbering 360 steps, lead to the water; and at one spot the tombs are shown of the Pathân lover of a Brâhmaṇ girl whom he sought to bear away, and of the horse who died in leaping down from the wall."[1]

On a stone slab in the Arjuna-Bârî, on the north-west side of the Sâmelâ lake, is an inscription in 46 lines on a slab 32 inches in breadth by 35½ in height, commemorating the building of the walls of the town by Kumârapâla Solañki, in Saṁ. 1208 (Sept. 1152 A.D.).[2] It was composed by Śrîpâla, the court poet, and traces in grandiloquent terms the history of the Solañki dynasty; then it proceeds —"This earth, that is blessed in being enjoyed by that king (Kumârapâla), bears a sacred settlement of Brâhmaṇs, rich in men of noble caste, called Nagara... Hence the gods gave to this (*town*) its second name Anandapura . . . There the Brâhmaṇs, descended from the Nâgara race, protect the king and the realm and guard them by sacrifices that ward off evil and cause prosperity. Nevertheless, lest this Brâhmaṇ town, though thus given up to difficult austerities, should suffer harm, the king, full of devotion, ordered a rampart to be built for its protection. . . . The crest-jewel of the Chaulukyas adorned this whole town with a rampart, desiring to benefit the Brâhmaṇs," &c.

Abul Fazl in the *Âîn-i-Akbarî* (*circa* 1590 A.D.), describes Baṛnagar or Vaḍanagar[3] as "a large and ancient city and containing 3,000 pagodas, near each of which is a tank; it is chiefly inhabited by Brâhmaṇs." Even including the smallest shrines this estimate must have been far in excess of the fact; but it indicates clearly enough that the city abounded in temples even in the sixteenth century, though during the Musalman rule of the preceding three hundred years, we can hardly suppose that they had not often suffered. Still we find even now temples to Somanâth Mahâdeva, to Mahâkâleśvara, Jâleśvara Ajapâla, Dhaneśvara Mahâdeva, to Ambâji Mâtâ, and to Âshâpurî Mâtâ, none of them perhaps very ancient; besides, there are two Jaina temples, and a more recent one of Svâmi Nârâyaṇa, with others too insignificant for enumeration.

During the reign of Muzaffar Shâh II, or about 1520, when Sañgram Siñgh of Chitor was insulted by Mubâriz-al-Mulk, he attacked and defeated him, ravaging

[1] *Bomb. Gaz.* vol. VII, p. 624.
[2] This has been translated in *Epig. Indica*, vol. I, pp. 293-305.
[3] Jarret's *Âîn-i-Akbarî*, vol. II, p. 242.

the province, but he spared the Brâhmaṇs of Vaḍnagar, whilst, finding the neighbouring town of Visalnagar defended against him, he took it by assault, slaying the Muhammadan governor.[1]

The chief temple is to the west of the town, picturesquely placed below the walls, with a high and massive śikhara. It is dedicated to Hâṭakeśvara Mahâdeva—the special divinity of the Nâgara Brâhmaṇs. Of considerable size, it is profusely ornamented with carving, and the figures are noticeably quaint and suggestive. The Jainas have two temples conspicuously placed, in the older of which is a large stone figure of an elephant.[2]

Of the older remains of Vaḍanagar, the chief are two magnificent *kirttistambhas* or triumphal arches, that must once have been connected with a great temple of which not a vestige now remains. They stand outside the walls to the north of the town, and are identical in size and design—the more easterly of the two being in much better preservation than the other, which stands parallel to it but to the north-west. It seems probable that the first stood before the main or east entrance to a temple and the other to the north of that entrance—much as that still left does at the Rudramahâlaya of Siddhapura (Plate XXXVIII). Both of them face the east, and houses now occupy the intermediate space between the arches.

They are built of red and yellow sandstone without mortar or other cementing material, and to give stability to such structures, the bases of the pillars are relatively of considerable dimensions: in fact, the base of each pillar occupies a square of 7 feet 4 inches—excepting the rebates at the corners; in other words, the areas covered by the bases are each exactly 53 square feet. Their construction is purely trabeate, the two pillars supporting a deep architrave and pediment (Plates LVII and LIX). The *toraṇa* or arch is not constructive but decorative, springing from the bracket capitals of the pillars, which form its support, and touching the soffit of the lintel. From the western *stambha* the *toraṇa* is now gone.

Here again the mouldings of the pillars follow those of the *mandovara* of the walls of a temple: first a complete *piṭha* or base with three *bhaṭas* or plinths, the upper carved with a lozenge ornament—which on comparison with the *piṭha* of the Moḍherâ temple (Plate XLIX) it will be seen that they are identical. Secondly, over this, the *kumbha* or sur-base has groups of figures added on the faces as in the Sûṇak, Ruhâvi, and Motâb temples (Plates LXXXI, LXXXIII, XCIII and CI). The large figures, in panels, above this correspond to the *jaṅghâ*; and beyond this the mouldings agree very closely with those of the pillars at Moḍherâ. The double capitals are an elegant feature and, with the lower brackets, form needful supports to those figures which the workmen were so fond of introducing both on the necks of pillars and in the roofing of domes. The sur-capitals with their stilted shafts are close copies of the lower cap and neck of the pillar; and this portion of the column may be compared with the mouldings above the *jaṅghâ* on the walls of the temples at Ruhâvi, Gorâd, Motâb, and the small

---

[1] *Râs Mâlâ*, vol. I, p. 384.

[2] *Bomb. Gaz.* vol. VII, p. 625.

temple at Delmâl (Plates XCIII, CI, CII, and LXVIII). In the last will be seen the groups of figures above the cornice, corresponding to those over the lintel of the *kîrttimukha*. The square blocks carved with figures, vertically above the pillars, again are the analogues of similar ones over the corners of temple cornices, where they are known as *kûṭas*. These may be noted in the Gorâd and Ruhâvi temples (Plates XCIII and CII). The only addition on the pediment is the cusped *toraṇa* over-arching the central sculpture and issuing from *makara* heads.

Most of the bracket figures have been destroyed and the little circles of perforated work that filled the hollows between the cusps of the *toraṇa* with the small guttæ at the points, have nearly all disappeared.

There is another arch like this at Kâpadvanj, standing on the bank of a tank in the town, but it is not so lofty, being scarcely 23 feet high, whilst this one is 35½ feet, nor is it so fine a piece of work, and is apparently later in style.

In a small and partly ruined temple in the town, though otherwise of no particular interest, are two well-carved roof panels. One of them (Plate LVIII, 2) is on a slab 2 ft. 7 in. square, carved—apparently—with *kîrttimukha* faces and flowing arabesque work in the corners,—three of which are destroyed, and with a circular panel covering the breadth of the stone, having a border of round blossoms. Inside this border are sixteen male figures, arranged like the spokes of a wheel, each with a sword in his right hand, held horizontally behind his head, whilst with his left hand he grasps the wrist of his next neighbour. Their feet are towards the centre of the circle, and the legs interlaced in an unsymmetrical way, but owing to the contraction of the space, the whole number could not be introduced, though the arrangement prevents this being noticeable until we attempt to count them.

The other panel, represented on Plate LX, is on a rectangular slab measuring 3 ft. 6½ in. by 2 ft. 7½ in., and is of exceedingly chaste design. Two cross ribs each way enclose a central raised area 12½ inches by 20½ inches, and leave narrow sunk strips at the sides and small 2½-inch squares at the corners. In the centre panel is cut a lozenge-shaped compartment filled with rich arabesque—spreading out from a central oval boss. In the corners outside the lozenge-border are four different figures with floral appendages: in two opposite corners they are perhaps Gandharvas, in a third the *kîrttimukha*, and in the fourth or opposite corner a peacock. The ribs and marginal panels are carved with various florid arabesques and the crossings of the ribs with rosettes. The whole is deeply chiselled and effective. Both these slabs are of the ordinary close-grained and durable sandstone so universally used in Gujarât in the building of temples.

Outside the east gate of the town, and with an old tank close by, is a small enclosure in which are the ruins of what—if we may judge from the fragments lying about—was once a small but very ornate shrine. Round it are five cells (Plate LXI, 1)—four behind and one to the right of the entrance. The half-plan and elevation of the left side of one of those behind is given on Plate LXII. From the style of what remains of the *śikhara*, and from the pillar at the entrance of it, we may suppose that it belongs to about the early half of the thirteenth century.

Built into the wall surrounding the courtyard are two curious gargoyles (Plate LXI, figs. 2, 3). One is the figure of a very obese dwarf with his mouth wide open, who holds one hand on his forehead and the other on his stomach, as if in the qualms of sickness. The other represents a man canting over a water-vessel which he holds between his knees.

The entrance of the right-hand or north cell of the four is given in detail on Plate LXIII, together with one of the pillars of the porch. The figures of Varâha, Narasiṁha, &c. on the jambs might seem to indicate that this temple had belonged to the Vaishṇavas. On the lintel are represented the nine *grahâ* or planet *devatas*,[1] and above them a frieze carved with *kîrttimukhas;* but on the centre of the lower fascia of the architrave is a figure of Gaṇapati — the usual representative of Śaiva worship. At each end of the front step is a low square pedestal, on which apparently, there was a tiger's face.

Built into the sides of the small tank, at a short distance from these remains, are several old sculptures (Plate LXIV, 1). One of these is a slab 30 inches broad by 29 high, containing two compartments filled with dancing musicians, male and female, the middle figure in each being probably a goddess.

Another carving (fig. 2) about 2 feet square, represents an elephant at full trot, ridden by a *deva* (or a râja) with numerous attendants, male and female, in the air. The elephant seems to be seizing a small figure on horseback, who is brandishing a sword. Parts of the sculpture, however, are chipped off, and the allusion is not clear.

A third sculpture, nearly 4 feet long by 18 inches high, represents Kâmadhenu, Kâmaduh, or Surabhî—the cow which grants desires belonging to the sage Vasishṭha, and here attended by eight ascetics. The Ṛishis are usually spoken of as only seven, though the *Vâyu Purâṇa* gives eight names — Marîchi, Atri, Aṅgiras, Putaha, Kratu, Pulastya, Vasishṭha and Bhṛigu; and the *Vishṇu Purâṇa* adds Daksha and calls them the *nine* Brahmarshis.

[1] Conf. the door of a shrine at Anjar in Kachh,—*Arch. Sur. Westn. Ind.* vol. II, pl. lxi, at p. 210.

CHAPTER IX.

DELMÂL, KAMBOI-SOLANKI, VÂGHEL, &c.

PLATES VIII, AND LXV TO LXXI.

THE village of Delmâl or Dilmâl lies about 16 miles S.S.W. from Pâṭaṇ and 10 miles W.N.W. from Moḍherâ. If we may judge from the number of small shrines, now more or less ruined, lying in its vicinity and extending for some distance to the south and south-east of the village, it must at one time have been a place of considerably more importance than at present it can claim to be. Upon slight mounds some distance apart are five temples, partly ruined, and there are other knolls that bear indications of having been the sites of as many more.

Within the village, enclosed in a rectangular court measuring 92 feet by 58 feet, and surrounded by a high wall, is the principal temple—that of the goddess Limbojî Mâtâ, the presiding deity of the place (Plates LXV to LXIX).

Limbojî is one of the Śaktis or Mâtâs—the mother goddesses—so largely worshipped in Gujarât: thus we have Ambâ, Ambâjî or Ambâ-Bhavânî, whose great shrine is in the Ârâsur hills; Âdgâ or Hajârî-mâtâ the goddess of the Jhâlâ tribe, whose shrine is at Halwad; Âshâpurâ-mâtâ or Ashâpurṇâ—the wish-fulfiller of the Lâd Vâṇiyâs and Jâḍeja Râjputs, whose temple is at Mahar in Kachh; Asir-mâtâ, worshipped by the Sonis; Bahucharâji or Becharâji-mâtâ, whose shrine is on the border of the Aḥmadâbâd district, 11 miles S.S.E. from Delmâl; Bhut-mâtâ, whose temple is at Aruej near Koṭ; Bhilaḍî-mâtâ of the Shenvâs, who is represented by a cocoanut; Châmuṇḍâ, worshipped by the Châvaḍas and Vâghelâs; Devlî-mâtâ of the Gâmtâs; Hinglâj-mâtâ of the Vêgûs, Bhâvsars, Darjis, Khatris, &c., whose shrine is in Sindh; Kâlikâ-mâtâ, Kâlî, or Chaṇḍî of the Kansârâ caste; Khodiâḍ-mâtâ of the Gohils, whose temple is at Râjapura near Sihor; Mandavrî of the Parmârs, with a temple at Mûli; Merî-mâtâ of the Mângs; Randel of the Lohânâs; Revalî-mâtâ of the shrine at Vadâli, 12 miles north of Îdar; Samudrî of the Kapols with her shrine at Sundrî in Dhrângadra; Sitalâ-mâtâ, the small-pox goddess; Vâgheśvarî, the patron goddess of the Śrîmâli Vâṇiyâs and Sonis; Vindhyavâsinî of the Jethvâs, whose shrine is at Nâgamâtâ near Navanagar; and others too numerous to mention.

This Delmâl temple of Limbojî-mâtâ is of comparatively modern date, but occupies the place of a much older shrine, a portion of the materials of which has been built into the later one. The surrounding smaller shrines, which were appendages to an older central temple, still remain in good preservation and, by their careful finish and abundant detail, show that they were constructed at a period when Hindû architecture was in the zenith of its excellence.

The image of Limbojî-mâtâ was originally enshrined in an old temple, which is now in ruins on the bank of a tank to the east of the village, and will be noticed below. The present temple (Plate LXV) has been built on precisely the same lines as the old one, but in larger dimensions,—the figures on the walls of the latter being literally copied upon the former—but are of inferior workmanship. Like the old shrine, the new one faces north, which is said to be the direction that temples should look which are dedicated to Vishṇu, the goddesses, and some minor *devatas*.

The *nimb* or *limbdo* tree (Melia azadirachta) is regarded as the home of Vishṇu in the form of Jagannâtha, and is worshipped in cases of small-pox.[1] And the image in this temple is called Nîmbdojî, Limbadâ or Limbojî-Mâtâ, because, it is said, it was originally discovered under a *nimb* tree. She is represented with four arms, and her head surmounted by a snake hood: in her upper right hand she holds a *triśula*, and the lower is open with the palm turned outwards and the fingers pointing upwards, or in the *varada mudrâ*; in her upper left hand she holds a bell (*ghaṇṭa*) and in the lower a pot (*kalasa*). And at her right and left sides are a tiger and a lion; thus, apparently, representing a form of Durgâ, rather than a Vaishṇava goddess. Round the *vedi* are some indecent figures.

Nearly the whole of the main temple has apparently been rebuilt and white-washed. The sculptured figures on its walls are rather coarsely carved, somewhat in the style of the seventeenth and eighteenth centuries. Some parts of the maṇḍapa are rebuilt with the material and sculpture from the original temple. The interior is plain, the roof domical with figure-brackets, and the floor paved with irregular slabs of mottled marble. The *pîṭha* or basement of the temple has no *narathara* nor *gajathara* bands of moulding.

On Plate LXVII are given some further details of this temple: fig. 1 represents a pillar on the screen-wall round the Maṇḍapa; fig. 2 shows the mouldings on the plinth or basement of the temple; and figs. 3–5, the doorway into the shrine, with Gaṇeśa on the lintel, designating the shrine as a Śaiva one. The dwârapâlas and other figures on the jambs and frieze of the door—all belong to the mythology of this sect—and more especially to the Śakta form as followed by the Dakshinâchârîs who belong to the Śaivas.

Inside the courtyard, round the central temple, are smaller shrines and other buildings (Plate LXVI). Behind the temple, in the south-east and south-west corners, are two neat little shrines, both alike save in the figure sculpture. Plates LXVIII and LXX represent that in the south-west which is now dedicated to Lakshmi-Nârâyaṇa, whose image, dated in Sam. 1532, occupies the shrine,[2] whilst on the east wall of the same is a figure of Vishṇu upon Garuḍa (Plate LXVII). The corresponding temple in the south-east corner was dedicated to Sûrya. Both are genuine examples of good old work and are exceedingly neat and complete little structures—chaste in design and ornament. The *gajathara* and *narathara* bands of sculpture have been left out of the base to reduce its height and suit the small size of the shrine. The *śikhara* is complete in both cases.

A somewhat curious sculpture occurs on the west face of the south-east shrine (Plate LXIX and LXXI, 7): in one figure the four divinities Vishṇu, Śiva, and Brahmâ—or the Trimurti—with Sûrya, appear blended; or shall we

[1] *Bomb. Gaz.* vol. IX, pt. i, p. 385.

[2] See the inscription No. 7, *Epig. Indica*, vol. II, p. 27.

PLATE VIII.

DILMAL: OLD TEMPLE AT THE TANK, EAST OF THE VILLAGE.

rather say it represents a Vaishṇava Trimurti, with Sûrya-Nârâyaṇa as the central figure, seated on his *vâhana*—Garuḍa? The figure had eight arms, of which several are now broken off, and three faces. The boots, *viyaṅga* or belt, and the two lotuses represent Sûrya; Nârâyaṇa's hands are now broken off; but Garuḍa is his vehicle; the triśula or trident and triple-hooded cobra belong to Śiva; and the left hand holding the *kamaṇḍalu* or drinking vessel, and right hand open, belong to Brahmâ as does the vehicle—the *Haṅsa* or swan, just below the sculpture; whether the other animal is intended for the seven-headed horse of Sûrya or the Nandi of Śiva is hard to say. The face of Brahmâ is that on the spectator's left hand, the central one is of Sûrya (as often represented) with a flat-topped *mukuṭa*, and the third face, over the snake, is Rudra or Śiva's.[1] Our usual text-books on Hindû mythology say nothing about such an image—but they are lamentably defective.

In the shrine of this small temple are two images that are probably not original: one of them is of Sûrya about 2 feet high, and the other a female figure. Gaṇeśa—the usual symbol of a Śaiva temple—presides on the centre of the door architraves of both these little shrines.

Besides these, there are two structures in the north-east and north-west corners of the court, each containing three cellas; also two very small isolated shrines on the west of the main temple[2]; and a small cell against the east wall, dedicated to Pârśvanâtha.

In one of the three shrines in the north-west corner is a carefully carved figure of Brahmâ represented on Plate LXXI, 6. He is bearded, with very large ear-rings, three faces are seen; he has four hands—the two left holding the *Vedas* and *kamaṇḍalu;* the lower right probably held the rosary of *rudrâksha* beads, and the upper holds a wooden libation spoon (*sruch*). At his left foot stands his vehicle the *Haṅsa* (Tamil, *Annam*), from which he is called Haṅsa-vâhana or Annavûrti; and two Ṛishis with their wives (or are they divinities?) attend him. He wears the *yajñasûtra* or *yajñopavita*—the sacred cord of the Brâhmaṇs, and a richly jewelled head-dress, necklace, belt, anklets, &c.

Under the figure of the Jaina Tîrthakara—Pârśvanâtha, in the cell on the east of the court, is a short inscription recording its dedication in Saṁvat 1285[3] (A.D. 1228–29), but as this shrine differs in style from the others and runs into the wall of the enclosure, it is not unlikely that it was there before the others were built, and was afterwards enclosed when the wall was erected.

Before the principal temple is a *chhatri* or pavilion on four pillars, and in front of this again, abutting on the court wall, is a *kîrttistambha*[4] under which is the entrance. On the west of the temple stand two pillars supporting a plain

[1] The *Vâyu Purâṇa* makes the Trimurti consist of Brahmâ, Agni, and Vishṇu. On the Śaiva Trimurti, see *Rock Temples of Elephanta* (Bombay, 1871), § 21, and note 31.

[2] In one of these, on the seat of the image, is a short inscription in three lines, dated Saṁ. 1532, dedicating an image of Vishṇu. *Epig. Indica*, vol. II, p. 26, No. 6.

[3] The hundreds figure of this epigraph is almost obliterated, and is read with doubt. *Epig. Ind.* vol. II, p. 26, No. 4.

[4] On one of the pillars of this is an inscription in twelve lines, but so abraded that no connected statement can be made out; perhaps it was dated in Saṁ. 1512. *Epig. Ind.* vol. II, p. 26, No. 5.

lintel, possibly for the swinging of the goddess on certain festival occasions (Plate LXV).

The original shrine of Limbojî-mâtâ—already mentioned as a ruin outside the village, to the south-east (see Plate VIII)—is now said to be devoted to Pârvâdevî. It is of exactly the same plan as the larger temple in the village—which is a copy of it—even to the sculpture, but the work on this older shrine is vastly superior to that on the later one. The carving is deep and crisp, the cornice projects more and is much more elegant; the pillars are well conceived and executed in the style of those at Moḍherâ, Kasarâ, and Sûṇak; and the upper ledge of the screen wall (or *kakshâsana*) is deeper and better proportioned than that of the newer temple.

In front of the temple are portions of two pillars that once supported a *Kîrttistambha* such as stands before Limbojî's temple in the village. All the figures on the *vedi* are Devîs, and on the middle of the east wall of the shrine—the only one standing—is a figure of Mahîshâsura-mardinî—the slayer of the buffalo-formed Asura. The only male figures observed were Îśvara and Indra—two of the eight *dikpâlas* or guardians of the quarters.

To the east and south-east of the village are three old shrines, partly ruined, but similar in construction to those in the south end of the courtyard of the Mâtâ's temple first described, and they have in their basements both the *gajathara* and *narathara* mouldings, which are wanting in the others. In addition to these are two similar ruined temples, and sites of others, scattered over the plain on the east and south-east of the village.

On the south of Delmâl village, built into a long platform are twenty-six *pâliyâs* or memorial stones—known in the south as *vîrgals* or *vîrakallus*.[1] These commemorate the deaths of certain individuals between the dates of Saṁvat 1513 and 1891 (A.D. 1457-1835). A panel on the upper portion of the slab is supposed to portray the individual himself arrayed in his best, sometimes mounted on horseback, at others standing beside his wife, whilst the date is inscribed below. The sculptures are exceedingly crude, and the carving being shallow, these bas-reliefs form a great contrast with the much better work on the old shrines. They are entirely void of expression or of the slightest animation of pose. Five of them are represented on Plate LXXI. The sun and moon—the first symbolised as a lotus blossom—must appear at the head of each as the great witnesses. The first and second examples commemorate the *sati*—of two wives in the first case, and of one in the second—the others are of local heroes.

Speaking of such memorials, the author of the *Râs Mâlâ* remarks[2] that—"Gujarât is covered with monuments, more or less permanent, pointing out the spots whence mortals have departed to Swarga. These are sometimes merely unhewn stones, smeared with red lead, or heaps . . . loosely thrown together, but more usually engraved headstones, either standing alone, or covered by the pavilions called Chhatris and not unfrequently temples of greater or less size which enclose an image of the Deva.[3] The sculptured monuments are called *pâliyos*. They bear

[1] *Ind. Ant.* vol. XX, p. 69.
[2] Vol. II, p. 435, 436, or reprint p. 691.
[3] Across the river to the north-east of Pâṭaṇ and near the river bank, is a group of these Pâliyâs, where each is in the form of a diminutive shrine. At Maṅgrol in Kâṭhiâwâḍ, near the shore, great numbers of Pâliyâs are set up in memory of sailors drowned or who died at sea.

a rude representation of the deceased warrior, mounted upon his war-horse or driving his chariot, according to the circumstances which may have attended his fall. The pâliyo of the Sati is distinguished by a woman's arm adorned with marriage bracelets. A dagger piercing the heart or throat of a man often shows the spot where a Bhât has slain himself in *trâgâ*. Beneath the sculptured bas-relief is written the name of the deceased, the date of the death, and usually an account of the circumstances which preceded it. These funeral monuments, frequently in great numbers, fringe the reservoirs of water, or cluster around the gateways of the towns. At each pâliyo the relations of the deceased worship once a year, either on the anniversary of the death, or on some other day appointed for festival, and, when a marriage takes place in the family, thither the bride and bridegroom repair, to pay obeisance to their beatified ancestor.

"Some of these monuments attain insensibly to a high degree of sanctity. If a person who has made a vow at one of them chance to obtain the object which he had in view, his gratitude leads him to spend money in entertaining Brâhmaṇs at the pâliyo, or even in erecting a temple there. In either case the fame of the Deva is spread by those who are interested in maintaining it, and others are attracted to the now general worship."

About three miles north-east from Delmâl is the village of Kamboi-Solaṅki, where is the old temple of Sandaleśvara, in the middle of the village, and still in use, having a liṅga in the shrine. The temple faces west, is rather plain, and appears to have been clumsily rebuilt at some remote period. The basement is buried beneath the present surface of the ground, and the śikhara has a shattered look.

At Itoḍâ or Itodrâ, about two and a half miles east-south-east, from Delmâl, under a grove of trees on the bank of a tank, is a small shrine about 7 feet square outside, with the ruins of four still smaller ones round it. It also faces west. These are in the usual style, much like the smaller shrines at Delmâl; but neither the temple at Kamboi-Solaṅki nor this at Itoḍâ appears to be of much interest.

Vâghel or Vyâghrapalli is about four and a half miles west from Delmâl and in the Râdhanpur territory. It was the principal village in a grant of land made by Kumârapâla to his cousin Ânâka, the grandfather of Vîra Dhavala who established the Vâghela dynasty, A.D. 1243. At this village, says Mr. Forbes,[1] "is a temple similar in style to those which have been described" (Moḍherâ, &c.) "but of smaller dimensions. It consists of a single open maṇḍapa, one storey in height, with pyramidal roof, three porticoes and an adytum surmounted by a spire." This no longer exists, not even a vestige of its foundations remains. The villagers say it was broken down and the materials carried off about 1865–70, to be used in the construction of a new tank at Râdhanpur. Thus do Hindûs destroy and obliterate the best remains of their ancient art and the evidences of their past history; they can hardly upbraid the conquering Muhammadans for wrecking their shrines as their religion bade them, when, to save a trifle of

[1] *Râs Mâlâ*, vol. I, p. 255, or reprint p. 196.

extra expense, they allow, without protest, an ancient monument to be destroyed by some local contractor, and its richly carved material employed for the most vulgar of common-place purposes. Vandalism without a motive is the most pitiable form of ignorant destruction, and the perpetrators do not realise the loss thus caused.

There are here some interesting pâlîyâs with spirited, deep-cut carvings on all four sides, and with tops cut in the form of temple śikharas.[1]

At Vâghel is a large multilateral tank with an island in the middle of it; but it has fallen into ruin and most of its surrounding stonework has disappeared. Hindû tradition tells that, when Râ Khangâr of Girnâr had carried off the beautiful Râṇikadevî who had been betrothed by Siddharâja—though he had sixteen râṇis already—the latter called to his assistance his familiar spirit Bâbaro the *bhûta*, and bade him accompany him as he was going to Girnâr to fight with Râ Khangâr. On the march the king was joined at Vâghel by this Bâbaro, who had collected five thousand two hundred *bhûtas;* and at Siddharâja's order they constructed the talâv there in one night. And of every old reservoir or temple in Gujarat, a story is told tracing it to the great Solaṅki king. On this same march the forts and tanks at Jhanjhuvâḍa, Viramgâm, Wadhwân and Saylâ are all said to have been constructed by Siddharâja.[2]

---

[1] *Bom. Gazetteer*, vol. V, p. 350.

[2] *Râs Mâlâ*, vol. I, p. 162–64; 2nd ed. p. 125 f.

CHAPTER X.

MUNJAPUR, LOTEŚVARA, ŚANKHEŚVARÂ, &c.

PLATES LXXII–LXXVI.

MUNJAPUR, a village in the Râdhanpur state, six miles south-west from Vâgel and twenty-four south-west of Pattana, is said to have been founded during the reign of Mûlarâja by Muñja Râja or Vâkpati II of Mâlava (*cir.* A.D. 974–95) when on a penitential pilgrimage to this part of the country which is traditionally called by the Brâhmaṇs Dharmâraṇya. Whether such a legend has any other basis than to account for the name of the place it would be hazardous to affirm; more probably it derives its name from the *muñja* grass used to form the Brâhmanical *mekhalâ*.[1]

Towards the east side of the village is the old Jâmi' Masjid, which has been constructed, like most of the early mosques, of the materials from older Hindû temples,—the figures being chipped off the pillars and lintels, in accordance with the mandates of Muslim iconoclast principles. This building is still in a fair state of preservation (see Plate LXXII and plan on Plate LXXIII, 1). On the north side of the court-yard are the remains of a porch or *maṇḍapa*, which appears to have been part of a temple left *in situ*, to serve the purpose of an entrance porch to the court-yard.

To obtain the requisite height, the pillars of the mosque (Plate LXXIII, 2, 3) have been stilted by the introduction of a second shaft and capital over the principal column. This contrivance was at once suggested by the old Hindû system of brackets on the shafts of pillars to support *toraṇas* and figures, as we see in the Sûrya temple at Moḍherâ; and here some of the pillars employed may even have been so stilted in the temples from which they were reft. But in a mosque, where there are no *toraṇa* arches, much less images, to support, these under-bracket capitals become meaningless.

The large central dome of the roof is carved in the usual leaf pattern, arranged in concentric circles. In the apex of it is inserted a cusped rose pendant, such as we find so often in Hindû and Jaina domes. The rest of the roof is covered by seven small domes and twelve areas roofed by flat slabs cutting off their corners with others over these.

The three *miḥrâbs* are plain, and the *mimbar* is provided with seven steps. Over the central *miḥrâb* is a Persian inscription, and built into the wall to the south of it is another, under a small window. On a lintel, in the north end of the mosque is a Sanskrit inscription in three short lines, but very much abraided.[2]

---

[1] Manu. II, 42, 43; Stewart's *Panjâb plants*, p. 261. In Gujarât the spirit of a thread-girt and unmarried Brâhmaṇ youth is called *Muñja* and is to be appeased by pouring water on the roots of the Pipala or *Ficus religiosa*, sacred to Vishṇu. *Bom. Gaz.* vol. IX, pt. i, p. 385.

[2] The date "Saṁvat 1217, Vaiśâkha śudi 5" is all that can be read with any certainty. *Epig. Ind.* vol. II, p. 28, No. 9.

The perforated stonework (Plate LXXIII, 4) that fills the windows—of which there are three in each end and four in the back wall—has been taken from the maṇḍapa of an old Hindû temple, where it would perhaps be used to close in the space between the *kakshâsana* or ledge on the screen wall and the edge of the drip or lintel under it—occupying the space where the wood and bar lattice work is seen in the view of the Delmâl temple on Plate LXV.[1] The drip cornice has also belonged to an early temple.

About a mile and a half to the west of Muñjapur is a group of modern temples with some fortifications at a place called Loṭeśvara. There is here a kuṇḍa or rather a well of a very curious plan (Plate LXXIV, 2). Four rectangular cisterns, each approached by a flight of steps, form four branches or arms to the central well, which is circular—the whole being in plan like a Greek cross. The surrounding cisterns are connected with the central well by openings through the intervening walls.

The water in this peculiarly shaped well is exceedingly filthy, yet once a year there is a great *melâ* or religious fair held here, when some thousands assemble to bathe in the sacred, if insanitary, waters of this well. On these occasions certain individuals practise exorcism and persons possessed are brought here from all parts of the country to be cured.

Saṅkheśvara[2] lies seven miles south-west from Muñjapur, and is also in the Râdhanpur territory. It appears to have been an old *tîrtha* or sacred place of the Jainas, and there still remains in the middle of the village the court of an old Jaina temple of Pârśvanâtha, surrounded with cell shrines built of brick. The temple itself however has entirely disappeared, probably during last century.

The brickwork is similar to that of the temple at Sarotrâ, and is very carefully put together, the bricks being moulded—not cut—to the shapes for the various string-courses and other mouldings. Even the small brackets under the cornices of the larger shrines are of brick—each moulded and burnt in one piece. This work has been covered with fine plaster, cut whilst wet into the most delicate geometrical patterns (see Plate LXXVI). But all this has suffered grievously from the weather, the greater part of it having peeled off.

Upon the stone lintels over the doors of the cells are numerous short inscriptions ranging in date from Saṁvat 1652 to 1686 (A.D. 1596 to 1630). The image of Pârśvanâtha that belonged to the temple is said to have been transferred to a modern temple which has been built hard by; and the inscription upon the base of the image being dated Saṁvat 1666 (A.D. 1609–10) seems to agree with this. On the new temple the only inscription is dated Saṁ. 1868 (A.D. 1811–12), recording the donation of five thousand rupees towards its erection. This modern temple is of the present Jaina style, and is noways noteworthy.

The enclosure of the older temple measures over all 135 feet in length by 102 in breadth, and inside—between the fronts of the cells—about 121 feet by 70 feet. Two larger shrines project out from each of the enclosing side-walls, and one

---

[1] This sort of screen suggests the origin of the enclosure to the entrance of the gallery in Aḥmad Shâh's masjid at Aḥmadâbâd. *Arch. Sur. Wn. Ind.* vol. VII, pl. xvii.

[2] Can this be the Śaṅkhapura of Merutuṅga? *Prabandha-chint.* p. 202; *Râs Mâlâ*, vol. 1, p. 246.

from the end opposite to the main entrance. This last occupies the space of three cells, and from the right side of it to the corner about four cells have been broken down. On the left side of the court there is also an entrance which occupies the space of two cells; and opposite it, and on both sides of the court, the continuation of the pillars of the portico is broken: otherwise it runs round the quadrangle. Exclusive of a very narrow closet on each side, the number of cells is forty-six in line and five larger ones standing back, and which are properly temples. Inclusive of the principal shrine there are thus the favourite fifty-two in all.

The style of this building, as may be seen from Plates LXXV and LXXV[B], belongs to the sixteenth century, and it was doubtless erected soon after Akbar's conquest of Gujarât in 1572, when the Jainas had gained favourable consideration from the emperor, and being released from the pressure of the iconoclastic Aḥmad Shâhi sovereigns, they would feel encouraged to resume their zeal for the restoration of their fanes.

The local insignificance of Śaṅkheśvara, the cost of stone and marble brought from great distances, and their previous oppressed condition, would naturally tell with the local Śrâvakas in favour of using brick as the cheaper convenient material, and lead to its adoption for their temple. Lintels, pillars, door-jambs, and roofing slabs they could provide, and, with the best brickwork they could secure—carefully faced with the finest plaster—they produced a shrine that must have done credit to their religious devotion and liberality.

Six miles south from Śaṅkheśvara and eleven north-east of Jhiñjhuvâḍa, situated in the extreme south of the Râdhanpur state, on a dry, flat, treeless plain, anciently known as Vaḍhîyâra, is the village of Pañchâsar or Pañchâśara, —traditionally at least—one of the oldest towns in this part of Gujarât. For it was here that the heroic Jaya-Śekhara was besieged fully eleven hundred years ago by the invading army of Bhûdeva, and where four of his queens threw themselves upon his pyre to be consumed with his body.

Pañchâsar has nothing left above ground to commemorate its traditional fame. It is now an insignificant village of no importance. Ancient bricks of large size are sometimes unearthed by the inhabitants, these and a group of old battered sculptures in the village are the only evidence of there having been any temple in the place.

Groups of pâliyâs and *sati* stones are found round the place and on the burning-ground at some distance from it, but none of them go back more than seven centuries, and of that age there are only five with much abraided epigraphs. It is handed down that over the spot where Jayaśekhara's body was burnt a temple to Gujaradeva, the tribal god of his clan, was erected[1]: there is a common little Linga shrine here, but it is comparatively modern, and we do not know whether it marks the spot spoken of in the legend or not.

To the east of the village are some mounds from 20 to 30 feet in height, but these are said to be merely accumulations of village refuse. A mile to the west, in a little modern shrine, are placed some mutilated images that may have belonged to some temple of about the thirteenth century.

[1] *Râs Mâlâ*, vol. I, p. 34.

CHAPTER XI.

CHANDRÂVATÎ, ROHO, AND SAROTRA.

CHANDRÂVATÎ[1] is now a small village at the junction of the Śivâlan with the Banâs river, near the south end of Mount Âbû and in the Sirohi state, but at one time it must have been a place of no small importance. Until about the beginning of the fourteenth century it was the capital of the Paramâra chiefs of Âbû, who were feudatories of the Solaṅki sovereigns of Aṇahilavâḍa. After 1303 it was held by Chauhân chiefs, who perhaps paid but a scanty obedience to their paramount suzerain.

In A.D. 1209 the Mâṇḍalika under Bhîmadeva II was the Paramâra Dhârâvarshadeva, with his brother Prahlâdanadeva as Yuvarâja.[2] In 1230 the Mahâmâṇḍalika was Somasiṁhadeva, and his son Krishṇarâjadeva.[3] But in A.D. 1321 we find Śrî Ludhaga ruling at Bâhunda, near to Chandrâvatî; and in 1331 we have an inscription of the Châhumâna Tejaḥsiṁha of Chandrâvati, and in 1338 one of his son Râja Kâṇhaḍadeva.

Colonel Tod, on his way home from Rajputana, in June 1822, was unable to visit Chandrâvatî, though he camped at Girwar only 6 or 8 miles to the north-west. But he entered with his usual enthusiasm into the vicissitudes of the history of the place, deploring the vandalism of the petty chief of Girwar, "the depredator and salesman of what time and the ruthless Turk had spared of its relics"—who "despoiled, sold, and converted into lime," the toraṇas and sculptures, "probably to cement some structure ignoble as the spoiler."

The city itself he says was "overgrown with jangal; its foundations and wells choked up, its temples destroyed, and the remains daily dilapidated by the Girwar chief, who sells the marble materials to any who have taste and money to buy them." And he quotes the following extract from the journal of Mrs. Colonel William Hunter-Blair, who followed in his own footsteps a year and a half later, and made the sketches from which his work was illustrated.[5]

"The ruins of Chandrâvatî," she says, "which was anciently the capital of the Paramâra Râjas, are situated about twelve miles from the foot of the Âbû mountain, on the banks of the Banâsa, and in a fine well-wooded country. The city is said to be mentioned in ancient legendary tales and poems, but until the beginning of the year 1824 . . . it had never been visited by Europeans, to whom it was scarcely known even by tradition. . . The city, to judge from

---

[1] Lassen, *Ind. Alterth.* Bd. III, S. 574, 575. [2] *Ind. Ant.* vol. XI, p. 221.

[3] *Asiat. Res.* vol. XVI, p. 302; *Bhâvanagar Inscr.* pp. 174, 218; *Râs Mâlâ*, vol. I, p. 274.

[4] *Asiat. Res.* vol. XVI, p. 285; *Arch. Sur. Westn. Ind.* Miscell. Mem. No. 2, app. p. xv; *Ind. Ant.* vol. II, p. 256.

[5] *Trav. in Westn. India*, p. 134. To Chandrâvatî three of her sketches are devoted; one of these is reproduced as a woodcut in Fergusson's *Ind. and Eastn. Arch.* p. 238, and another in the accompanying illustration, No. 9.

CHANDRÁVATI: GENERAL VIEW OF THE RUINS

the fragments of marble and stone strewn over an extensive plain, must have been of considerable size, and its pretensions to great refinement and riches may be admitted from the beautiful specimens still remaining of its marble edifices, of which twenty of different sizes were discovered when the spot was first visited by His Excellency Sir Charles Colville[1] and his party in January 1824." The

9. Chandrâvatî : ruined Temple, &c. in 1824.

one represented (fig. 9) she describes as "Brahmanical, and adorned with rich sculptured figures and ornaments in high relief, those of the human form being nearly statues, and only attached to the building sufficiently for their own support. They are executed with a degree of excellence scarcely equalled in Indian sculpture, and which would not in some instances disgrace more cultivated artists. Of these images there are one hundred and thirty-eight. The smallest are two feet high and placed in niches of the most elegant workmanship. The principal figures are a Triad, or three-headed statue, with a female seated on his knee, sitting on a car, with a large goose in front:—Śiva (?) with twenty arms:—the same with a buffalo on his left, the right foot raised and resting on a small figure resembling Garuḍa: a figure of Death (? Bhairava)[2] with twenty arms, one holding a human head by the hair; a victim lying beneath, and a nymph on each side; one seems drinking the blood falling from the head:—with many others, surrounded by different attributes in various postures: but the most admirable are the dancing nymphs, with garlands and musical instruments, many being extremely graceful and well executed. This building is entirely formed of white marble, and the prominent parts have retained their lustre; but those which recede are become dark from the influence of weather and atmosphere, adding to, rather than diminishing, the effect of the rich carving.

[1] Commander-in-Chief, Bombay; 1819-1824.
[2] Conf. *Arch. Sur. W. Ind.* vol. V, pl. xxii, 2.

"The interior of the temple and centre dome is highly finished; but the roof and exterior of the domes have lost their outer coating of marble. The pillars in the foreground of the drawing . . . are of marble, which material is strewn over the adjacent ground in great profusion, and columns, statues, cornices, and slabs, are tossed in heaps all around."

Mr. Kinloch Forbes gives no account of Chandrâvatî, and perhaps never visited it. The effect of weather and vegetation, with the carrying off occasionally of pieces of sculpture and even the burning of larger blocks into lime by neighbouring villagers, would all have their effects during the next fifty years, but much of interest remained when the author passed it in December 1872, and regretted that he had not the time for a few photographs. A decade later the Râjputâna-Mâlwâ Railway was constructed, and the devastation of the contractors ensued.

In 1884, Dr. Gustave le Bon, an eminent French archæologist, made a tour in India, and in one of his letters to *Le Temps* he thus wrote:—"We talk with reason when we say that nothing is more clearly written than what is written in stone: the history of India is traced as clearly as possible upon its monuments. These last, unfortunately, are disappearing with regrettable rapidity. The English pickaxe is unmerciful, and whenever any temple is found situated upon a road under construction, porticoes, columns, statues, fall under the pick of the demolisher to go and help to consolidate some embankment,—and the traveller who has painfully journeyed far to visit a temple described by some archæologist, on arrival finds it entirely demolished.

"I had recently made a long journey to Chandrâvati to visit a temple among several other remains. A lucky chance at the moment of starting made me aware that the temple had been recently reduced to fragments, by an engineer to pave a road!

"The few archæologists who are interested in ancient monuments have written numerous brochures urging their conservation, but it does not at all appear that any serious results have been secured . . . . . The protection of the Government is only exercised upon a small number of monuments of the first rank. The others continue to be completely overlooked and at the mercy of the first engineer who comes and requires stone to construct a road or a bridge."

When visited by Mr. Cousens, at a later date, he reported:—"Save portions of the basement of one temple, and a few blocks of the back-wall of another, nothing now remains of the beautiful shrines discovered in 1822, excepting one solitary column which, by its loneliness, accentuates the desolation around it. A short walk from this reveals one of the chief causes of this; for there, under the railway bridge, on each side of the stone piers, in the river bed, lie in heaps upwards of a hundred cart-loads of sculptured fragments and images,—the unused portions of the vast amount of marble carried off from these temples. It has been used wholesale on the railway, to build the piers of the neighbouring bridges and culverts and to break up for metalling the permanent way. Nor is this at all a solitary

[1] Four letters were translated in the columns of one of the Bombay newspapers in 1885.

instance of such wanton destruction by railway contractors and others: it has been only too common."[1]

The site of the old city and its extent are still indicated by the mounds of bricks that formed the foundations of these old temples—of which there are great numbers; and on the south side are portions of the ancient city walls which faced the river Śivâlan.

The lines of the old fortifications ran along the river face at some little distance from it. Below the wall, and between it and the river, are cultivated fields, whilst inside the walls, and on a much higher level, is the site of the city. Scores of mounds, thickly interspersed amid the jangal that has overgrown them, indicate the sites of old temples and important buildings—some of them up on the hill side, thirty to fifty feet above the rest. Judging from such images as still lie about, it would appear that the majority of the temples were Brâhmanical, and that they were built of white marble.

The general plan of what remains of one temple near the village (Plate LXXVII, 1) is arranged somewhat after the plan of the Śivâlaya temple known as Govindeśvara at Sinnar in Nâsik district, with its five smaller shrines round it. In this instance the central temple and two of the smaller ones have disappeared, but three of the latter, with the outline of the platform—80 feet wide by 112 in length, still indicate the arrangements.

The river Śivâlan runs round and skirts the south side of the city site; the east is bounded by the hills, and the railway appears to run along its north-western side, beyond which is the Banâsa river and a thickly wooded plain which trends away northwards to the Âbû hills.

Sarotrâ and Roho.

Roho and Sarotrâ are two small Bhil villages on the river Banâsa in the extreme north-west of the Pâhlaṇpur state, and about six and eleven miles respectively to the south-west of Chandrâvatî.

Beside the village of Sarotrâ stands an interesting old Jaina temple, built of white marble (Plate LXXVII, 2). The principal shrine stands in a rectangular court, measuring 54 feet by 90, over the walls; and inside, this was surrounded by a corridor with the favourite number of fifty-two small cell shrines. But the back or south end and a large portion of the east side have been demolished and cleared away since 1872. A portion of the sculptured walls at the south-west corner of the central temple has also fallen or been removed. The whole has been wrecked and all the images have been carried away.

From the number of spires on the corridor, on which there were flag-staffs when the temple was in use, it has received the name of Bâvanadvaja or Bâvandhaja. In plan it is almost identical with several other Jaina temples—such

[1] In 1882, for instance, the foundations of the very old Jaina temple at Mûrti in the Gamdhala valley, in the Panjâb, mentioned by Hiuen Thsang, were dug up by order of the Assistant-Commissioner to furnish materials for the bridge at Chaya Saidan Shâh.—*Vienna Orient. Jour.* vol. IV, p. 82.

as that at Bhadreśvara in Kachh,[1] of Neminâth on Girnâr, of Vimala Sâh on Abû, and of Seṭh Hathisingh at Aḥmadâbâd: there are of course divergencies in detail. The cells in such cases may really exceed fifty-two; but the extra ones belong to divinities that are subordinate to the Jinas, and are not counted.

The temple faces north, and the front half of the court, like the Bhadreśvara and Vimala Sâh examples, is roofed quite across by means of lintels connecting the front maṇḍapa with the pillars of the corridor. This maṇḍapa is roofed by a dome standing as usual, on an octagon of lintels over the pillars. Four steps—in three divisions—between the columns on the inner side of the maṇḍapa, lead up, as at Bhadreśvara and Âbû, to the pillared platform in front of the temple itself, which is also almost a copy of the Bhadreśvara one; and consists of a principal maṇḍapa supporting a dome on eight pillars attached to angles of the walls, with a small anti-chamber in front of the adytum.

The whole temple, as may be seen from Plate LXXVIII, stands on a raised podium or basement, and is approached by nine or ten steps under a projecting porch, and has a special shrine for the Yakshiṇi and Devata on each side the entrance—and which, like all the others, are entered from the court, but are walled off from the rest of the *bhamti* which is appropriated to the Jinas. Outside, on the north-east, is a small *chhatri* or pavilion upon four pillars, perhaps intended only for rest and shade to visitors, or possibly as a cenotaph.

The temple itself is shown on Plate X, as seen from where the corridor on the east side has been destroyed. In its structure, marble has been used throughout, except for the śikhara, which is built of brick and plastered. The filling in, or core, between the outer and inner facings of the walls is of brick and mortar.[2] The images have been removed from the principal niches of the maṇḍapa and vimâna, and the sculptures on the walls are much of the same sort as we find at Śatruñjaya, Bhadreśvara, and other Jaina temples—consisting of Yakshas, Devîs, musicians, dancers, and figures from Hindû mythology which the Jainas recognise and have worked into their legendary *Mâhâtmyas.*

The cells round the corridors are built entirely of brick, and on the outside, moulded bricks are used for the lines of horizontal mouldings. The pillars and roofs of the corridors, with the frames of the cell doors and the benches or seats for the images are all of white marble. All the doorways—save one—have little figures of Jinas carved over them: the exception being in the cell to left of the entrance, which has a figure of Gaṇeśa on the lintel. He is recognised by the Jainas under such Brâhmanical names as Heramba, Gaṇa, Vighneśa, Parśupâni, Vinâyaka, Dvaimâtura, Gajâsya, Ekadaṅshṭra, and Lambodara.[3] The other cell, or that behind the shrine, would be appropriated to the Yakshî who was the Śâsanadevî of the Tîrthakara to whom the principal shrine was appropriated.

The overgrowth of vegetation has long been sapping the walls both of the temple and corridors; and no one cares for a shrine, long disused, and partly

---

[1] *Arch. Sur. W. Ind.* vol. II, pll. xxxii and lviii.

[2] A soft sort of mortar in which apparently brick dust was used. Marble is found in the neighbourhood, and may have supplied the material for the mortar.

[3] Hemachandra, *Abhidhâna-chintâmaṇi, Sl.* 207.

PLATE X.

SAROTRÂ: TEMPLE OF BHAVANADHVAJA

destroyed within the last quarter of a century, and carried away for some vulgar purpose. The columns figured on Plate LXXIX show sufficiently the care and elaboration bestowed on the original work.

Over the doorways of the cells in the corridors are short inscriptions engraved on the lintels, ranging in date from Saṁ. 1656 to 1690 (A.D. 1599 to 1634), and one on a pillar of the maṇḍapa is dated Saṁ. 1685.[1] These record gifts of *chhatris*, &c., and it is to be noted that they commence not long after Akbar's conquest of Gujarât and his grant of toleration to the Śrâvaks. For three centuries previous to that the temples had been at the mercy of the Muhammadan rulers, and few shrines could then have immunity for any length of time; a more humane government appeared with Akbar's conquest, and the old shrines began to be repaired and images were again installed on the deserted *âsanas*. When persecution and dangers threatened, towards the end of the seventeenth century, they would again be taken away and hidden.

Roho is about four and a half miles north-east from Sarotrâ, and has a step well with four short Sanskṛit inscriptions on its pillars and pilasters. The structure is entirely of white marble, apparently taken from older temples. It is now in a somewhat ruinous condition and has fallen into disuse (Plate LXXX).

At the entrance to the well are two small shrines—one on each side, and from the platform on which they stand steps descend to another platform about 6 feet broad: this is on a level with the roofs that cross the well at three equal distances and brace the side walls. A stair of nineteen steps descends to the second platform, nearly 8 feet broad, and roofed over. The next stair is of steeper gradient, and, by seventeen steps, descends to the next lower stage; from which the third flight of steps leads down another storey of 10 feet to the stage that looks into the well shaft. To the roof of this storey a stair also leads down, in the body of the side walls, from the ground level above. The well shaft is octagonal. The style of some of the columns employed in the well is illustrated by the two examples on Plate LXXX, 3.

In one of the inscriptions, measuring 8½ by 6 inches and of thirteen lines, we are told that Châmpâ, the wife of Râja Śrî Mânaji, and her daughter Sajjabâî, built the two shrines and the well at a cost of Piroji(?) 51,000.[2] This was in Saṁvat 1616 or A.D. 1560. An image lying in one of the two ruined shrines is dated apparently in Saṁ. 1676 and again gives the name of Châmpâbâî, but is much abraided.[3]

Two other small inscriptions at the top of the well evidently belong to some temple from which the materials were taken; they are dated Saṁ. 1259 and and 1299 (A.D. 1213 and 1243) respectively, and the second mentions the dedication of an image of Neminâtha in a chaitya of Ṛishabhadeva.[4] The fourth inscription seems to be a portion of a larger one and as a fragment is unintelligible.

---

1 Ten of these are given in *Epig. Ind.* vol. II, pp. 30–33, Nos. 17–26.

2 Perhaps *Mahmudis*, and so would be about 24,500 rupees. See *Epig. Ind.* vol. II, pp. 29, 30, No. 15. The date is doubtful and may be Saṁ. 1674.

3 *Epig. Ind.* l.c. No. 16, p. 30.

4 Nos. 13, 14, in *Epig. Ind.* vol. II, pp. 28, 29.

Not far from the well are the ruined remains of a Jaina temple constructed of white marble. On a pillar of the *Chhatri* of this temple is an inscription of which the date, Saṁ. 1259, is about all that is legible[1]; and on the base of an image of Pârśvanâtha lying here, is another epigraph, but much abraided. Close by this again are the decaying walls of a very substantially built railway engineer's or contractor's banglâ, in the outer gateway of which have been used the columns of some old temple. Was the remainder of the same shrine used for railway purposes—just as the temples of Chandrâvatî were carried off to railway bridges and culverts?

---

[1] *Epig. Ind.* vol. II, p. 28, No. 12.

CHAPTER XII.

SÛṆAK AND KASARÂ.

PLATES XI, LXXXI–XCII.

SÛṆAK or Soṇak is a village in the Pâṭaṇ division of the Kaḍi prânt of the Baroda territory, lying nine miles south-south-west from Siddhapur and five west from Uñjhâ. In the village is an old temple of Nîlakaṇṭha Mahâdeva, that is, of Siva with the blue or black throat—so discoloured by his swallowing the poison produced at the churning of the milky ocean in order to obtain the *amṛita*.[1] This temple is still in use; and on the bank of the tank to the north-west of the village is a small temple now in ruins.

The Nilakaṇṭha temple contains the usual Śaiva Liṅga; but whether this is the original it is impossible to say. The doorway of the shrine, on the lintel of which the dedicatory symbol is carved, has been reconstructed, and, in fact, much of the temple appears to have been rebuilt. As it now stands, it consists of the shrine and an open hall or maṇḍapa with an entrance porch before it, facing the east. (See Plate LXXXII, 1.)

There is an inscription in nine short lines on one of the pillars dated in Saṁ. 1356, and another on the base of an image, but very defective, dated "Saṁ. 1596, Śrâvaṇa vadi 13, Monday."[2]

The Sikhara is fortunately complete to the finial, and the roof of the maṇḍapa together with the porch are also intact (Plates LXXXI and LXXXIII). It is thus a fairly complete example of this style.

The roof of the hall is supported by sixteen columns or a square of twelve, flanked on the north and south sides by two additional pillars in projecting bays. And here, as to Kauoḍâ and other small-sized temples in Gujarât, the arrangement of the eight inner pillars, in order to give sufficiently wide central openings on the four sides, is not such as to yield a regular octagon; for in this case, the middle openings would be only of 4 feet. To get over this, the width of the maṇḍapa over the pillars is divided into five parts, one of which is the distance between centres of the corner pillar and the next on the adjoining sides of the square: thus, if the extreme dimension over the corner pillars be—as in this case—13 feet 4 inches, and the diameter of the pillars about 12 inches, the distance between the centres of the corner pillars and the next on each side will be 32 inches, and between their centres across the corners will be 53¾ inches, whilst between centres of the middle pairs on each of the sides the opening will give a clear passage of 6 feet: the sides of the octagon thus formed by the

---

[1] Hence he is also called Śitikaṇṭha—dark-necked; Nîlalohita—blue and red; Nîlagrîva—blue-necked; Śrikaṇṭha—beautiful-necked.

[2] *Epig. Ind.* vol. II, p. 33, Nos. 27, 28.

lintels will then be as 25 to 16—those across the corners of the square being the shorter. To reduce this to a regular figure for the dome, a second architrave or frieze has to be placed over the first, projecting more over the corner lintels than over the side ones. If the first lintels were all laid accurately, then the upper ones on the corners would require to project 8 inches farther in than those at the sides, and would really rest upon the ends of the lower side lintels; and as the diameter of the octagon between the lower architraves will be 11 feet, each side of the regular figure will be 54⅝ inches, as on Plate LXXXVI. The lower lintel is carved with *grasaḍa* or *kirttimukha* faces and scroll work, with projecting blocks masking the corners; and the frieze is ornamented with figure sculpture. (See section on Plates LXXXVI and LXXXIV.)

In this example the dome is very richly sculptured and has had twelve *devatas*, supported by brackets projecting from a deep vertical tier of upper frieze. These figures are about two feet high, and the brackets are carved with human or demon supporters: but six of the *devatas* are now wanting.

The mouldings on the outside of the shrine walls are similar to those on the Moḍherâ temple, only the sculptures are Śaiva — that seen in the principal niche on the north face (Plate LXXXIII) being an image of Kâlî, but much defaced. The figure in the niche to the west—the back of the temple—represents Śiva as Nâteśa or in the *tâṇḍava* dance[1]—while on the south side is Bhairava: these are represented on Plate LXXXV, 2.

The mouldings are more decorated, however, than on the Moḍherâ temple. Here there are two *bhaṭas* instead of one (Plate LXXXII, 2, 3), and their upper edges are chamfered off in curves. The *jâdamba* above these is very richly decorated (Plate LXXXV, 8); the *kumbha*, over the *pîṭha*, is covered with groups of little figures in relief, which are absent in the Moḍherâ temple, and it is among these sculptures that indecent figures are usually found. Above this the *kalása* or torus is overlaid with surface ornament, now much weatherworn. On the upper edge of the lesser cornice or *chhâjali* is an ornament repeated continuously along, and also over the figures on the *jaṅghâ* or wall area, which is a survival of a form as old as Buddhist art. If we compare it, for example, with the arch in the façade of the Viśvakarma cave at Elura,[2] we note at once the resemblance between the two, and the human figures on each side the Buddhist arch are here represented as busts. But essentially the same ornament may be traced from the early Buddhist work at Barâhat, through mediæval Jaina

---

[1] Burgess, *Elephanta.* §§ 68–72 and note 98.

[2] *Arch. Sur. Wn. Ind.* vol. V, p. 9, fig. 3. This decoration is locally known as the "ass hoof" pattern, and is ascribed to Gardabhailla (or Gandharvasena ?) the father of Vikramâditya, who is said to have ruled at Ujjaina B.C. 74-61, and to have had this carved on all his buildings—the legend telling that he had the form of an ass during the day, but resumed that of a man every night. *Bom. Lists of Antiq. Rem.* 1st ed. p. 171; *Bom. Gaz.* vol. V, p. 342; *Ind. Ant.* vol. II, p. 363. The famous Vikramâditya, his son, also has the epithet of *Gardabharûpa*—"having the form of an ass"; and the small coins found in Gujarât, with very debased representations on them, are known as *Gadhiya kâ paisâ*, and are erroneously ascribed to Gardabhailla or to the Gardabha or Gardabhilla dynasty, of which the *Vishṇu-purâna* says there were ten princes to be placed between B.C. 74 and A.D. 78, a period of 152 years. The Gadhiya paisâ, are, really, of mediæval date: see *Jour. Bom. B. R. As. S.* vol. XI, p. 334; vol. XII, p. 325; *J. R. A. S.* 1900, p. 118 f.; Rapson, *Ind. Coins*, in *Grundriss der Indo-Arischen Philol.* p. 34.

PLATE XI.

KASERĀ: OLD TEMPLE FROM THE NORTH-EAST.

and Hindû temples to the pediments over windows and *miḥrâbs* of the Musalmans in the fifteenth and sixteenth centuries.[1]

On the shrine wall the *jaṅghâ* is very simple as compared with that of the Moḍherâ temple, which is covered with figure sculpture. Above it, at all the corners, are imitations of the capitals of pillars with the *grasapaṭṭi* band round their necks, which is not the case at Moḍherâ. In the latter, too, the greater mass of the decoration belongs to the pillared hall or *chauri*; here and at Sûṇak the *jâdumba* is the more fully decorated. In the *vedi* of the maṇḍapa we seem also to have another survival of Buddhist art—the rail with its pillars slightly projecting and the cross-bars with their discs represented by the scroll ornamentation between them. This *vedi*, and those at Kasarâ and the old temple at Delmâl, present a more pleasing proportion to the projecting *kakshâsana* over it than it does in the Moḍherâ temple, where it is rather too high, whilst the *kakshâsana* is rather stunted. The projecting cornice or *chaju*, too, is wanting in relief, and is not so pleasing as it is here and at Delmâl.

The temples of Sûṇak, Delmâl and Kasarâ have, on the whole, an older appearance than that of Moḍherâ; are not so elaborate in plan, and may possibly belong to the century previous to the date of the last.

The construction of the roofs of the halls of Hindû temples has never been fully elucidated. There were, probably, several methods employed, which could only be illustrated by carefully prepared sections and descriptive accounts of different types. This Sûṇak temple appears to be of a similar type with that at Amaranâtha near Kalyâṇa in the Koṅkaṇa,[2] and a comparison of the section on Plate LXXXIV with the half plan of the śikhara on Plate LXXXII, fig. 4, may help somewhat to illustrate the construction of that roof.

Some twelve or more years ago there was found at Sûṇak a copperplate grant of Karṇadeva I, Trailokyamalla (A.D. 1063–93),[3] dated from Aṇahilapâṭaka on 5th May 1091, making a land grant, on the occasion of a lunar eclipse, to maintain a tank (*vâpî*) at Sûṇaka. The land was at Laghu-Ḍâbhî, a village still existing about a mile south of Sûṇak, and it was bounded on the north and west by the village of Saṇḍera—which is a large one about 4 miles south-west of Sûṇaka. The grant was addressed to the royal officers of "the prosperous Ânandapura," the chief town of a division containing one hundred and twenty-six villages. This is clearly the modern Vaḍnagar.

Kasarâ.

Plates XI, LXXXVII–XCII.

Kasarâ or Kasrâ is a small village in the Tharâ estate of Kâṅkrej, to the east of the Banâs river and about fourteen miles west-north-west from Pattan. The old temple here is of a type we occasionally find elsewhere—three shrines, dedicated to the separate divinities of the Trimurti—Śiva, Vishṇu and Brahmâ—

[1] See Cunningham, *Bharhut Stûpa*, pl. xi; Burgess, *Elephanta*, note 95; *Arch. Sur. W. India*, vol. vii,—*Muham. Archit. of Ahmadâbâd*, pll. lxxxi, 3; xc, 1; cii, 2, 3.

[2] See drawings in *Ind. Ant.* vol. III, p. 319, Nos. ii. and iii.

[3] *Epig. Ind.* vol. I, pp. 316–18.

grouped round a central hall or maṇḍapa on its north-west and south sides (Plate LXXX, 1). The front porch, that formed the entrance from the east side, has entirely disappeared, and the whole building, which was profusely covered with sculpture, has been badly battered and injured. It has long ago been desecrated and has since been used by the villagers as a cattle shed. Almost every figure on the walls has been defaced, and even the corners of the walls themselves have been roughly knocked about (Plate XI). The red and grey sandstone of which the temple is wholly built is of a brittle texture, and this rendered it more liable to injury.

It is not of great size; the central maṇḍapa is only about 10½ feet square, or 13 feet to 13 feet 4 inches over the pillars that support its roof; and this is about the same as in the Sûṇak temple, so that the arrangement of the pillars is exactly the same. Behind the two middle pillars in front of each shrine, and only 5½ inches from them, is a second pair, and beyond them the entrances into the shrines. These face east, north and south; and the doorways (see Plate XCII, 1–6) are all of one pattern, but the shrines belong to different divinities. On that central door, belonging to the west cella (Plate XCII, 1) the figures are all Śaiva; those on the north one are Vaishṇava (figs. 4, 5); whilst those on the south belong to Brahmâ (figs. 4, 6); these being the divinities of the Hindû Trimurti or triad.

The original images have been taken out of the sancta; but one of them—that of Vishṇu—lies outside, battered and broken in two (Plates XI and XCII, 7). In the north and south cellas are *vedis* or *âsanas* for images, but in the west or central one there is not, and it probably was occupied by the Liṅgam or emblem of Śiva.

In this west cell there are now two white marble figures of Sûrya—represented on Plate LXXXVIII, figs. 4 and 5. They figure the divinity quite in accordance with the early descriptions of how he ought to be delineated. On the first is a minute representation of his seven-headed horse—which is quite grotesque. The villagers say these were found in a well, and it is quite evident they had no connection whatever with this temple.

On the outer walls of these cells the figures in the principal niches correspond with those of the doorways. On the Vaishṇava shrine to the north (Plate XCI) are images of Lakshmî-Nârâyaṇa with Garuḍa, Varâha, Vishṇu, the Vâmana-avatâra, &c. Round the west or central adytum are Mahâkâlî, Bhairava, Mahiśâsuramardinî, and Naṭeśa; while on the walls of the south shrine are Brahmâ with Sarasvatî on his knee, repeated in the three principal niches, and Brahmâ standing. The "ass-hoof" ornament, though now broken off in most places, was originally of as frequent occurrence here as at Sûṇak.

The figures sculptured on the walls appear to have been carved in high relief and with considerable spirit, and in this respect are perhaps more of the character of older work than that on some of the other temples which may fairly be ascribed to the same or a later age. But exceptions in such details are not uncommon—being dependent on individual capacity or taste on the part of workmen.

The central hall, surrounded by twelve pillars—all standing on the low screen that encloses it, has a double architrave resting on the lintels that lie over the bracket capitals of the pillars; and as at Sûṇak it is the second that forms the regular octagon on which the dome rises in concentric circles of plain leaf mouldings, round the outer edges of which depend serrated fringes or "drops." A lotus pendant hangs from the apex of the dome.

The pillars are all of one pattern (Plates LXXXVIII and LXXXIX, 3); the ornamentation on the shaft naturally reminds one of the pillars in some of the Brahmanical caves at Elura, but the bracket capital carved with four armed dwarfs differentiates them, and closer comparison makes it manifest that there is no indication here of relative age. This Kasarâ temple and that of Sûṇak are of the same period, and they can scarcely differ in age by more than fifty years from the Delmâl and Moḍhera temples; the pillars on the screen wall of the *chauri* in the latter (Plates VII, VIII, LIII, LXXXV) are quite of the same style as here—but they alone would scarcely be a safe guide, and we have to take into account the whole style of the structure. The curves of the Śikhara are much the same as those on the Sûṇak temple, and the arrangement of the plan and roof of the maṇḍapa is quite the same.

In many places about this temple—on lintels, mouldings, under images, &c. —are carved names and letters, such as Madana, Pâvaḍa, Prâlaḍa (?), Ajaḍa or Âjaḍa, &c.; but, from the fac-similes taken these do not appear to be of very early date, though it is impossible to say exactly to what age—later than the twelfth century—they may belong: they are probably the names of workmen or masons, if not of visitors.

The basement is mostly covered by an accumulation of earth, about 3 feet deep, round the temple; but a sketch and section of its mouldings to a scale of 1-20th is given on Plate LXXXVIII, 2.

In the Kâṅkrej state on the north of the Baṇâs river, about twelve miles south-west from Dîsâ, and eleven north of Vâyad is the village of Bhilaḍi or Bhilḍi, three miles south of it is Mudeṭhâ or Mundeṭhâ, and about four miles south-west of this again and fourteen miles north of Kasarâ is Khemâna. At all three villages there were old marble temples about forty years ago; but in 1890 Mr. Cousens found that the Bhilaḍi temple "had not only been razed to the ground but its foundations had even been dug out and the whole of the material carted away to be converted into lime." The same fate has befallen the old shrines in the neighbouring villages of Mudeṭhâ and Khemâna, where "a few forgotten fragments, lying near the pits, out of which these temples had been rooted, were sufficient to show that the architecture was of that same high class that once adorned Chandrâvatî."[1]

[1] *Ante*, p. 29; and conf. *Progress Report, Bombay Govert.*, 1889-90; *Revised Lists of Antiqu. Remains, Bombay* (1897), p. 234.

CHAPTER XIII.

RUHÂVI, SAṆḌERA, MANOD, DHINOJ, &c.

PLATES XII, XCII–CIII.

RUHÂVI is a village about three miles south-west from Sûṇak. Here is the shrine of an old temple of Nîlakaṇṭha Mahâdeva, perched upon a high artificial brick mound (see Plate XCII). The maṇḍapa has been destroyed and cleared away except a portion of the basement. The temple faced the east, and has been of the same style as that at Sûṇak; its better preservation perhaps helps to give the work the appearance of having been somewhat superior in style; but the whole of the walls are covered with whitewash.

In the principal niches on the north, west, and south faces respectively are figures of Brahmâ with Sarasvatî, Śiva and Pârvatî, and Lakshmî-Narâyaṇa. Under these, on each side, are pairs of erotic figures. The doorway of the shrine, which is much encrusted with whitewash, has a figure of Gaṇeśa on the lintel, with the members of the triad—Brahmâ, Rudra and Vishṇu above him; and a linga occupied the centre of the floor of the shrine.

The brick foundation is an evidence of the early age of the temple, but there is some reason to suspect that the śikhara above the shrine walls has perhaps been rebuilt at a later date: it is more tapering in form than spires of the same age as the walls; the finial is larger and clumsy like; and just under the *âmalasara* or circular cap, are added a face on each of the four sides. These were added on later temples to ward off evil spirits, and are to be seen on nearly all the more modern temples in Gujarât, as at Śatruñjaya, &c., but are not found on older temples, as for example on the small shrines left behind the Rudra-mâlâ at Siddhapur (fig. 4, p. 68), those behind Limboji Mâtâ's temple at Delmâl (Plate LXVIII), at Saṇḍera (Plates XCIV and XCV), or on the Sûṇak temple, which was possibly also rebuilt but on the pattern of its first tower. Here it seems to have been re-erected after the style of the later temples, and these faces added at the top.

At Saṇḍera, a village about two and a half miles west from Ruhâvi and between four and five south-west from Sûṇak, are two small disused but interesting old temples (Plates XCIV, XCV). Beside them is a modern temple of Saṇḍerî-Mâtâ—one of the numerous Śakti goddesses.

The larger of the old temples is identical in plan and detail with that of Nîlakaṇṭha Mahâdeva at Sûṇak, only smaller, being 28½ feet in total length from east to west. It faces the east, and the basement is buried to a depth of about two feet in the soil. In the carving here, as in the old shrine at the tank at Delmâl (Plate VIII) the crispness and depth even of the surface ornament is noticeable, and, though weathered by centuries, it still strikes the eye by the rendering of light and shade.

Over the shrine doorway, Gaṇeśa is carved on the usual projecting block, whilst above are Brahmâ, Vishṇu, and Śiva. In the dome of the maṇḍapa are eight female dancing bracket figures—where at Sûṇak there are twelve.

Outside, in the principal niche in the back or west side of the shrine, is a figure of Śiva; on the north side is Vishṇu, and on the south Brahmâ.

The other and smaller shrine is somewhat peculiar and rather more archaic in appearance. The squat square tower reminds us of the temples in Orissa, which have been ascribed to the sixth century. Above the shrine door is a figure of Gaṇeśa, and over him, on the frieze, are the *nava-graha* or nine planets, as we have them also over the doorway of the small shrine at Vaḍnagara (Plate LXIII); on an old doorway at Anjâr n Kachh,[1] and elsewhere.

Two and a half miles south of Saṇḍêra and four south-west of Sûṇak is the village of Mâuod, Mânuṅd or Manoj, at which is a small old temple, still in use, but enclosed all round by houses (see plan on Plate XCVI, fig. 1). Like so many others it consists of a small shrine with a porch or maṇḍapa before it On a roof panel in the latter is a curious sculpture representing Vishṇu seated on Sesha, whose tail, and those of two attendant snake devîs, interlaced and knotted together, form the border of the panel (ill. No. 10). The tails in crossing from one side of the border to the other enclose eight somewhat oval spaces round the circle, and in these are small sculptured figures, among which it is easy to recognise the Narasiṁha and Varâha avatâras of Vishṇu, but the other six are not apparently of the same class.

10. Roof Panel in the Temple of Nârâyaṇa at Mânod.—Scale 1-10th.

Śesha or Ananta, the couch and canopy of Vishṇu while sleeping during the intervals of creation, is here represented as the *vâhana* or vehicle[2] of the god and portrayed with a human face, having a canopy of three snake-hoods, and with hands joined in reverence. This is more like the Buddhist representation of Nâgarâjas than anything Hindû: indeed it seems as if the original motif had been Buddhist. He has very large ears and heavy earrings and necklets. The Nâganîs on each side have a single snake-hood each over their heads, with similar earrings and necklets, and are also in the attitude of worship. Śesha's wife is Anantaśîrsha; is she represented twice here simply to preserve uniformity in the design?

---

[1] *Arch. Sur. Westn. Ind.* vol. II, pl. lxi, 2.

[2] Vishṇu is also represented in the Bâdâmi caves as seated on Śesha; *Arch. Sur. Westn. Ind.* vol. I, pl. xxx.

Vishṇu's right foot and left knee rest on the shoulders of Śesha, whilst the left foot is turned up towards his elbow. He is represented here as Chaturbhuja—four-armed, but the symbols he holds are not the usual ones. The upper right holds the *chakra*, but the lower has the *śaluṅka* or Śaiva *liṅgapîṭha*, and it is not quite clear what the symbols in the left hands are. All round, from behind Vishṇu and Śesha project what seem to be large flower buds.

Dhinoj or Dhenuj is fully five miles south of Manod and about eight west-north-west from Mehsâna. It is a village of considerable size, and around it are remains of buildings, tanks, and step-wells of former times. Among these is the old temple of Vyâghreśvarî—whose vehicle is the tiger (*vyâghra*)—the patron goddess of the Sonis or goldsmiths and of the Meśri Śrimâli Vâniyâs. (See plan on Plate XCVI, fig. 2, and photograph on Plate XCVII.) It stands to the south of the town above the bank of an old tank.

This temple faces the east and seems also to have been rebuilt, the portions of the original left undisturbed are the low screen wall round the maṇḍapa and the pillars, which are of an old pattern. The dome is in the Muhammadan style. The course in the basement, usually filled by a close line of elephants, is here almost plain but divided up by half pillarettes into small spaces, in a very few of which are carved the head and fore-quarters of elephants (Plate XCVII). The screen wall or *vedi* is very richly carved with a variety of florid patterns arranged vertically and broken by compartments containing Śaiva figures (Plate XCIX). The *kakshâsana* over this, forming the sloping seat-back, is in a more modern style than the rest, and only the corner blocks seem to have been finished.

In the front porch there is also a finely-carved roof of geometrical design, which can best be explained by the drawing and section on Plate XCVIII. Near Dhinoj are the remains of the supply sluice of an old tank consisting of three large circular openings through which the water was admitted into the reservoir, which has long since disappeared (Plate C).

Kanoḍâ, Motâb, Gorâd, &c.

Plates CI–CVIII.

Kanoḍâ is a small village on the Rupen river about four miles to the south-west of Dhinoj. Close to it, upon the south side of the village tank are the ruins of what must once have been a very pretty little temple. The maṇḍapa is left, but the shrine has all but disappeared—only part of the foundations now remaining: sufficient, however, to show its size. Its door frame has fallen within it and lies in pieces—the two jambs and the lintel.

The hall, though of much the same style and workmanship as the temple of Nilakaṇṭha Mahâdeva at Sûṇak, is arranged somewhat differently—having three porches to the maṇḍapa (Plate XCVI. fig. 3). The style of pillars is much like the others already described, and, as at Sûṇak, we have the *chaitya*-window ornament on the basement of the screen wall. The basement or *pîṭha* itself is less in height in proportion as the temple itself is smaller than at Sûṇak, and

PLATE XII.

KANODÂ: OLD TEMPLE OF SOMEŚVARA FROM THE NORTH-WEST.

accordingly the two upper mouldings, usually filled with elephants and with human figures, are both omitted to reduce the height.

The domical roof of the hall has been decorated in the usual way, but instead of a central pendent ornament, it has a flat rosette or lotus, and there are sixteen brackets round the dome to support as many dancing figures and musicians.

In the middle of the shrine lies a large stone head measuring 12½ inches from the chin to the top of the forehead, looking like the head of a gigantic *dwârapâla;* and beside it is a fragment with a *devi* sculptured on it, which the villagers call "Bormarana-devî."

Motâb is a village about three miles south of Dhinoj, and not far up the river from Kanoḍâ. On the east side of the village tank is a neat little shrine, of which the maṇḍapa has quite disappeared, and a great part of the outer facing of the back wall has fallen (Plate CI). The temple faces the east. On the plinth or *kumbha* of the wall are many more pairs than are usual of highly erotic figures. The elephants on the basement are somewhat larger than is common on small temples, and at each outer corner is a very obese kneeling figure with his shoulders thrown back and the hands laid together as if in worship. Among the female figures on the wall face or *jaṅghâ* is one in the act of applying something to her eye with a stick or brush, while she holds a cup or pot in her right hand; another arranges her hair with the right hand and holds a mirror in the left.

In the shrine is a high altar or *âsana* against the back wall on which is placed a large-headed bust with long pendent ears. It is much battered, but occupies the principal place among other slabs carved with figures which are placed here. This temple is known locally as Jakrad Vîr.

Gorâd is a village on the Pushmâvatî river, about three miles north-east of Dhinoj. Here is a small old sculptured temple in a walled enclosure, dedicated to Someśvara Mahâdeva. Part of the basement is now buried below the present ground level; the porch appears to have been rebuilt, and is not bonded with the masonry of the shrine, and the prominent mouldings of its base are 10 inches below the corresponding ones of the shrine. It faces west (Plate CII).

The principal figures on the outer walls of the shrine are Mahâkâla on the north, Nateśa on the east, and Bhairava on the south, whilst over the shrine door is Gaṇeśa. These figures are well carved and remind one somewhat of the Elura cave images. The jambs and lintel of the doorway are much encrusted with layers of whitewash.

In the porch is a neat flat ceiling (Plate CIII). The śikhara or spire is entire, though it has been mended and possibly rebuilt. The roof of the porch is evidently quite modern.

Half a mile west by north of Gorâd is the village of Vîrtâ, in which is also a neat little temple of Nîlakaṇṭheśvara, of which the shrine is similar to that of Gorâd, but it has the addition of a maṇḍapa (Plate XCVI, fig. 4). The pillars are not so richly sculptured or so well finished as those at Sûṇak and Saṇḍera. The domed roof of the hall resembles that at Sûṇak, but it has only three bracket figures left—out of the twelve that once adorned it.

In the three main niches of the shrine walls are the same figures as at Gorâd; over the shrine door is the representation of Gaṇeśa; and the temple faces west. There can be no question then of its being originally a Saiva shrine.

In the hall there is a loose black stone image of Vishṇu, about 2 feet 10 inches high, in a standing attitude, which must have come from some other temple.

Vâyad and Mândwâ.

Vâyad is a small village about two miles south of the Banâs river and fourteen miles north-north-west from Pâṭaṇ. It is regarded as being the ancient Vâyuvaṭa of the *Vâyu Purâṇa*, and the present village still possesses a celebrated image of Vâyu, for which an annual *jatra,* or fair, is held. It is said that the original image, mentioned in the *Purâṇa,* was thrown into the old well, and the present one installed in its place.

Here is one of the old step wells of Gujarât which Hindûs were so fond of constructing as meritorious works for the public good (Plates CIV–CVI). It is about forty yards in length and 12 feet 8 inches between the side retaining walls.

The structure is of five storeys in depth, and, except at the bottom of the fourth storey downwards, the landing platforms are unusually narrow—at the bottom of the third stair the landing being little over two feet in breadth. Along the side walls run wide ledges at each stage. As usual, it ends in a circular draw-well, about 13 feet in diameter at the top and diminishing to about 10½ feet below. At the head of this is the usual *moṭ* for drawing up water by means of bullocks for irrigation.

The pillars supporting the roofing slabs over the platforms of each landing are of two patterns: an older, in which the shaft changes from square to octagon and higher to round (Plate CVI, fig. 1), and one with a square shaft (fig. 2), quite of the pattern adopted in the Muhammadan mosques from the fourteenth century downwards. Possibly this may be due to some restoration of this well; or it may not be of great age. On one of the pillars of the older type is a much abraded inscription that seems to be dated in the thirteenth century of the Vikrama-samvat era.

In a panel on the wall is a figure of Śiva or Rudra in the Bhairava manifestation (Plate CVI, fig. 4)—four-armed, with the hide of an elephant behind his shoulders, and in the favourite attitude of spearing a victim as represented in the sculptures at Elephanta and Elura.[1]

Another well of a different type may be taken along with this. It is close to Mândwâ, the principal village of a small chiefship on the left bank of the Wâṭrak river, about five miles south of Amalyâra. Constructed in the bank of the river, a little to the north of the village, it is built of brick and consists of a circular shaft about 25½ feet in diameter at the top and somewhat less below.

---

[1] Burgess, *Rock-Temples of Elephanta,* 800 ed. pp. 35-38, and *Archæol. Surv. Westn. India,* vol. V, p. 24 and pl. xxii, 2.

A narrow arch is thrown across the mouth of the shaft, for the apparatus necessary for drawing up the water; and in one side of the well, chambers are built in three storeys (Plate CVII). It is thus of the type of the Bhamaria well at Maḥmûdâbâd.[1]

A passage, in the thickness of the wall, goes round the upper part of it and descends into one of the rooms; and at the north side another stair descends to the rooms in the first storey. On this upper floor there are three rooms in front and three smaller ones behind; and in the two lower storeys there are only three front rooms. The central front apartment on each floor is the larger and has an arched window looking into the well, whilst one of the smaller corner rooms contains the spiral stair connecting the floors. The walls are largely occupied by small recesses in which vessels for food or other articles might be placed—so that these cool retreats could be occupied in comfort during a hot, sultry day.

The water in the well was supplied by percolation from the adjoining river, and therefore it was necessary that it should be sunk somewhat deeper than the bottom of the river bed. The structure is quite Muhammadan in conception and is not, probably, more than four centuries old—possibly less.

[1] *Arch. Surv. Westn. India*, vol. VI, p. 46, 47, and pll. lxxvi, lxxvii.

CHAPTER XIV.

TÂRINGÂ, &c.

Plates CVIII–CXI.

TÂRINGÂ is one of the Jaina tîrthas or sacred places of pilgrimage. It is situated[1] among the hills on the west of the Sâbhramatî river, in the Gadhwâḍa district of the Mahi-Kâṇṭha, about twenty-six miles east-north-east from Siddhapur and three and a half north-west from Hadol. It is approached from Dabhora—from which it lies about five miles to the north-east—through three miles of flat scrub-covered country, then up a mountain torrent bed under large banian trees, up a steep slope of loose sand for half a mile, then over a roughly paved ascent and through a large arched portal, and finally down a very gentle descent into a basin among the hills, in the middle of which and surrounded by an extensive paved court-yard stands the temple of Ajitanâtha—the second of the Tîrthakaras—built by Kumârapâla (1143–1174) in his later years.

It retains, according to the *Râs-mâlâ*,[2] "more of the venerable appearance of age than either of the shrines of Pâlitânâ, though, like them, it has suffered much from the modern innovator; it is surrounded by several small temples of recent date, and in its vicinity are, as usual, reservoirs of the purest water. On the hill there remains a shrine to the Devî Târanamâtâ, from which is derived the name of Târingâ; it is associated with the times of Veni Vachharâja,[3] and his Nâgaputrî consort, and the site was probably occupied by a building long before the royal convert of Aṇahilawâḍa installed Śrî Ajitanâtha. A jangal of the thickest character, surrounds the hill on all sides, and renders access difficult to all, and nearly impracticable to a party unprovided with a guide, much more to an invading enemy. Two easily defensible paths alone give access to the plateau on which the temples stand, and which like that at Îdar, is fortified by the filling in of the few gaps nature had left exposed. On three of the surrounding peaks are built little whitened chhatris or pavilions, which, from their exceeding brightness, when a glimpse of them is now and then obtained through black ravines and tangled forest, serve as lanterns of the day, pointing out to the way-worn prilgrim the site of the holy dwelling of the 'Invincible Lord.'"

The Jainas make pilgrimages to this shrine, particularly at the full moons of the month of Kârtika and Chaitra—the first and sixth months of the saṁvat year in Gujarât which follows the *amânta* reckoning, or from new moon to new moon.

---

[1] In lat. 23° 59′ N., long. 72° 49′ E., near the small village of Timba.

[2] Vol. I, p. 369.

[3] Mentioned in an Âbû inscription, as of the Agara race, and who, in conjunction with Soma (the moon) started the Chandravaṁśa and Vachhya families.—*Asiat. Res.* vol. XVI, p. 134.

The temple measures about a hundred and fifty feet in length by a hundred across, inclusive of the porches of the maṇḍapa (see plan on Plate CIX). It is built of white sandstone and brick, and the labour in bringing the stones through the forest to the top of the hill must have been enormous.

The arrangement of plan is explained by the drawing on Plate CIX, in which it will be noticed that the maṇḍapa is entered from three sides, with porches on the north and south supported by two advanced columns; but on the front the porch is greatly enlarged, having ten columns. This occupies a platform measuring about 38 feet by 23, and the central pillars of the first and second rows are connected by arches—probably an alteration on the original structure. On each side of the entrance to the hall is a small shrine—possibly to Mahâyaksha and Ajitabalâ-yakshî.[1] The maṇḍapa has eight octagonal columns, arranged in a way that we do not meet with in earlier temples, or perhaps even in later ones. Its genesis is this: if we place, one across the other, two parallelograms each of whose dimensions are three and two, and divide the longer sides of each into three—then the eight corners and these points of division give sixteen points of support for the roof. In this case the parallelograms are 36 feet 9 inches by 24 feet 6 inches, and the distance between the middle pillars on each flank of the inner octagon is 12 feet 3 inches, and between its corners 8 feet 8 inches from centre to centre. The outer corners of the parallelograms are all occupied by attached pillars except the two toward the shrine; and behind them are four others symmetrically arranged, with an arch inserted between the middle pair. Close behind the last, stand other four connecting the screen that shuts off the shrine. The cell is about 18¼ feet square and has a recessed bench or *vedi* or *âsana* on each side as well as along the back wall. The plan here is also derived from two parallelograms measuring 18 feet 3 inches by 13 feet 4 inches laid crosswise so as to leave at each corner an angle projecting inwards about 2 feet 5 inches on each face. On the principal *âsana* a large figure of Ajitanâtha is seated: in the right-hand recess are three smaller images; in the left are four Tîrthankaras of various sizes; and at least eight others against the walls. There are also several in the maṇḍapa.

The *bhrama* or *pradakshiṇâ* round the shrine is well lighted by three large windows that advance out beyond the walls, and are shaded by projecting eaves. The pillars of the porches are illustrated by the drawing on Plate CXI, fig. 2.

The maṇḍapa is double storeyed and has an open arched entrance of Muhammadan style over each of the three doors.

The walls are cut up by horizontal mouldings as well as by numerous vertical angles leaving facets of various breadths; and round the whole, at about 14 feet from the ground, runs a belt of sculpture five feet deep, in which female figures in dancing and other attitudes predominate. About four feet higher is another belt of smaller figures of gods and goddesses, mostly single figures.

On the wall is an inscription in nineteen short lines recording a restoration, in which many alterations were doubtless made, in the time of the Emperor Akbar.[2]

---

[1] Hemachandra, *Abhidhâna-chintâmaṇi*, ślL. 41, 44.

[2] See the text of this in *Epig. Ind.* vol. II, p. 33 f., No. 29.

The spire or śikhara is of the usual style of the Gujarât temples, and might readily be taken as belonging to the sixteenth or a later century; the central tower is surrounded and overlaid by representations of the same on smaller scales.

Other Remains.

It is not to be supposed that all of the antiquities in the Baroda territories have been surveyed or are described among those noticed in the preceding pages. The northern province or prânt especially has been but little visited by Europeans, except along the main routes, and there are probably a number of interesting remains there as well as in the other districts.

A list of the places that have occasionally been mentioned as containing architectural antiquities — and respecting which enquiry might well be made — is appended here. Among them there may still be some of considerable importance that might yet be surveyed when opportunity permits. Many of them are mentioned in the published Lists[1] from the reports of inhabitants and of native officers, but such accounts are not authoritative as to age, style, or merits.

(1) At Nansâri is a Jaina temple of Pârśvanâtha with images of the twenty-four Tîrthaṅkaras; temples of Kṛishṇa, Mahâdeva, Âshâpurî-mâtâ, &c.; an old Pârsî fire-temple; dargahs of Makhtum Shâh and Sayyid Sa'adat; and a palace of the Gaikwâḍs.[2] (2) At Palsâna, 9 miles N.N.E. from Nausâri, two Hindû temples and a large tank are of some interest. (3) Mahâ or Mahuva on the Pûrṇâ, 14 miles east by north from Nausâri, has "a Jaina temple with a modest exterior," but which "is an excellent piece of architecture inside."[3]

(4) Variâv, about two miles from Surat, has two Hindû temples and a mosque. (5) At Kâmrej on the Tâptî, 11 miles N.E. from Surat, is a temple of Śri Nârada Brahmâ, with an image of superior ancient art in a subterranean shrine; also temples of Śrî Koṭeśvara and of Mokshanâtha Mahâdeva on the banks of the river; and an old temple of Kâlabhairava, half a mile to the north.

(6) Songaḍ in lat. 21° 10′ N., long. 73° 37′ E., near the Tâptî Valley Railway, has a notable native fort, with the ruins of a palace and some temples. And (7) at Sâlher in Bâglâṇa (lat. 20° 43′ N., long. 74° E.), about 40 miles S.E. from Songaḍ, are two other interesting forts.

(8) At Barodâ is the celebrated Navalâkhi step-well or Wâv. (9) At Sevâsi, 6 miles west from Barodâ, is also a fine step-well with an inscription.[4]

---

[1] The first draft of a list of these remains, as of those throughout Western India, was submitted by me to the Bombay Government in a *Memorandum on the Survey of Architectural and other Remains*, 24th August 1870 (see pp. 17, 18). That list formed the basis of the revised and amplified *Lists of the Antiquarian Remains in the Bombay Presidency, &c.* 1885 (pp. 166–171). This last was edited in the *Revised Lists* by Mr. Cousens, 1897 (pp. 225 ff.). The enumeration now given includes several additions of which no details are as yet available.

[2] *Baroda Gazetteer*, p. 564. This work has also been drawn upon in the following details.

[3] *Ibid.* p. 581.

[4] Forbes, *Oriental Memoirs*, 8vo. ed. vol. II, p. 101.

(10) Pâdra, 14 miles W.S.W. from Baroda, has a temple of Ambâ-mâtâ. And (11) Rânu, 4 miles south-west from Pâdra, has a temple of Tuljâ-mâtâ.

(12) Petlâd, 11 miles S.W. from Ânand, has temples of Râmanâtha, Gomanâtha, and Kâlkâ-mâtâ, with the dargah of Arjunshâh (died A.D. 1205), and two masjids. (13) Sojitrâ, 7 miles N.W. from Petlâd, has two wells "of ancient date and some pretensions."[1] (14) Bhâdran, 11 miles N.E. from Petlâd, has a temple of Bhadrakâli-mâtâ.

(15) At Valan, 5 miles south of Miyagâm,[2] (16) at Atâli also in the Choranda division; and (17) at Maṇḍâla, near Dabhoi, are step-wells. (18) Kârvân, 8 miles east from Miyagâm—the ancient Kâyavirohaṇa, a famous tîrtha—has remains of many old temples. (19) Karnâli and Châṇḍoḍ, on the Narmadâ, at its junction with the Or or Urî river, have noted temples of Someśvara, Kubera, and Pâvakeśvara in Karnâli, and of Kapileśvara, Seshaśayî, Kâśi-viśveśvara and Chaṇḍikâ-mâtâ, sculptured on the outer walls. And (20) at Ambâli village, close by, is the temple of Anasuyâ—a supposed incarnation of the Trimurti. (21) At Barkâl, also on the Narmadâ, is a temple of Vyâsa Muni. (22) Tên, between Châṇḍoḍ and Dabhoi, has a fine tank, octagonal in shape, with stone steps descending to the water, said to have been constructed by Visaladeva Vâghela under the charge of the architect of the Hîra gateway at Dabhoi. (23) Sinor, on the Narmadâ, 19 miles S.W. of Choranda, has temples of Bhadreśvara, of Angâreśvara Mahâdeva, &c.[3]

(24) Ancient remains have also been reported at Kathwâḍa, 8 miles E.N.E. from Aḥmadâbâd; at Vehelâl, 3½ miles N.E. of the last; at Bahiyal, 11 miles E. from Kathwâḍa; and at Lâwad on the Meśvâ, 6 miles N. of Bahiyal. (25) Vâghjipur, on the Meśvâ, 4 miles N. of Âtarsumba, has a very sacred temple of Utkaṇṭheśvara Mahâdeva, and (26) Atarsumba, on the Vâtrak, has a ruined but striking fort with a fine gateway.[4]

(27) At Satej, 9 miles N.W. from Ahmadâbâd; at Kâlol, on the Rajputana State Railway; at Nârdipur, 8 miles N.N.E. from Kâlol; and at Rupâl, 3 miles S.E. of the latter, remains are said to exist; also (28) at Chhatrâl, 4 miles N.W. of Kâlol, is a step-well dating from the time of Muḥammad Begaḍa. (29) At Kaḍi, 81 miles N.W. from Kâlol, are the Rang Mahâl and Supra Mahâl, the temples of Yudhiśvara Mahâdeva, of Khâkhi Bâwâ, and other remains; the Mandir of Gosâvi Mahârâja contains some elaborate carving.

(30–48) Between the Sâbhramati and Meśvâ may be named Dehegâm or Degam, 4 miles W.N.W. from Lâwad and 18 N.E. from Aḥmadâbâd; Isanpur, 5 miles N.W. of Dehegâm; Chhâla, 6 miles north of Isanpur; Wasna, on the Sâbhramatî, 4 miles west from Chhâla. And west of the Sâbhramati—Limboḍra, 8 miles N.E. of Nârdipur; Mânsa, 3 miles north of Limboḍra; Charâḍa, 4 miles north of Mânsa; Delwâḍa, 2¼ miles N.E. of Charâḍa: near Pilwai. 3 miles S.W.

---

1 *Baroda Gazetteer*, p. 540.

2 Pâlej,—near which are said to be some interesting old temples—is given in the *Lists* immediately after Moḍherâ, but without any indication of its position. There is a Pâlej a little to the north of Petlâd, and a Pâlaj 5 miles south of Kanoḍâ, but the place referred to is probably Pâlej, a village surrounded by Baroda territory, on the railway, 16 miles N.N.E. from Bharoch.

3 *Baroda Gazetteer*, pp. 554, 555.

4 *Ibid.* p. 591.

from Vijâpur; at 3 miles W.N.W. from Vijâpur and 2 east from Kolaṇḍa; Ubkâl, 8 miles west of Vijâpur; near Merala-vihâr, 2 miles S.E. from Ubkâl; Wasâi, 5 miles W.S.W. from Ubkâl; and Ghojariyâ, 4 miles south from Wasâi, and as far N.E. from Lânghnaj—are reported to have ancient remains; Sâldi, near Lânghnaj, has a temple of Mahâdeva; Vijâpur, has temples of Kâlikâ-mâtâ, Gaṇapati, &c., and the Khak Chauk, also some remains to the north-east; at Tâtosan, 7 miles W.N.W. from Vijâpur; between Kamona and Dadhiyâl, 5 miles south of Vîsalnagar; and at Vîsalnagar itself—indeed this whole district from Kâlol to Vîsalnagar is probably deserving of thorough examination.

(49) At Metrâna, 7 miles N.W. from Siddhapur, is a temple of Pârśvanâtha; (50) Daithali or Dadhisthala, on the Sarasvatî, 4 miles west of Siddhapur, where is Sandila-kunda, a temple of Vyâsa—bearded and holding a leaf of a book in his hand—and a group of old temples and cells[1]; near by is Mandikeśvara—a sacred place; (50) Uñjhâ, 8 miles south of Siddhapur, has a large temple of the Kaḍavâ Kunbis; (51) Athor, 3 miles south of Uñjhâ, has a noted temple of Gaṇapati, &c.; (52) Unâva, 3 miles west of Athor, has a dargah and temple of Mahâdeva; (53) Rânoj, 7 miles N.W. from Dhinoj, has some Jaina temples; and (54) Chânsama, 9 miles south of Pâṭaṇ, has a temple of Pârśvanâtha—the largest Jaina temple in the Baroda territory, said to have been built about seventy years ago at a cost of 700,000 rupees. It is built of Dhrângadhra stone, and very richly carved, with numerous spires. The interior is rich, and it is floored with marble.

There are possibly other remains of interest, but only a thorough exploration of the country could determine what is deserving of survey. Doubtless many epigraphs of historic value would also be found if sought for.[2]

---

[1] *Notes of a Visit to Gujarât*, p. 73.

[2] This list does not attempt to include the remains in the neighbouring districts of Mahikâṇṭha, Revakâṇṭha, Pâhlanpur, and parts of the Kaira and Ahmadâbâd zillas. "Akhaj," which Mr. Cousens has added to the first list, as "about 18 miles from Mehsâna," and having remains of a *kirttistambha*, I have failed to locate.

FINIS.

ANHILAWÂḌA PAṬṬANA: PILLARS AND ARCHITECTURAL FRAGMENTS.

FRAGMENTS OF STRING COURSES.

4-6, Scale—double that of figs. 1-3.

1. FROM THE RANI WAV.

MARBLE PILLARS FROM THE MUSALMAN TOMB NEAR THE KHAN SARUVAR.

SCALE TO FIGS. 1, 2, 3.

PLATE XIV

AṆHILAWÂḌÂ: TOMB OF SHAIKH FARÎD.

PLATE XV.

ANAHILAWÂḌA-PAṬṬANA: ROOF PANEL IN SHAIKH FARÎD'S DARGAH.

SCALE OF 12 1 2 FEET.

H. Cousens, supdt. S. J. Pashoshe, delt.

PLATE XVI.

ANHILAWÂḌA PAṬṬANA: CARVED CEILING AT SHAIKH FARÎD'S TOMB.

SCALE OF 12" 1 2 3 4 5 FEET.

ANAHILAPAṬṬANA: CEILINGS IN BHÂVÂ QÂZI'S TOMB.

SCALE OF 12' 1 2 3 4 5 FEET.

1. PERFORATED SCREEN FROM SHAIKH SARIFAH'S TOMB.

2

SCALE OF 12' INCHES

4

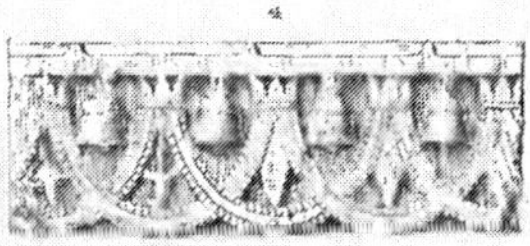

3

5

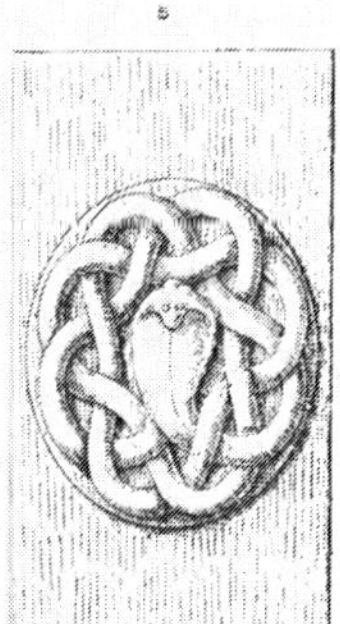

6

7

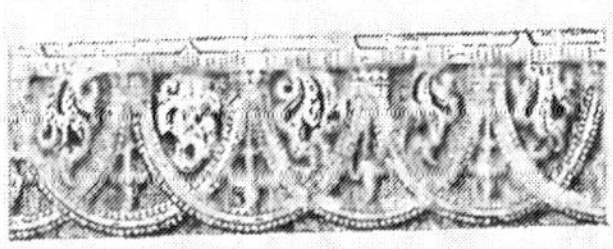

SCALE OF 12' FOOT.

ANAHILAPAṬṬANA: SHRINE OF ṚISHABHADEVA IN A JAINA TEMPLE.

SCALE OF 0 1 2 3 4 5 FEET.

H. Cousens, delin. Suyaj Rayhobe, etch.

ANHILAWÂḌÂ: SECTION OF THE MANḌAPA IN THE TEMPLE OF VÂḌI PÂRŚVANÂTHA.

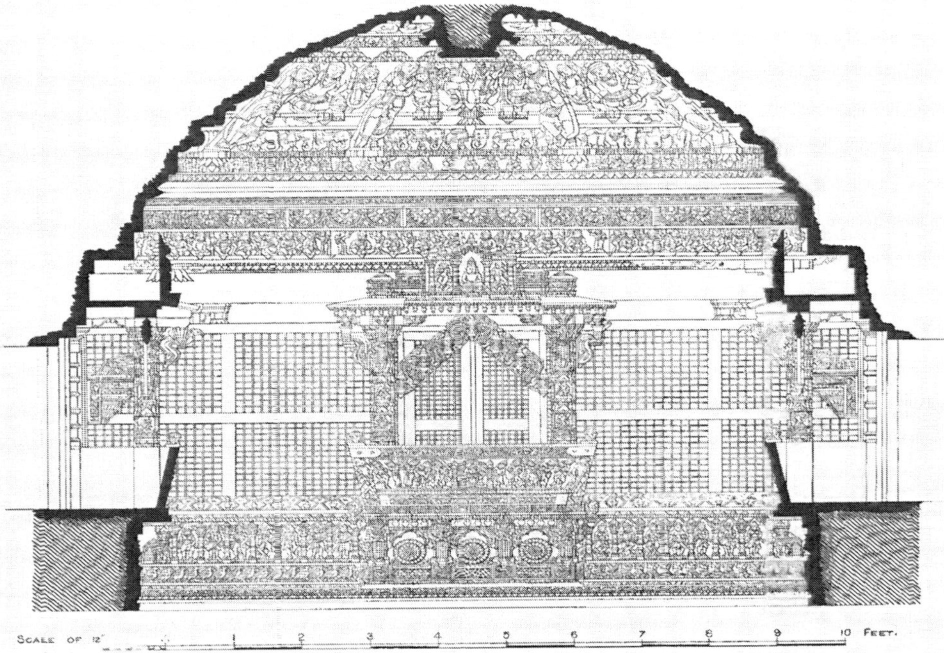

H. Cousens, mens.

Hari Gopal & Jayrâv Râghoba, delts.

ANAHILAPAṬṬANA: CARVED WOODEN CEILING IN THE TEMPLE OF VÂDI PÂRŚVANÂTHA.

H. Cousens, surv.

Hari Gopal, delt.

PLATE XXII.

AṆAHILAWÂDA WOOD-CARVING ON THE BHÂROT'S HOUSE.

PLATE XXIII.

ANHILAWÂḌÂ: GUMADA MASJID—PLAN, MINAR, AND BUTTRESS.

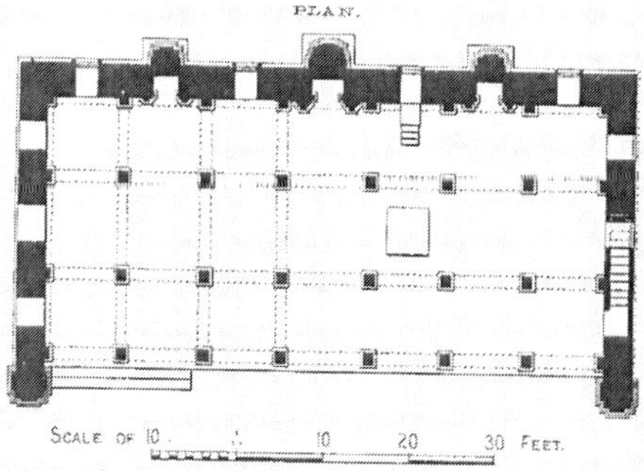

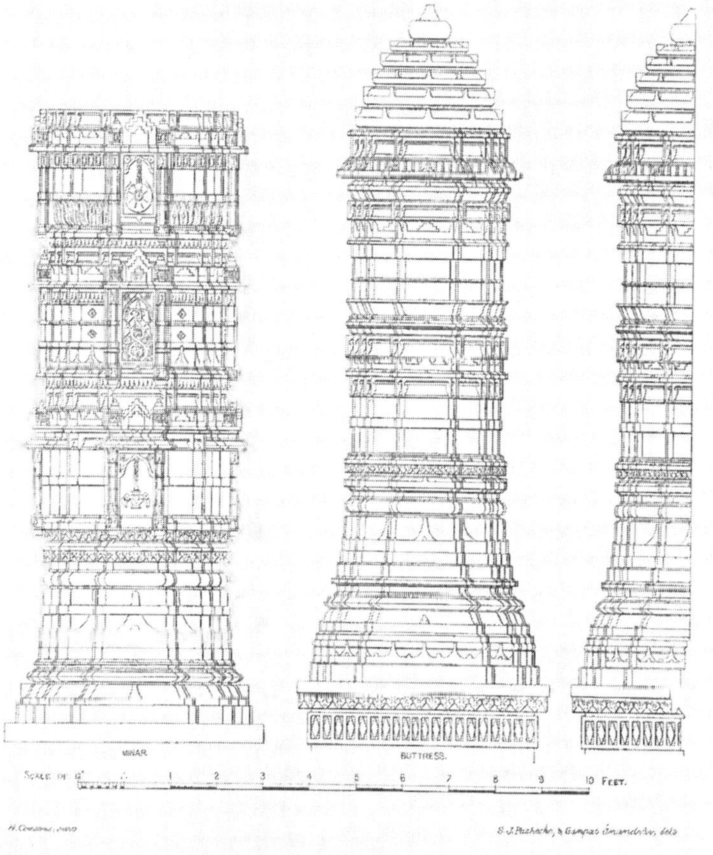

H. Cousens, direx. S. J. Pacheco, & Ganpat Anandrao, delt.

PLATE XXIV.

AṆAHILAWÂḌA: THE GUMAḌA MASJID

AṆHILAWĀḌA PAṬṬANA: GUMAḌA MASJID—DETAILS.

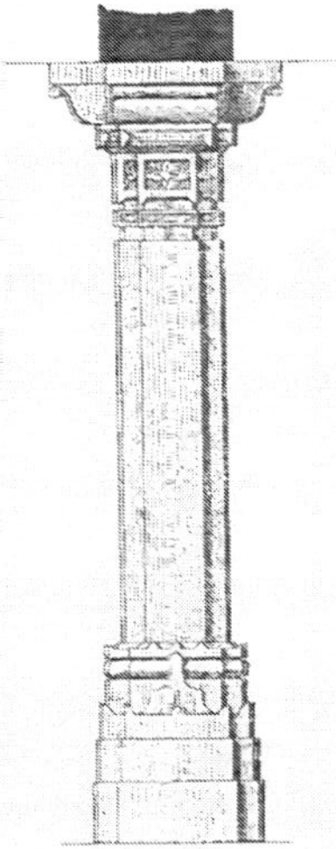

1. PILLAR.

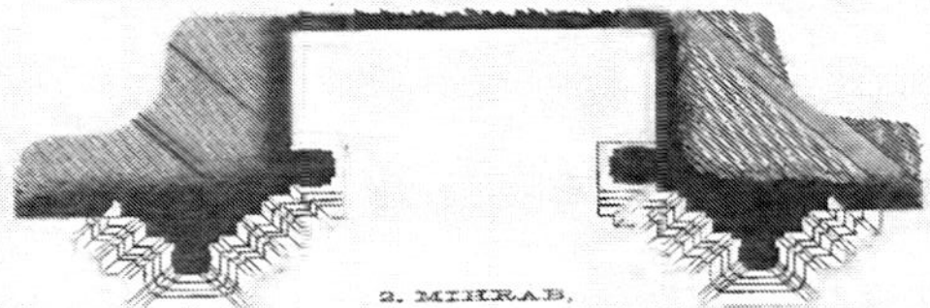

2. MIHRAB, ELEVATION AND PLAN.

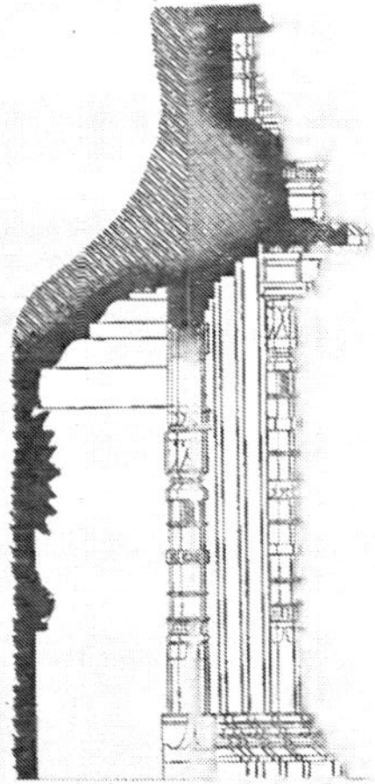

3. SECTION.

4

5

PATTERNS IN NICHES.

SCALE TO FIGS. 4, 5.

SCALE OF 12 0 1 2 3 4 5 6 7 8 9 10 FEET

H. Cousens, survr.

S. V. Pachcha, Jayrām Rāghuba } delt.

1 2

1, 2. WINDOWS FROM GUMAḌA MASJID.

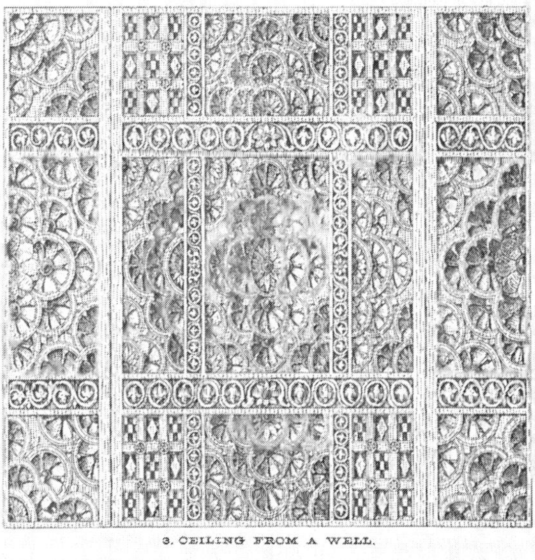

3. CEILING FROM A WELL.

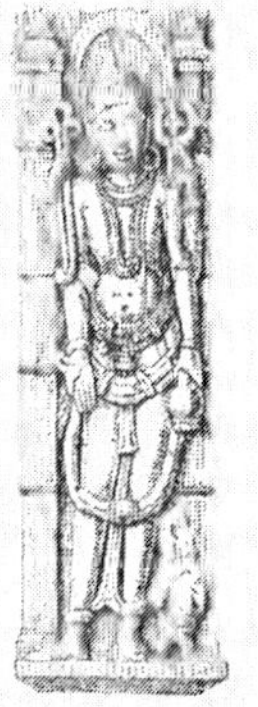

4. SCULPTURE AT KHÂN BAHÂDUR'S WELL.

SCALE OF 12" 1 2 3 FEET.

H. Cousens [illegible] Sayad Raghoba, del.

PLATE XXVII.

ANHILÁWAḌÁ PAṬṬANA: PLAN AND SECTION OF SHAIKH JODH'S MASJID.

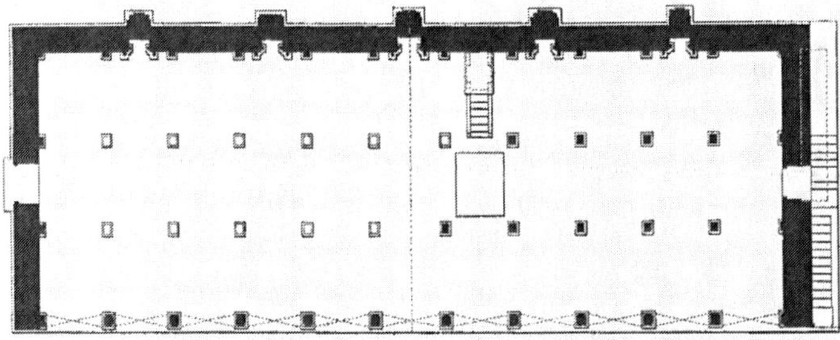

1. PLAN.

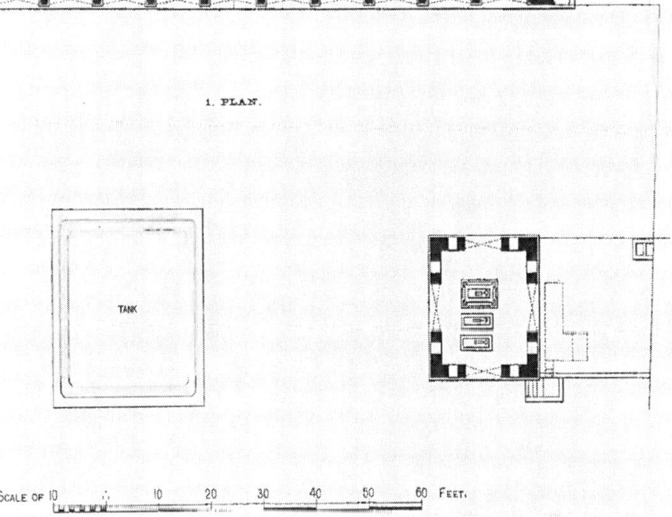

2. CROSS SECTION.

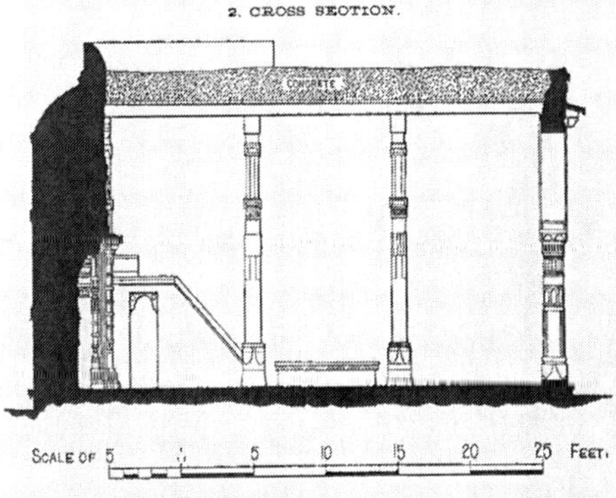

H. Cousens, direx.

Sitaram Dinkar & Ganpat Anandrao, delt.

ANHILAWÂDÂ: SHAIKH JODH'S MASJID—DETAILS.

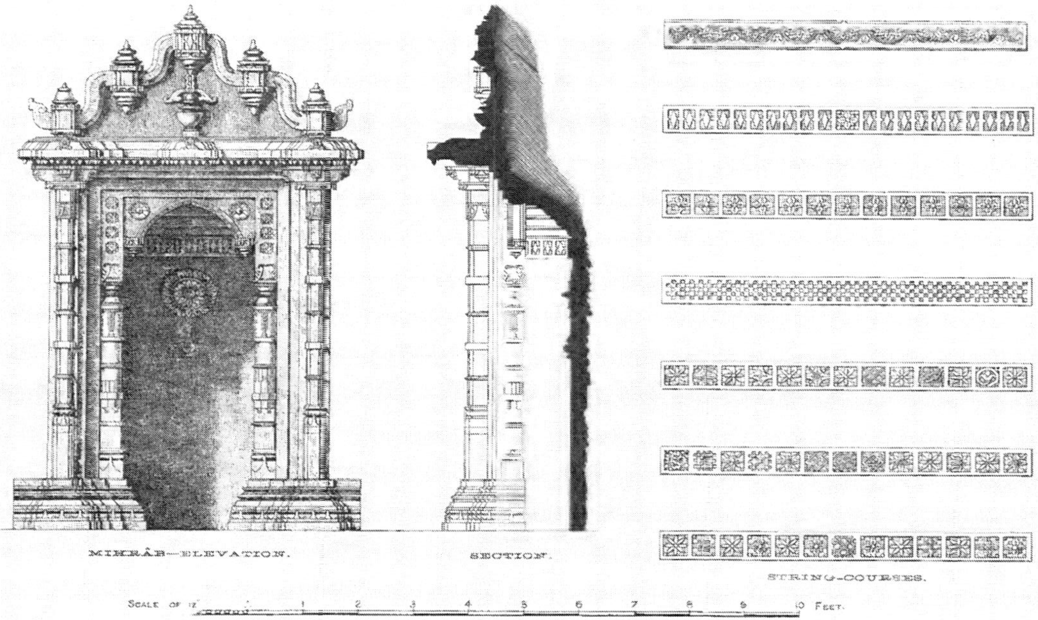

MIHRÂB—ELEVATION.

SECTION.

STRING-COURSES.

H. Cousens, direx.

Sitaram Dinkar, delt.

PLATE XLIX.

AṆAHILAWĀḌA: SHAIKH JODH'S MASJID

ANAHILA-PAṬṬANA: MUSALMAN TOMBS KNOWN AS MUHAMMAD TAHIR'S DARGAH.

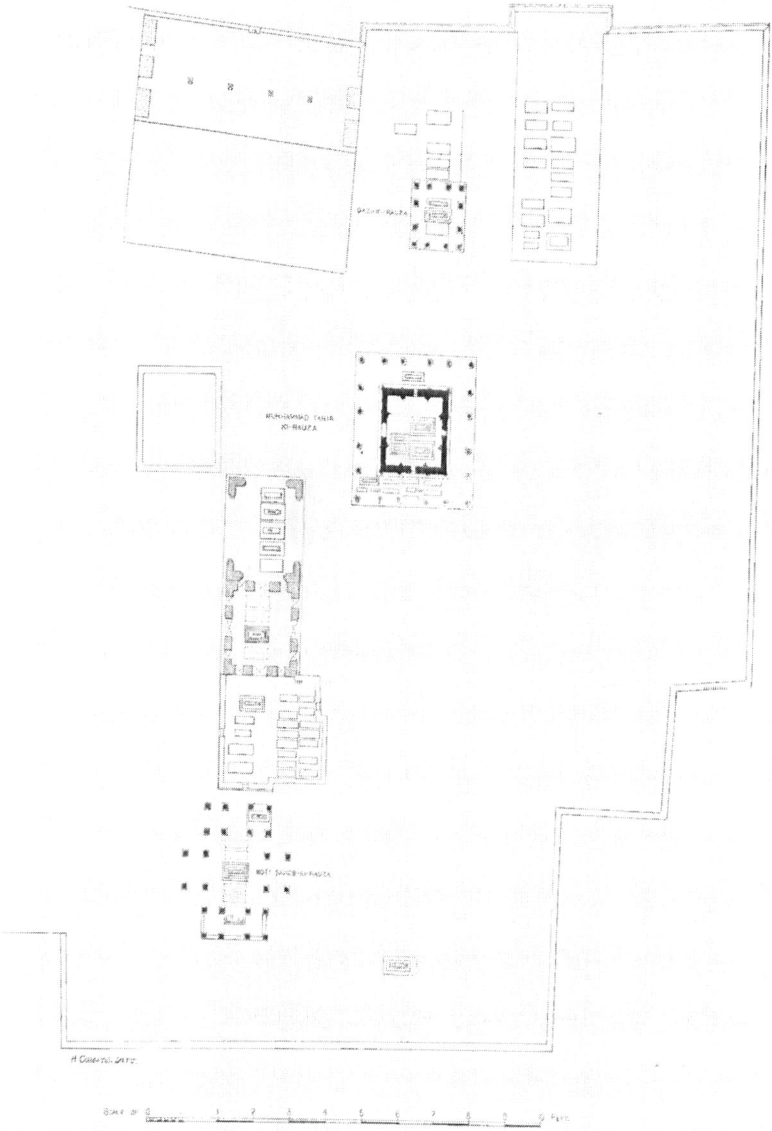

INLET SLUICE OF THE KHAN SAROVAR AT ANHILAWADA PATTANA.

PLATE XXXI.

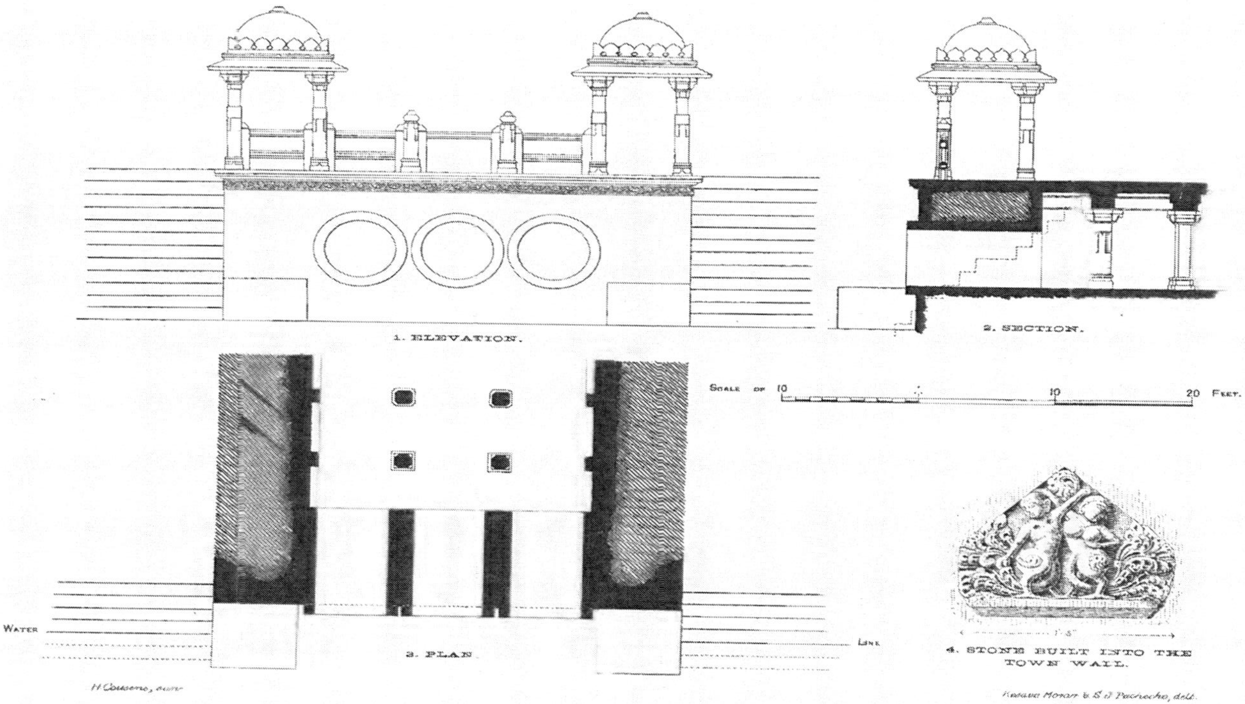

ANAHILAPATTANA: OUTLET SLUICE FROM KHÁN SAROVAR TANK

ANHILAWADA PATTANA: DETAILS FROM THE KHAN SAROVAR.

PLATE XXXIII.

1, 2. HINDU STRING COURSES.

FROM KHÂN SAROVAR

4. PILASTER FROM KHÂN SAROVAR.

SCALE TO FIGS. 5, 6.

SCALE TO FIGS. 1, 2, 3, 4.

AṆAHILAVĀḌA: FRONT OF INLET SLUICE TO THE KHÂN SAROVAR.

1

2

3

1-3 FRAGMENTS BUILT INTO WALLS.

4

5

6

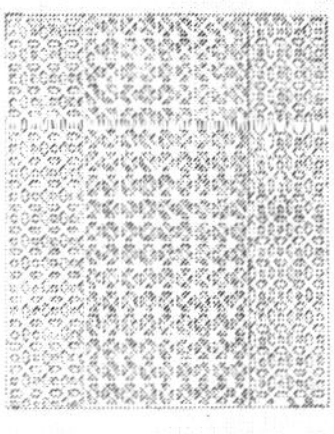

7

8

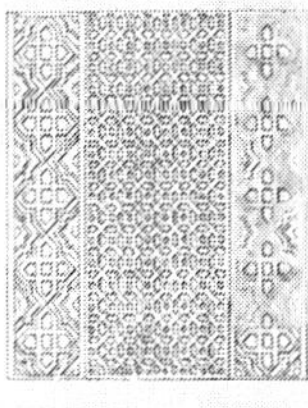

9

10

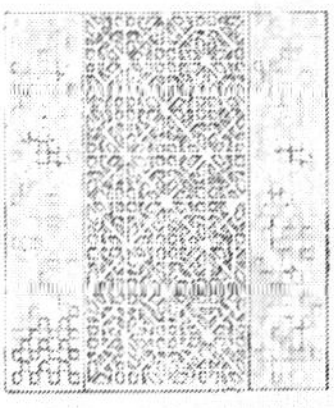

11

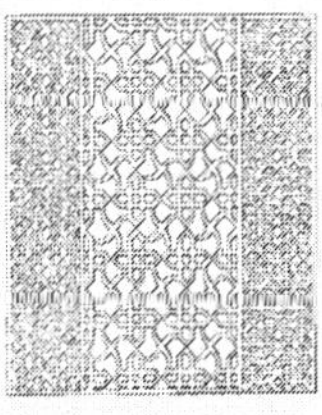

12

6-12. PLASTER ORNAMENTAL WORK FROM JÁLISVARA TEMPLE

SCALE OF 12" ½ 1 2 FEET

PÂTAN: OLD WOOD-CARVING ON A HOUSE FRONT.

SIDDHAPUR: RUDRAMAHÂLAYA—NORTH PORCH FROM THE EAST.

SIDDHAPUR: RUDRA MÁLÁ TEMPLE (RESTORED PLAN). PLATE XXXVIII.

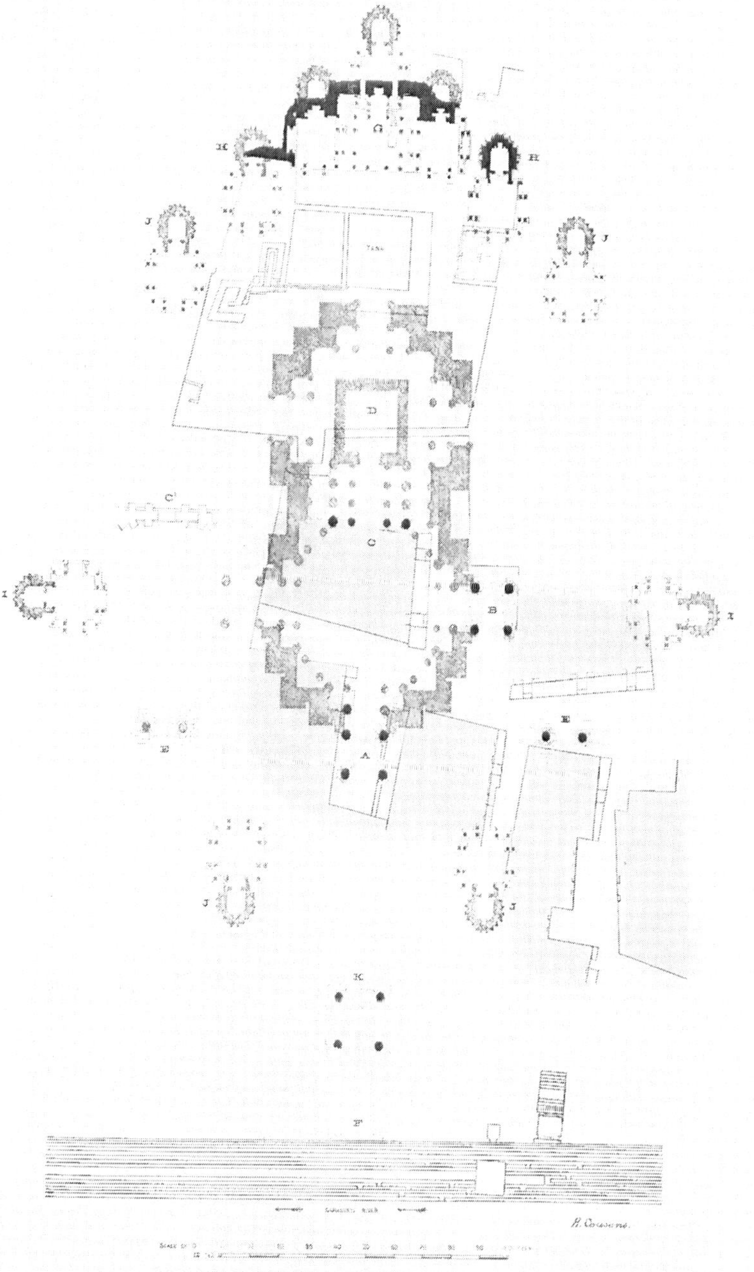

SIDDHAPUR: FRAGMENT OF THE RUDRA MÂLA. PLATE XXXIX.

SIDDHAPUR: ARCHITRAVE FROM THE RUDRA MÂLA TEMPLE.

PLATE XL.

SIDDHAPUR: ELEVATION OF THE NORTH PORCH OF RUDRA MÂLÂ TEMPLE. PLATE XLI.

SIDDHAPUR: ARCHITRAVES FROM THE PORCHES OF RUDRA MÂLÂ TEMPLE

PLATE XLII.

SCALE OF 12" 1 2 3 4 5 FEET.

H. Cousens, mens. *Sampat Ganpat & S. J. Pedvardeh del.*

SIDDHAPUR: RUDRA MÁLA.

PLATE XLIII.

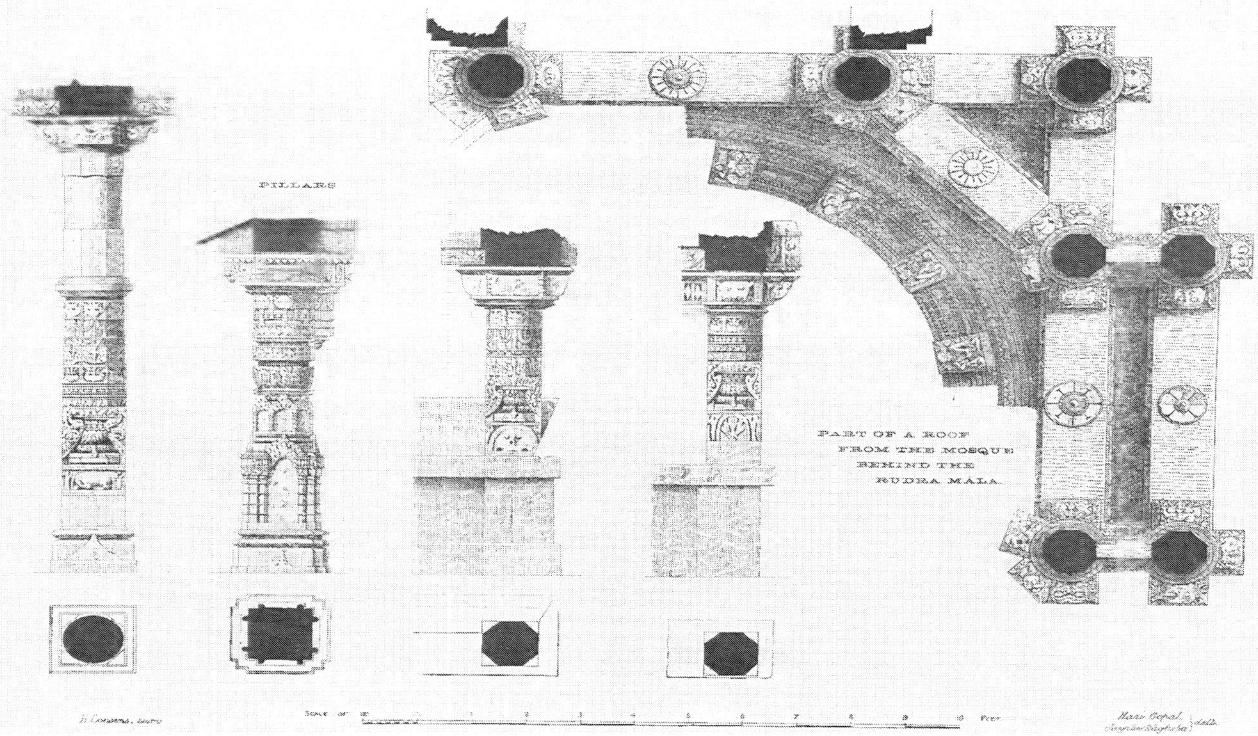

SIDDHAPUR; RUDRA MALA TEMPLE.

PLATE XLIV.

1. SCULPTURED BASE.

Scale of 1/12 Foot.

H. Cousens, del.

2. ELEVATION OF THE TORANA.

Scale six feet to one inch.

PLATE XLV.

SIDDHAPUR: JĀMI' MASJID.

PLATE XLVI.

SIDDHAPUR: CARVED WOODEN BALCONY WINDOW.

J. J. Purshoon, delt.

MODHERA: THE GREAT TEMPLE

MODHERÁ: GENERAL GROUND PLAN OF THE GREAT TEMPLE.

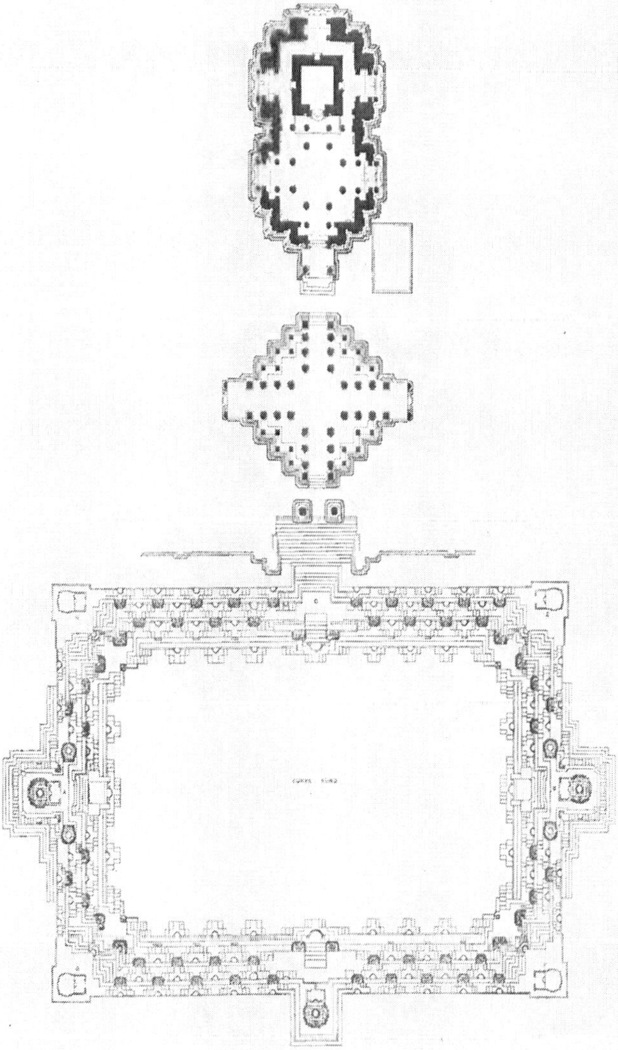

MODHERA: T

SOUTH S

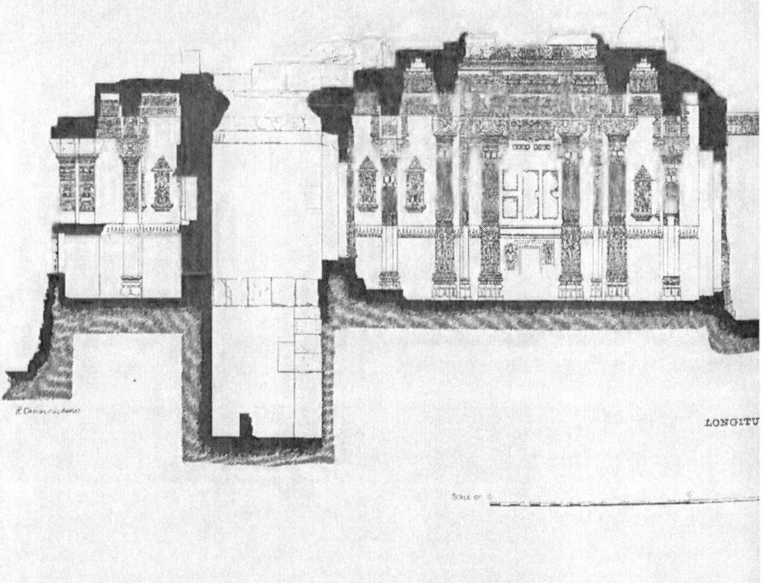

LONGITU

E GREAT TEMPLE

PLATE XLIX.

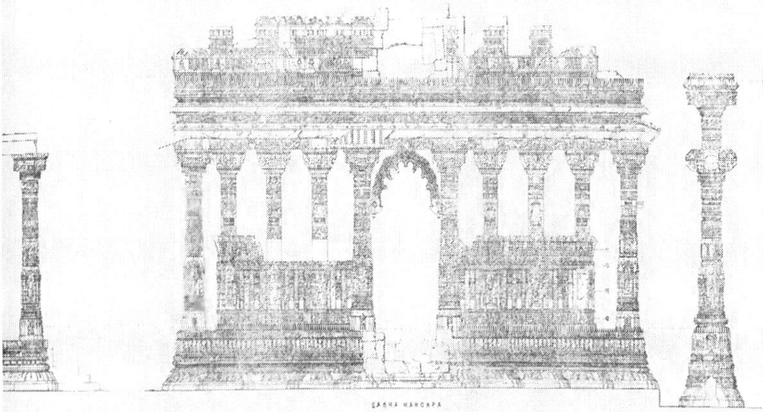

OE ELEVATION.

DINAL SECTION.

MODHERÂ: OPEN MANDAPA, IN FRONT OF THE GREAT TEMPLE, FROM THE S.W.

MAIN DOORWAY

H. Cousens, direx. Jayrdo Bághoté, delt.

MODHERÂ: DOORWAY OF THE TEMPLE.

MODHERĀ: PILLARS FROM THE TEMPLE. PLATE LIII.

H. Cousens, [illegible] [illegible]

H. Cousens, sup.

PILLARS AND PILASTER.

Jayaba Rāghobā, delt.

MODHERÂ TEMPLE: INTERIOR OF THE MAṆḌAPA.

SCULPTURES AT MODHERÂ.

PLATE LVI.

1

2

3

4

5. SURYA

6

7. SITALA

8. NAGA FIGURE

Scale of 12 6 1 2 3 Feet.

H. Cousens, direx.

Jayrâm Râghobâ, Hari Gopâl, Supat Ganpat } delt.

VAḌNAGAR: GREAT ARCH OR KIRTTISTAMBHA.

MODHERÂ.

1. LOOSE SCULPTURE.

Hari Gopâl, del.

SCALE OF 12" 1 2 FEET.

H. Cousens, surv.

2. VAḌNAGAR: CEILING PANEL FROM A HINDU TEMPLE.

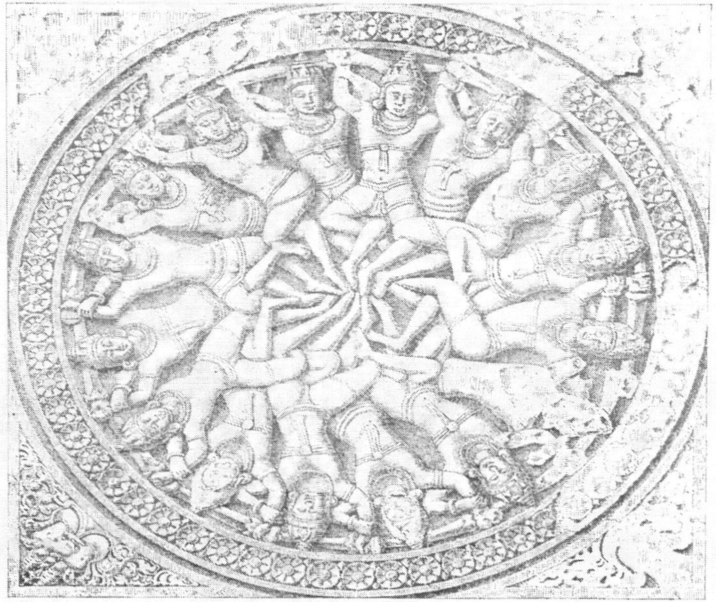

Jaysaw Ragnoba, del.

SCALE OF 12" 1 FOOT.

H. Cousens, surv. S. J. Pacheco, delt.

VADNAGAR: CEILING PANEL FROM A HINDU TEMPLE.

PLATE LX.

SCALE OF 12" 9 1 2 FEET

H. Cousens, direx.

Srīpat Gaṇpat & Hari Gopāl, deli.

VADNAGAR: PLAN OF AN OLD TEMPLE. PLATE LXI.

1.

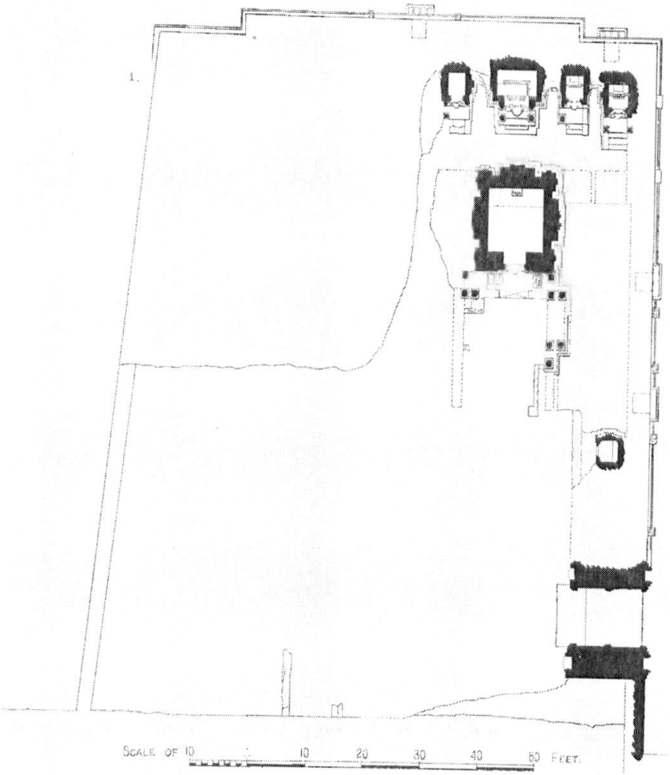

SCALE OF 10 0 10 20 30 40 50 FEET.

Sitaram Dinkar, delt.

2.

3.

SCALE OF 1 0 1 2 3 4 5 6 INCHES.

H. Cousens, surv. Keshav Nevai & S. J. Pacheco, dels.

VADNAGAR: A CELL OR SMALL SHRINE OF AN OLD TEMPLE.

ELEVATION.

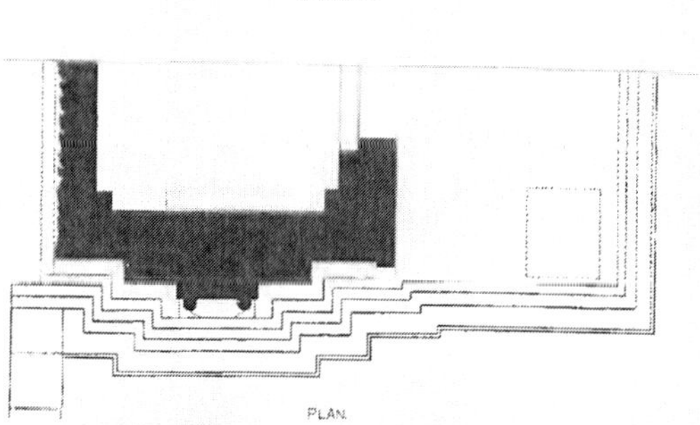

PLAN.

SCALE OF 12" 1 2 3 4 5 6 7 8 9 10 FEET

H. Cousens, direx. Hari Gopal, delt.

VADNAGAR: DOORWAY AND PILLAR FROM A CELL SHRINE OF AN OLD TEMPLE.

PLATE LXIII.

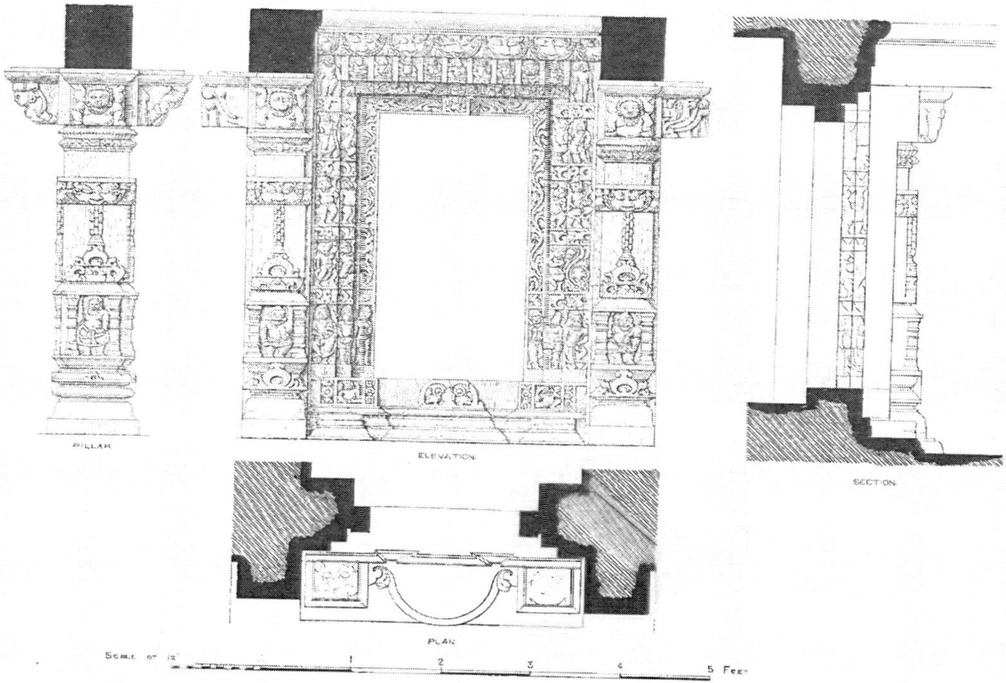

H. Cousens, surv.

Jayrâm Râghobâ, del.

PLATE LXIV.

VADNAGAR: SCULPTURED SLAB FROM AN OLD TEMPLE

1.

Kashav Morea & Jayram Raghoba dels

SCALE OF 12" — 1 FOOT.

2. LOOSE SCULPTURES

3.

SCALE OF 12" — 2 FEET.

H. Cousens, direx.

Kashav Morea, Jayram Raghoba } dels

DILMAL: TEMPLE OF LIMBOJÎ MÂTÂ—GENERAL VIEW.

DILMAL: TEMPLE OF LIMBOJI MÂTÂ.

PLATE LXVI.

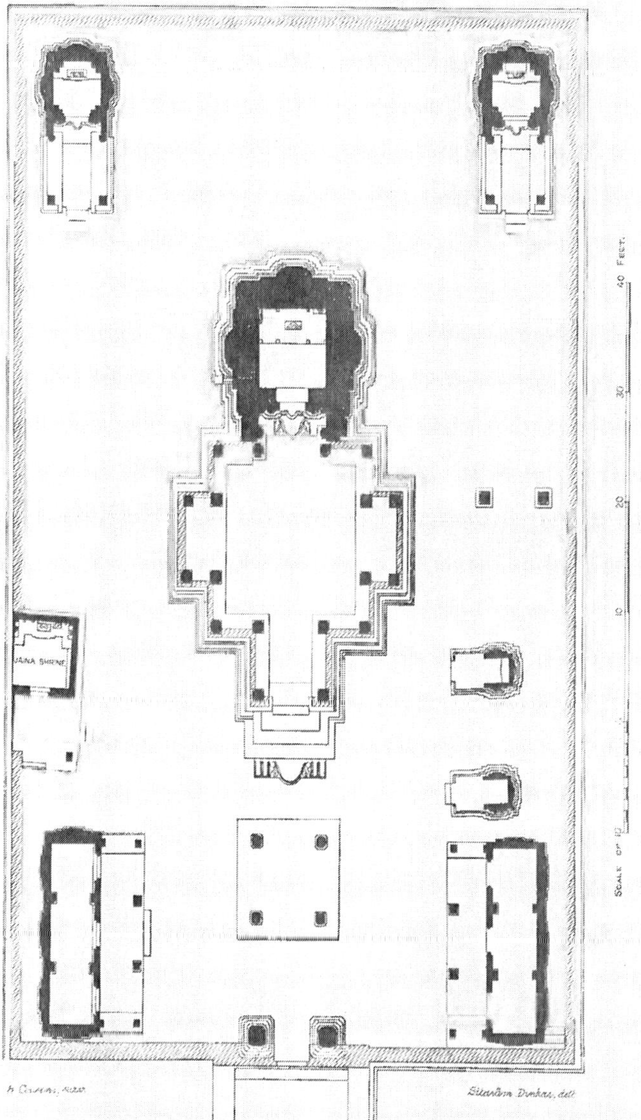

H. Cousens, Autor.

Sitaram Dinkar, delt

PLATE LXVII.

DILMAL: TEMPLE OF LIMBOJI MÁTÁ—DETAILS.

1. PILLAR. 2. PLINTH. 3. SHRINE DOORWAY. 4. SECTION. 5. PLAN.

H. Cousens, surr. Hari Gopál, delt

SCALE OF 12" 1 2 3 4 5 6 7 8 9 10 FEET.

DILMAL: SMALL SHRINE BEHIND THE TEMPLE OF LIMBOJÎ MÂTÂ.

DILMAL. VAISHṆAVA TRIMURTI ON SHRINE WALL OF LIMBOJÎ MÂTÂ'S TEMPLE.

DILMAL: TEMPLE OF LAKSHMI NÁRÁYANA.

PLATE LXX.

1. SIDE ELEVATION. 2. SECTION THROUGH PORCH. 3. SECTION THROUGH SHRINE.

SCALE OF 10 — 10 FEET.

H. Cousens, surv. Sitarám Dinkar, delt.

DILMAL: SCULPTURES FROM SATÎ MONUMENTS AND FROM TEMPLE OF LIMBOJI MÂTÂ.

SAT STONE. MEMORIAL STONES.

BRAHMA. COMBINATION FIGURE—SIVA, VISHNU, SURYA AND BRAHMA. ELEVATION OF OUTER WALL OF THE TEMPLE ENCLOSURE.

SCALE OF 12" 1 2 3 4 5 FEET

H. Cousens, direx Jagrâv Raghoba del.

PLATE XXXIX.

MUNJPUR: THE OLD MOSQUE.

MUNJPUR: OLD MASJID.

PLATE LXXIII.

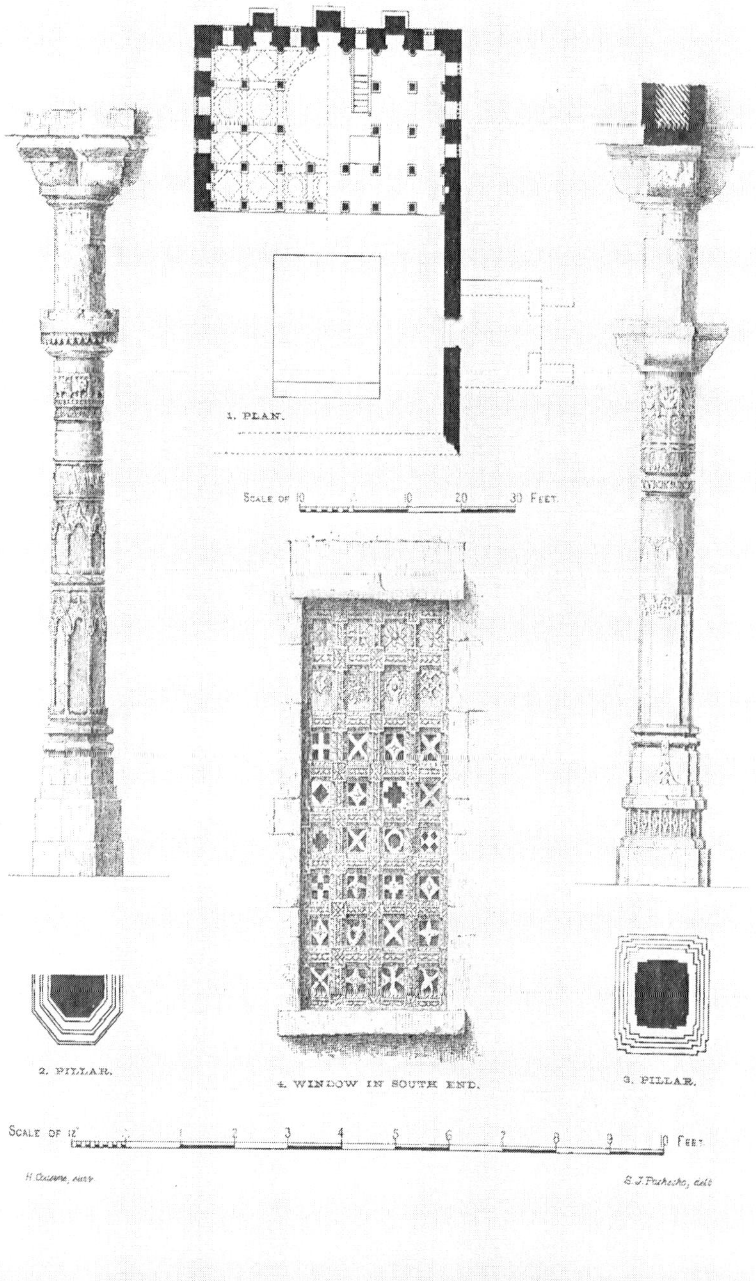

LOTEŚVARA AND ŚANKEŚVARA. PLATE LXXIV.

1. OLD JAINA TEMPLE AT ŚANKEŚVARA.

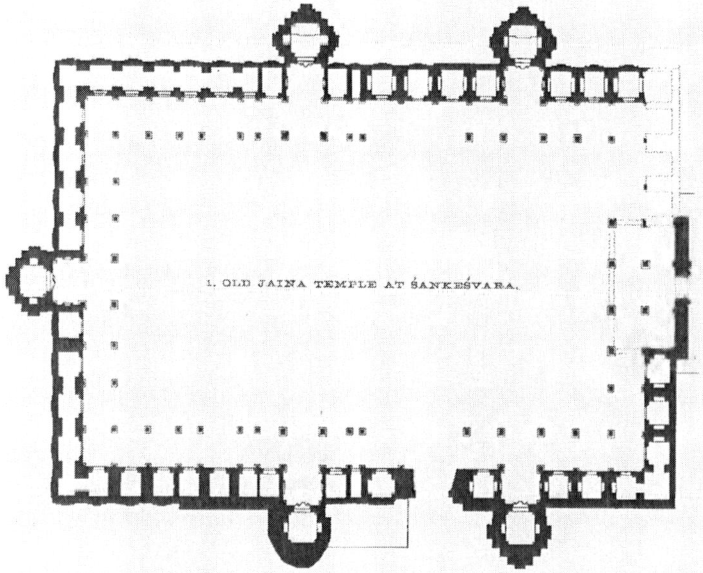

2. GANGUÂ KUND AT LOTEŚVARA.

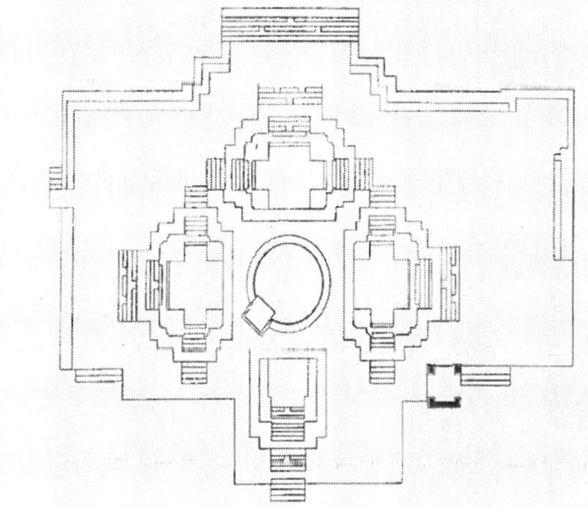

H. Cousens, surv. Sitârâm Dinkar, delt.

ŚANKEŚVAR: BACK OF THE OLD TEMPLE.

PLATE LXXV^{a}

SANKEŚVARA: OLD BRICK SPIRE OF THE TEMPLE OF PĀRŚVANĀTH.

SANKEŚVARA: PLASTER ORNAMENT FROM THE OLD JAINA TEMPLE.

PLATE LXXVI.

CHANDRAVATI AND SAROTRÂ.

PLATE LXXVII.

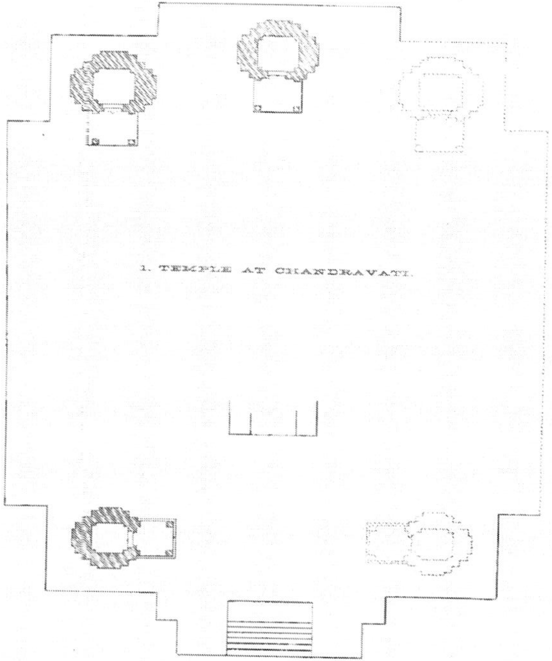

1. TEMPLE AT CHANDRAVATI.

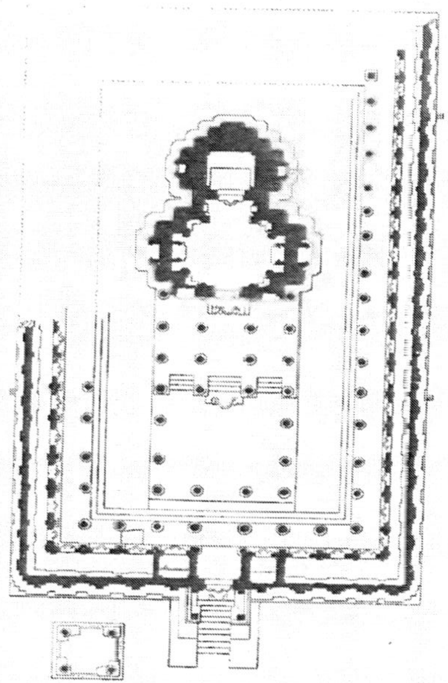

2. TEMPLE OF BÂVANADHVAJA AT SAROTRÂ.

H. Cousens, surv.

SCALE OF 10 . 10 20 30 40 50 FEET.

Sitârâm Dinkar, del.

PLATE LXXVIII.

SAROTRÂ: TEMPLE OF BÂVANADHVAJA FROM THE NORTH-EAST.

SAROTRÂ: PILLARS FROM THE TEMPLE OF BÂVANADHVAJA.

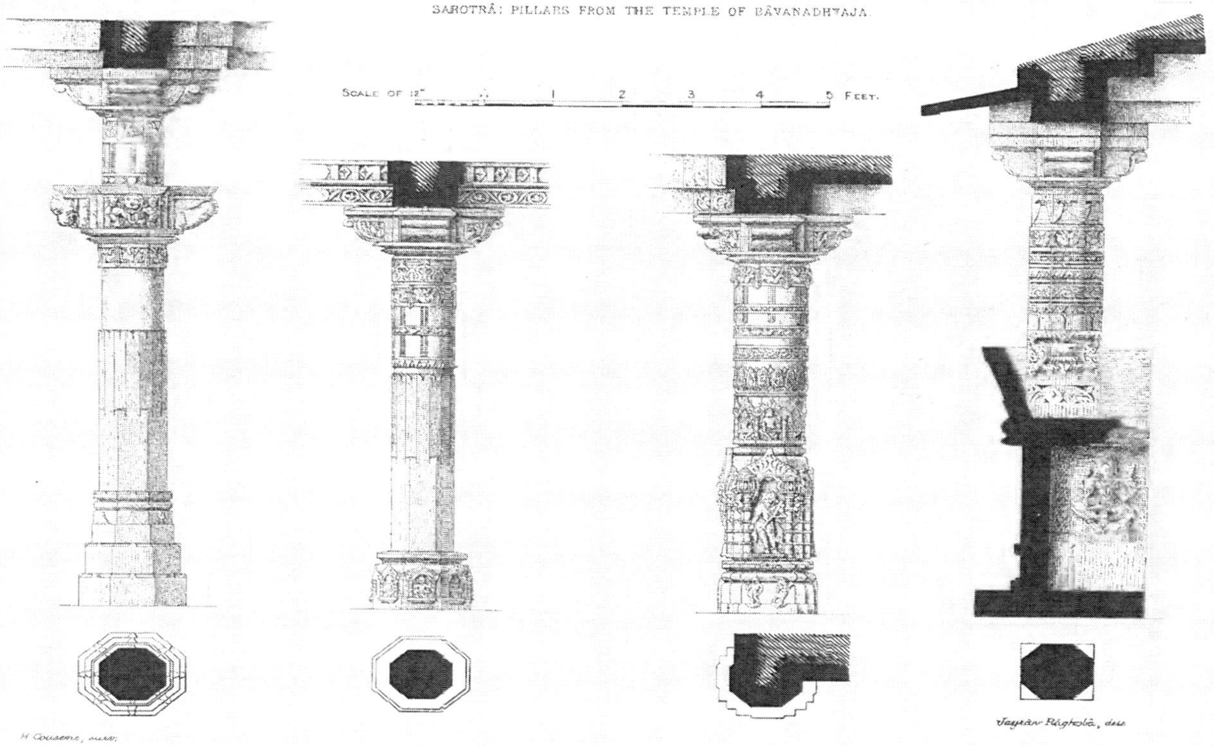

ROHO: STEP WELL.

PLATE LXXX.

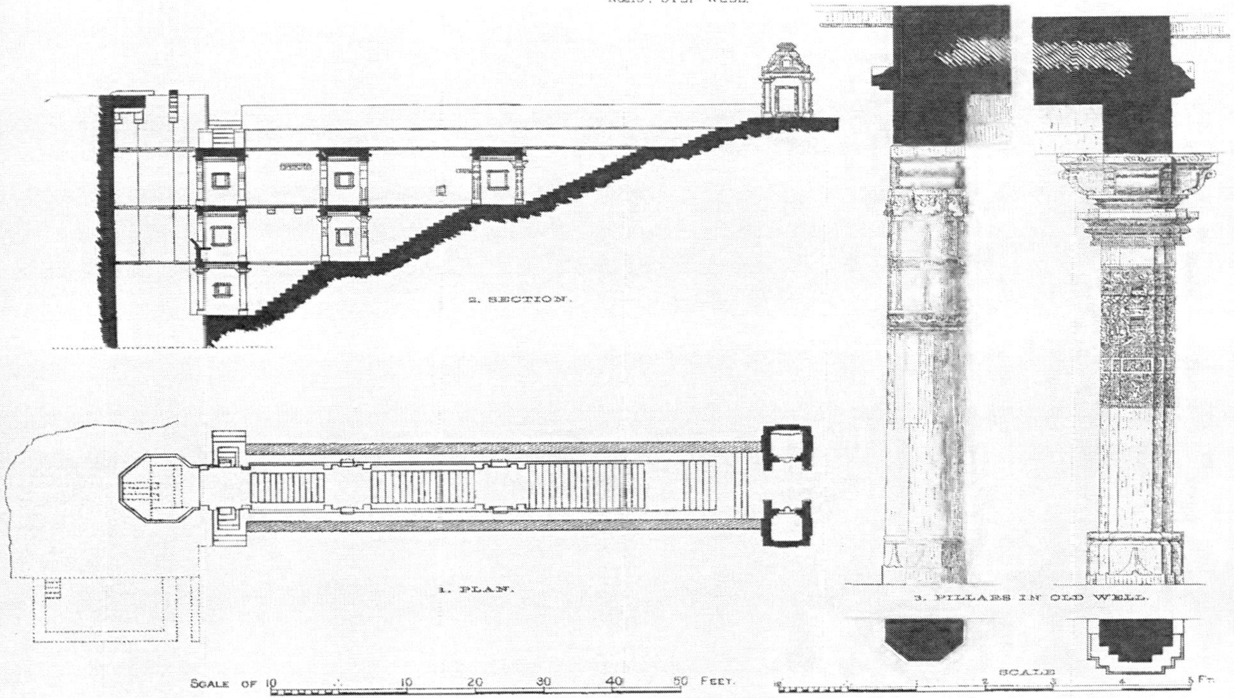

H. Cousens, curo

S. J. Pacheco
Sitaram Binkar } delt

Jayrao Bāgtoba, delt.

SÛNAK: NORTH WALL OF THE SHRINE OF NÎLAKANTHEŚVARA.

SUNAK: TEMPLE OF NÎLAKAṆṬHA MAHÂDEVA.

PLATE LXXXII.

1. PLAN.

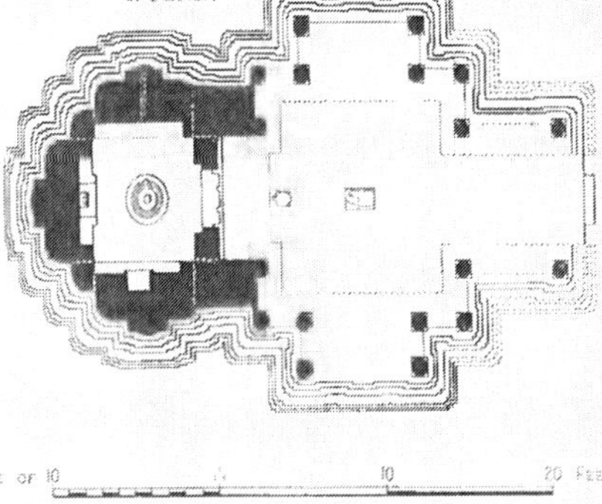

2. QUARTER PLAN SHEWING BASEMENT MOULDINGS.

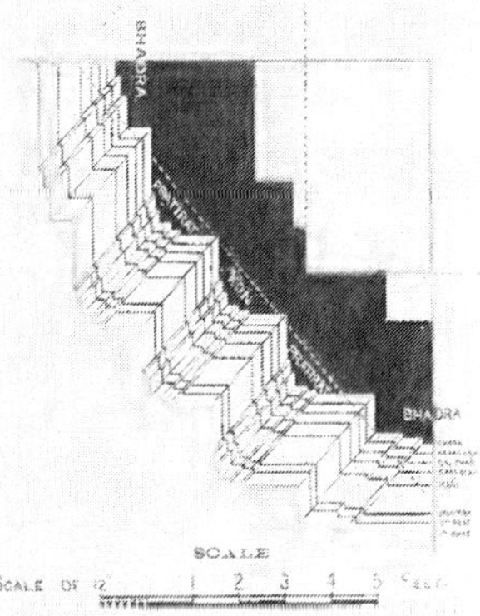

3. VERTICAL SECTION SHEWING MOULDINGS FROM GROUND TO CORNICE.

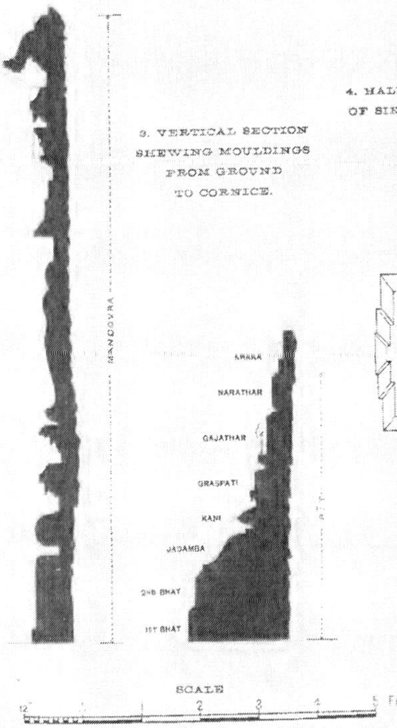

4. HALF PLAN OF SIKHARA.

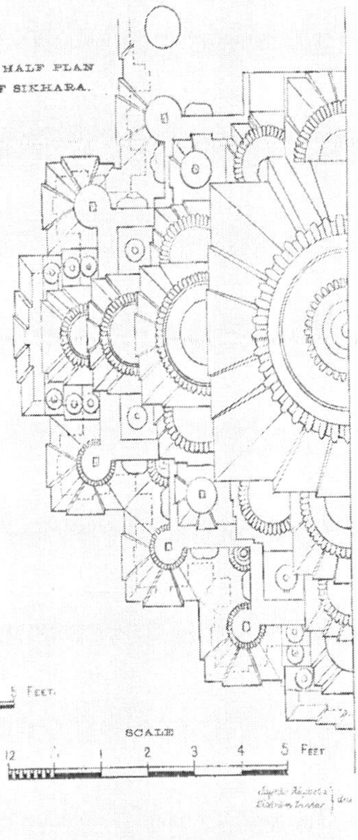

ELEVATION.

SCALE OF 10 — 10 — 20 FEET

H. Cousens, curv.

Sitârâm, Dinkar / Jayrâo Râghoba | del.

SUNAK: TEMPLE OF NĪLAKAṆṬHA MAHĀDEVA. PLATE LXXXIV.

SCALE OF 10 ... 10 FEET.

H. Cousens, surv.

LONGITUDINAL SECTION.

B. J. Pacheco
Anant Raghoba } del.

PLATE LXXXV.

SUNAK: PILLAR AND DETAILS FROM TEMPLE OF NÎLAKAṆṬHA MAHÂDEVA.

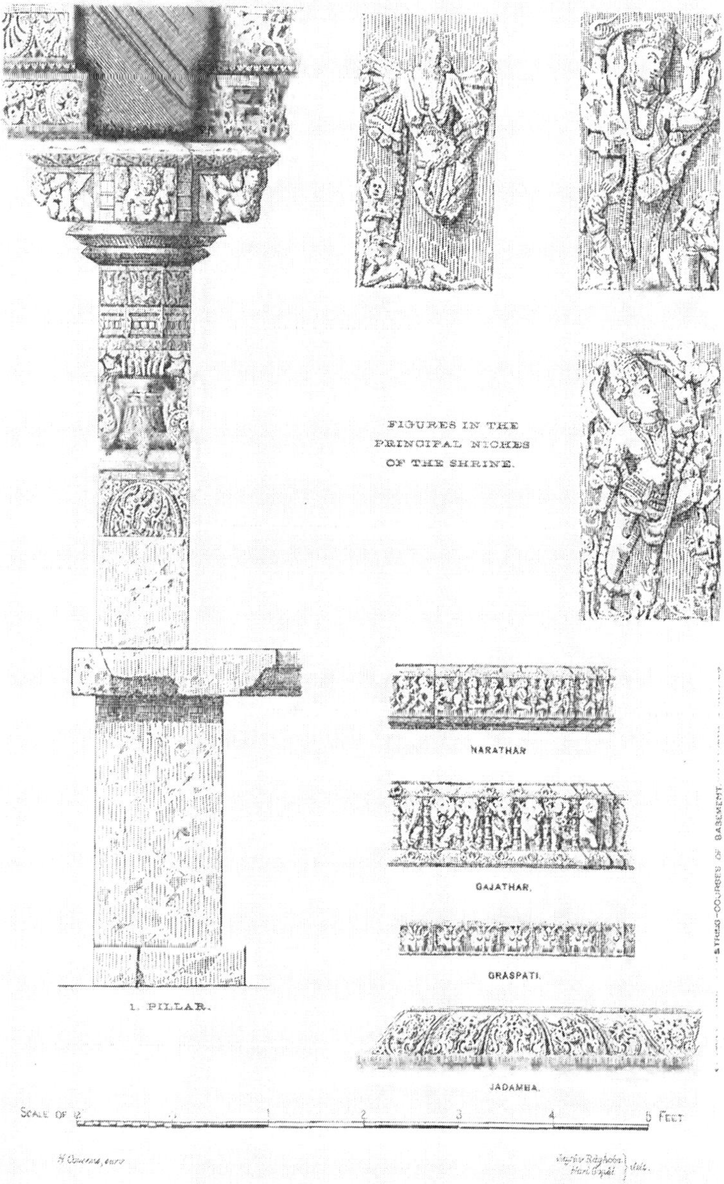

PLATE LXXXVI.

SUNAK: TEMPLE OF NÎLAKAṆṬHA MAHÂDEVA.

SCALE OF 12 . 1 2 3 4 5 6 7 8 9 10 FEET.

H. Cousens, surv. Hari Gopal dels.

PLAN AND SECTION OF THE DOME OF THE MANDAPA.

KASARa: THE OLD TEMPLE FROM SOUTH-WEST.

KASARÂ: OLD TEMPLE AND DETAILS. PLATE LXXXVIII.

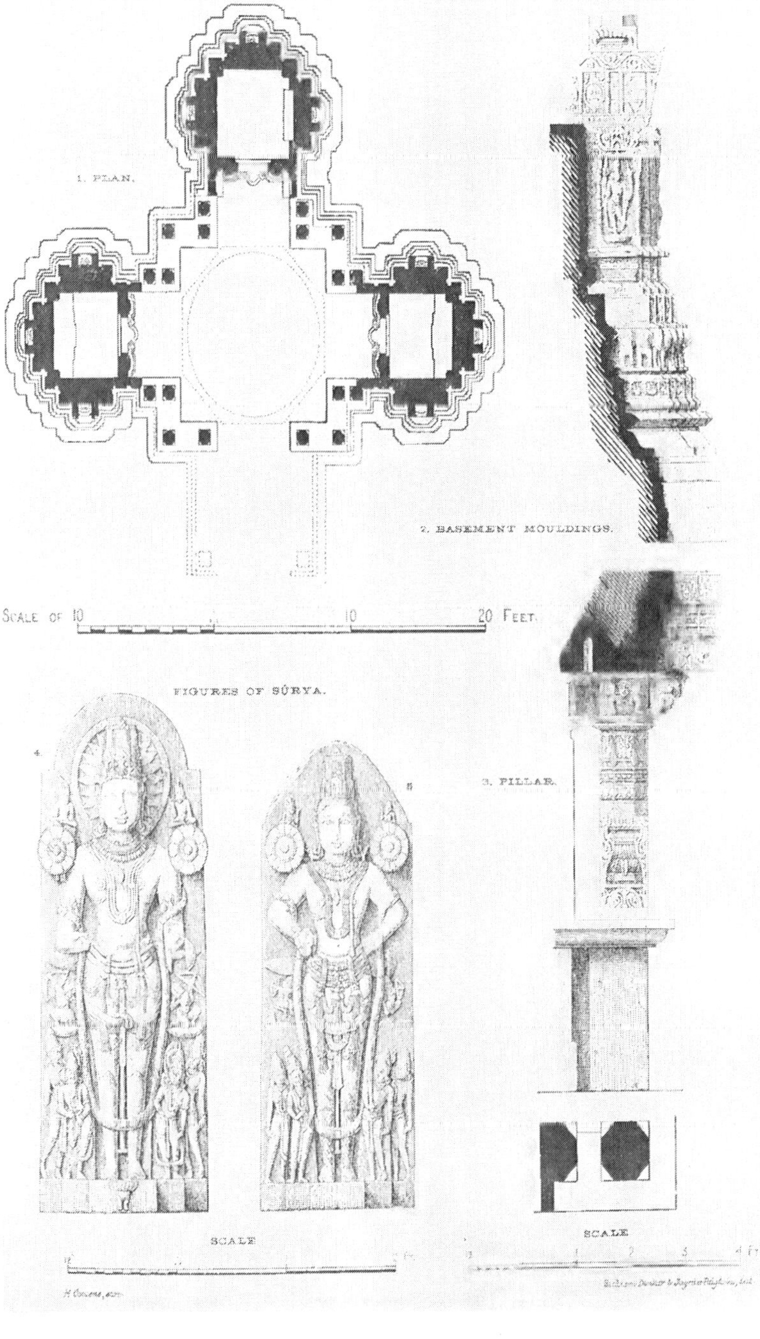

KASARĀ:-CROSS-SECTION OF THE OLD TEMPLE.

SCALE OF 10 — 10 FEET.

H. Cousens, surv.

Sitārām Dinkar, S. J. Pacheco, delt.

KASARÁ: OLD TEMPLE—NORTH SHRINE—FROM THE WEST.

KASARÂ: SIDE-ELEVATION OF THE SHRINE OF THE OLD TEMPLE. PLATE XCI.

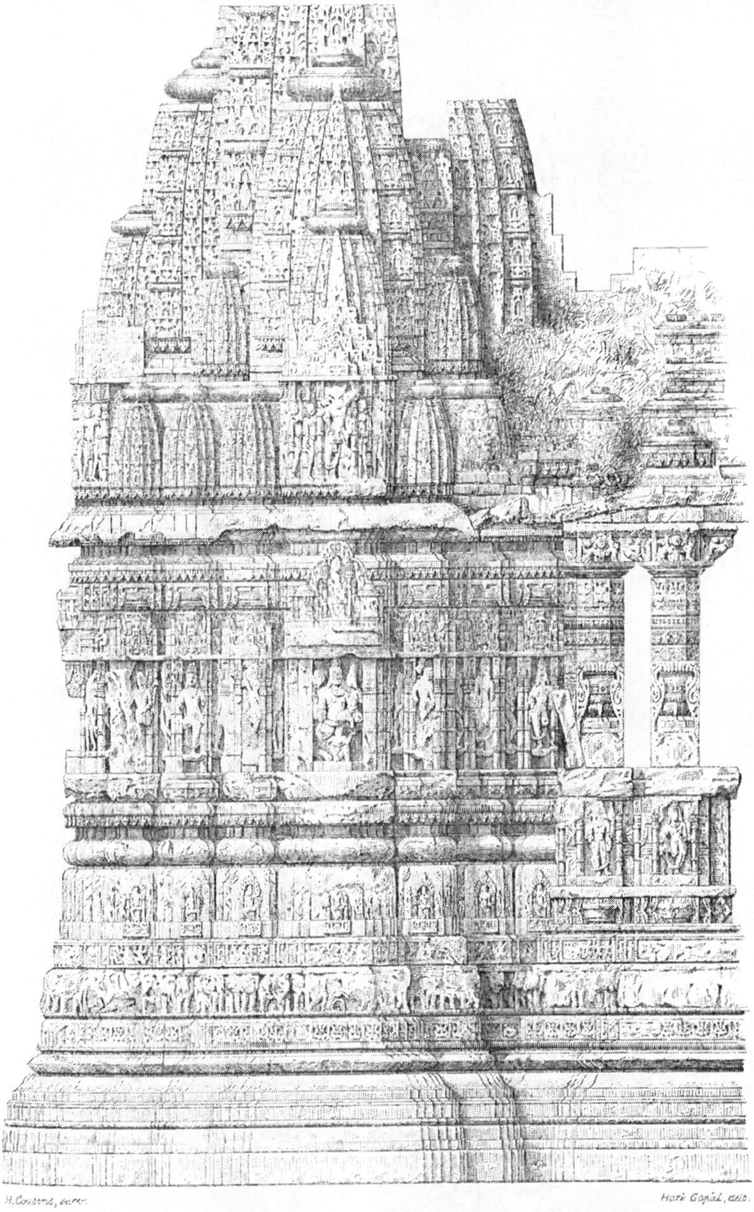

H. Cousens, direx. Hari Gopál, delt.

SCALE OF 2' 1 2 3 4 5 6 7 8 9 10 FEET.

KASARÂ: DOORWAY AND DETAILS OF OLD TEMPLE. PLATE XCII.

WEST DOOR.

1. ELEVATION.

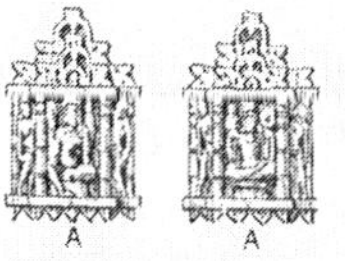

4. ON S. DOOR. ON N. DOOR.

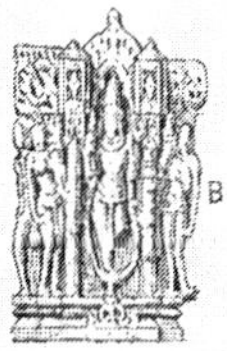

5. ON N. DOOR.

6. ON S. DOOR.

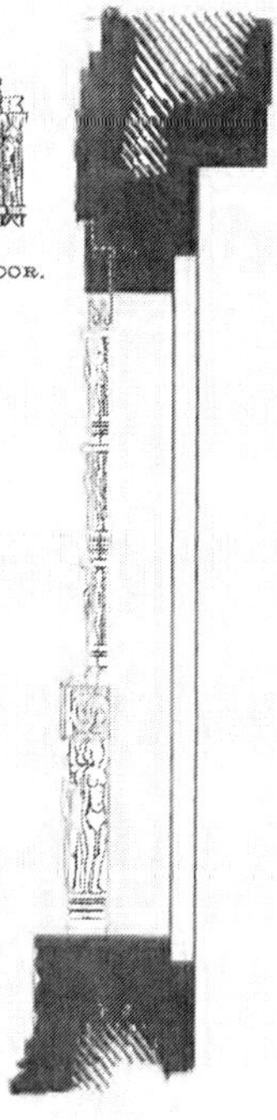

3. SECTION.

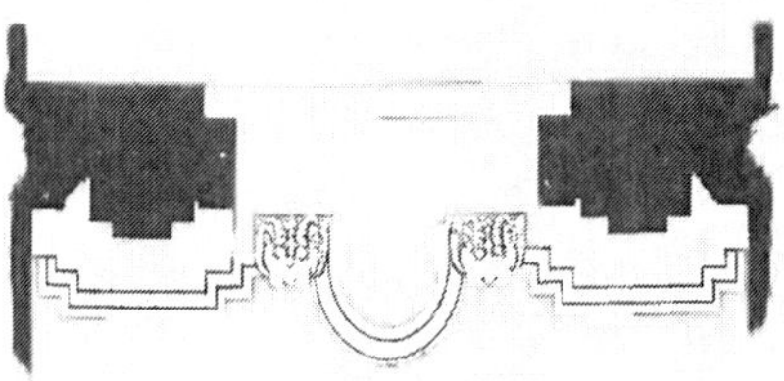

2. PLAN.

7. BROKEN IMAGE LYING OUTSIDE TEMPLE.

H Cousens, surv.

S J Pochase, delt

PLATE XCIII

LUHÀVI: TEMPLE OF NÍLAKAṆṬHA MAHÁDEVA.

PLATE XCIV.

SANDERA: THE OLD TEMPLE FROM THE SOUTH-EAST

SANDEEA: THE OLD TEMPLE FROM THE NORTH-WEST

PLANS OF TEMPLES AT MANOJ, DHENUJ, KANODÂ AND VIRTÂ. **PLATE XCVI.**

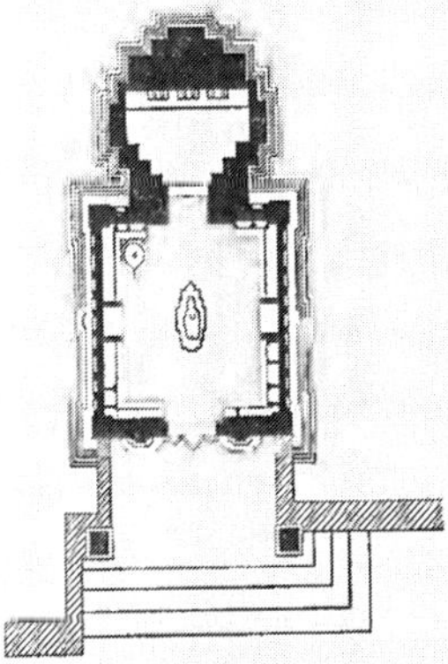

1. TEMPLE OF NARÂYAN AT MANOJ.

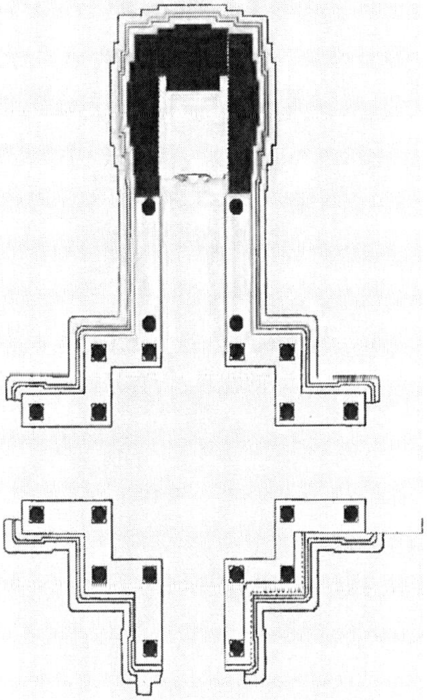

3. TEMPLE OF BAHUSARANA AT KANODÂ.

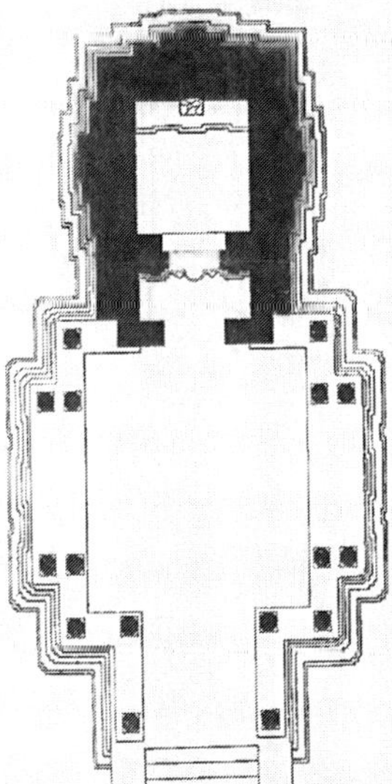

2. TEMPLE OF VYÂGHEŚVARI AT DHENUJ.

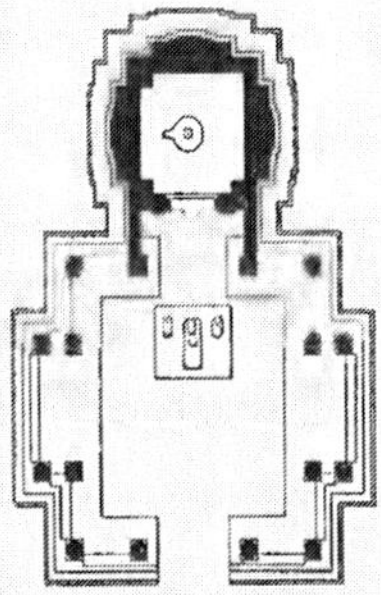

4. TEMPLE OF NILKANṬHEŚVARA AT VIRTÂ.

SCALE OF 10 · 10 20 30 40 FEET.

S. Dinkar & E. J. Pacheco, delt.

DHINOJ: TEMPLE OF VYĀGHREŚVARĪ.

PLATE XCVIII.

DHINOJ: PLAN AND SECTION OF ROOF PANELLING FROM THE TEMPLE OF VYÂGHESVARÎ.

SECTION

SCALE OF 12″ — 1 — 2 — 3 FEET.

H. Cousens, dir. — Hari Gopâl, delt.

DHINOJ: SCREEN WALL OR VEDI OF THE MAṆDAPA OF THE TEMPLE OF VYÂGHREŚVARI.

H. Cousens, curv. S. J. Pacheco, delt.

DHINOJ: SLUICE OF THE OLD TANK

MOTÁB: OLD SHRINE

PLATE CII.

GORÁD; OLD TEMPLE OF SOMEŚVARA.

1. PARAPET WALL AND PILLAR FROM THE TEMPLE OF NILKANTHEŚVARA VIRTÂ

2. CEILING FROM PORCH OF TEMPLE OF SOMEŚVARA AT GORÂD.

SCALE OF 0 1 2 3 4 5 FEET.

H. Cousens, dirx. Jayrâv Râghava, del.

VÂYAD: STEP-WELL AT THE VILLAGE.

PLATE CIV.

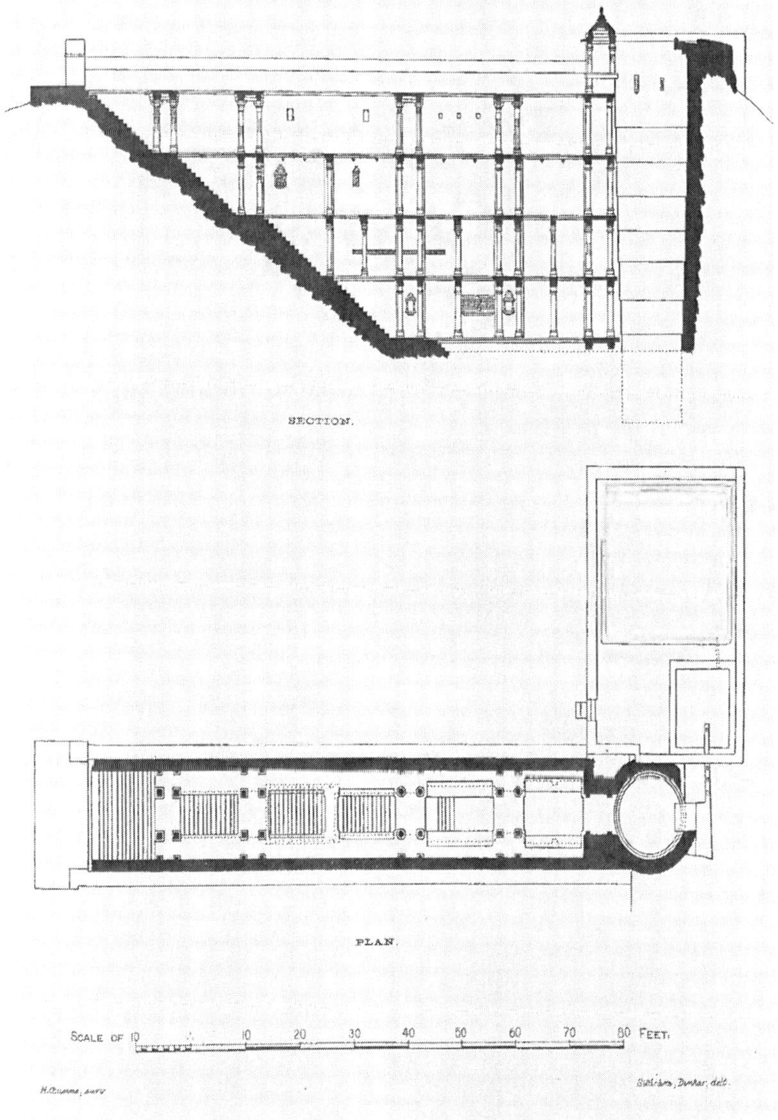

H. Cousens, surv. — Sitârâm Dinkar, delt.

VAYAD: OLD WELL

VÂYAD: PILLARS AND BAS-RELIEF FROM THE STEP-WELL.

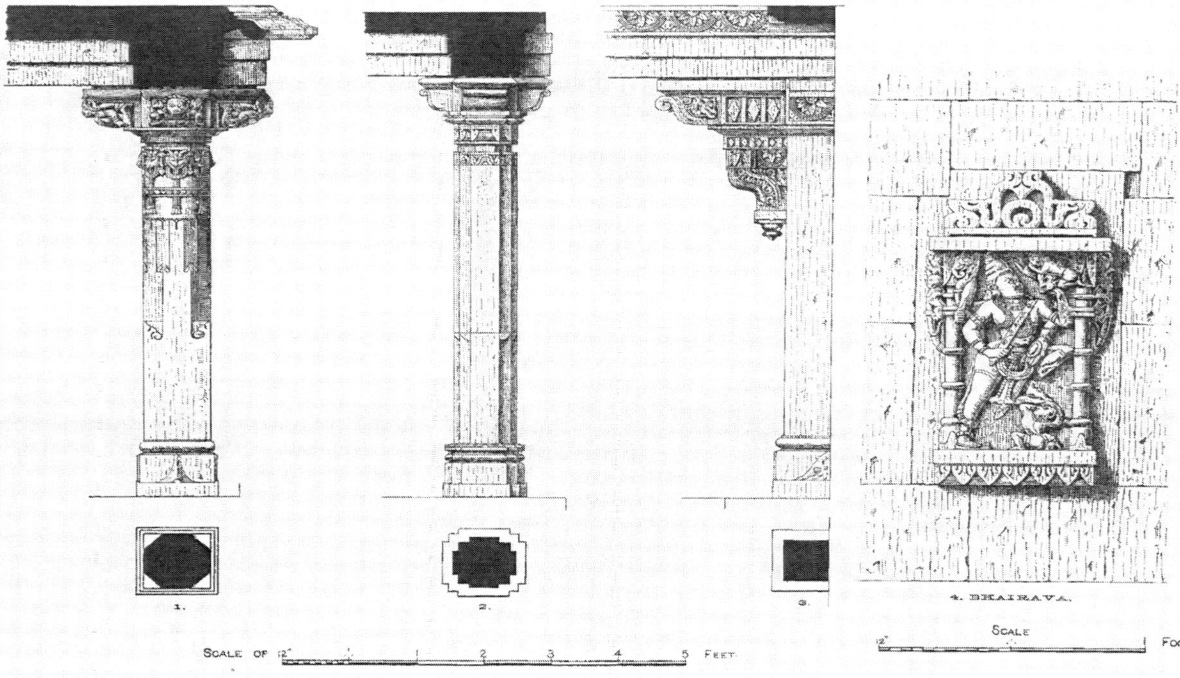

MÂNDVÂ: PLAN AND SECTION OF THE WELL.

PLATE CVII.

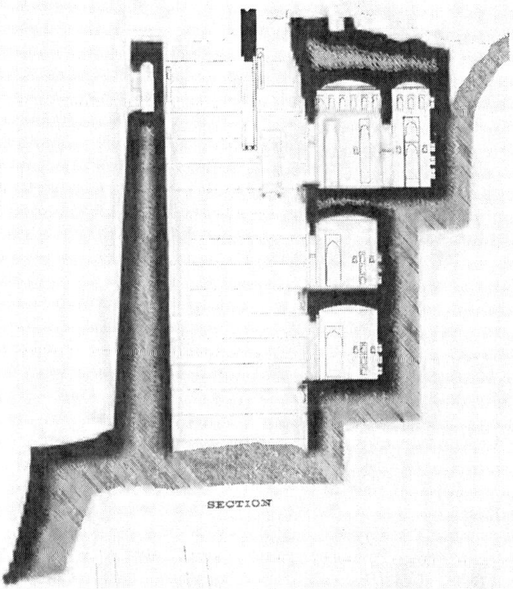

SECTION

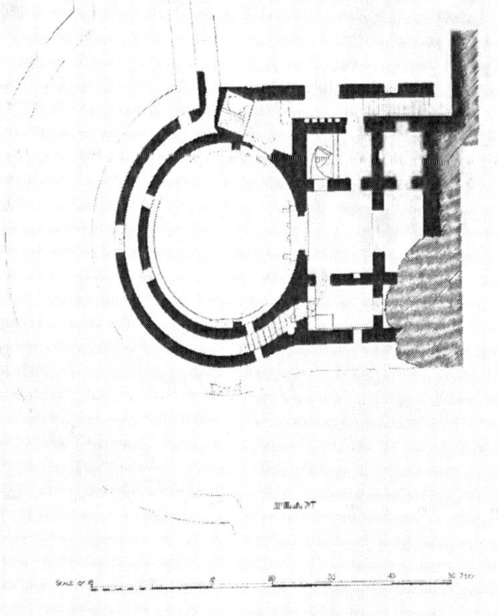

PLAN

TARINGA JAINA TEMPLE FROM THE SOUTH-WEST.

TÂRINGÂ: PLAN OF THE LARGE JAINA TEMPLE.

PLATE CIX

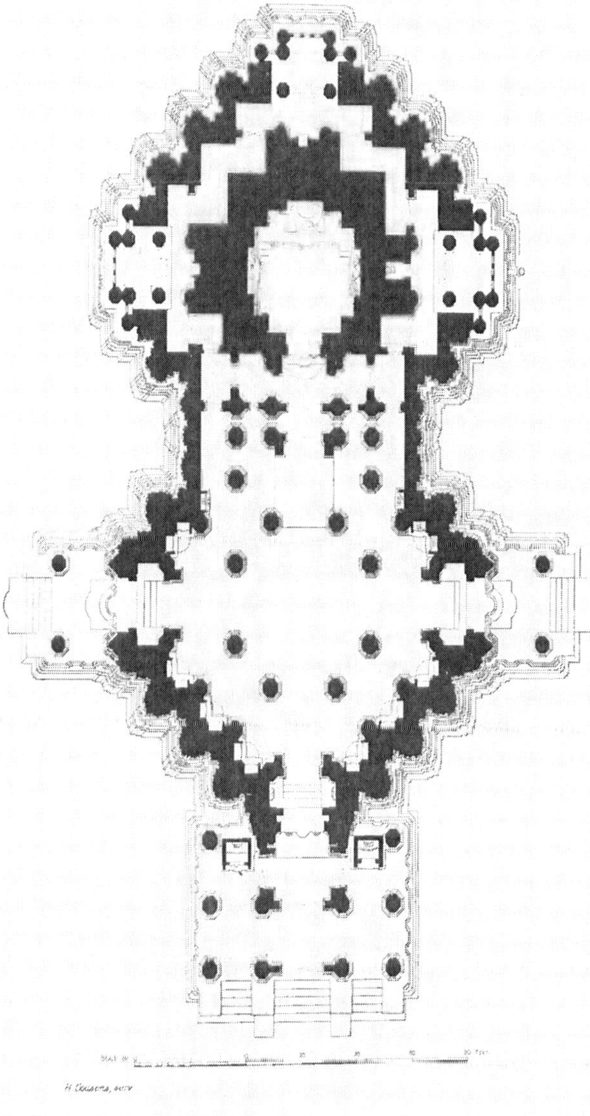

TARINGA JAINA TEMPLE FROM THE SOUTH-EAST.

1. SCULPTURE ON THE WALLS.

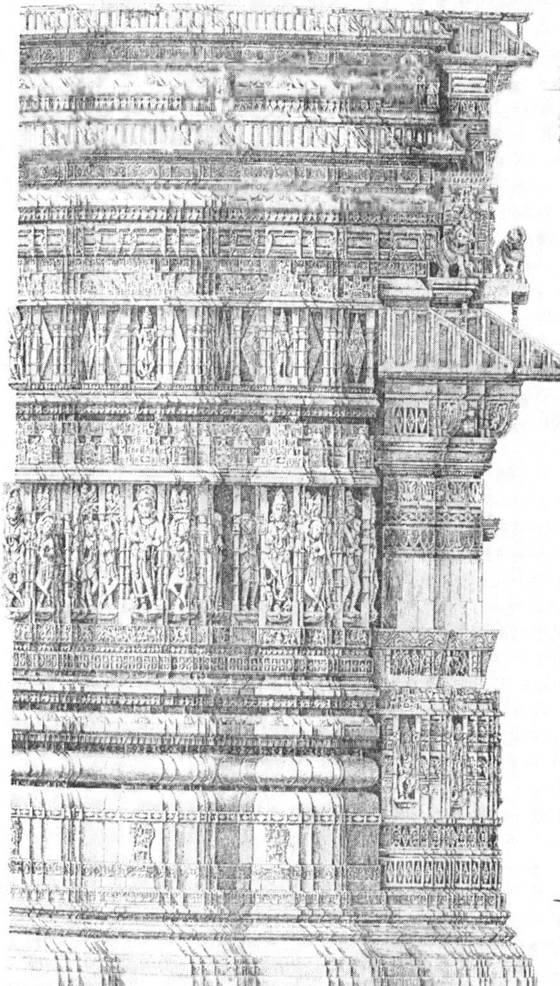

2. PILLAR.

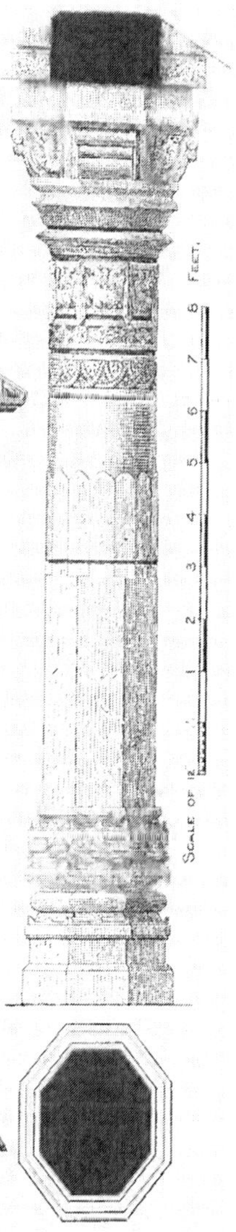

Published by order of the Secretary of State for India.

ARCHÆOLOGICAL SURVEY OF WESTERN INDIA.

REPORTS.

By JAS. BURGESS, C.I.E., LL.D., F.R.S.E., M.R.I.D.A., ETC.

Super-royal 4to, half morocco, gilt tops.

VOL. I.—REPORT OF THE FIRST SEASON'S OPERATIONS IN THE BELGAUM AND KALADGI DISTRICTS.

With 56 Photographs and Lithographic Plates and 6 Wood-cuts. 2*l*. 2*s*.

VOL. II.—REPORT ON THE ANTIQUITIES OF KATHIAWAD AND KACHH.

With 74 Photographs and Lithographic Plates, 242 pages. 3*l*. 3*s*.

VOL. III.—REPORT ON THE ANTIQUITIES OF THE BIDAR AND AURANGABAD DISTRICTS.

With 66 Photographs and Lithographic Plates and 9 Wood-cuts. 2*l*. 2*s*.

VOL. IV.—THE BUDDHIST CAVES AND THEIR INSCRIPTIONS.

With 60 Plates and 25 Wood-cuts.

VOL. V.—THE CAVES OF ELURA AND THE OTHER BRAHMANICAL AND JAINA CAVES IN WESTERN INDIA.

With 51 Autotype and other Plates and 18 Wood-cuts. The two Volumes. Price 6l. 6s.

LONDON:—KEGAN PAUL, TRENCH, TRÜBNER, & CO.

VOL. VI.—THE MUHAMMADAN ARCHITECTURE OF GUJARAT:—BHAROCH, CAMBAY, DHOLKA, &c.

With 76 Collotype and Photo-Lithographed Plates. Price 20s. nett.

VOL. VII.—THE MUHAMMADAN ARCHITECTURE OF AHMADABAD.

With 112 Collotype and Photo-Lithographed Plates and 11 Wood-cuts. Price 31s. 6d.

LONDON:—KEGAN PAUL, TRENCH, TRÜBNER, & CO.; B. QUARITCH; LUZAC & CO., ETC.
CALCUTTA:—THACKER, SPINK, & CO. BOMBAY:—THACKER & CO. (*Limited*).

THE CAVE TEMPLES OF INDIA.

By J. FERGUSSON, D.C.L., C.I.E., F.R.S., V.P.R.A.S., and JAS. BURGESS, LL.D., C.I.E., F.R.S.E., F.R.G.S., ETC.

Super-royal 8vo, half morocco, gilt top, pp. xx and 536, with Map, 99 Plates, and 76 Wood-cuts. 2*l*.

LONDON:—LUZAC & CO., *Gt. Russell St.*

THE BUDDHIST STUPAS OF AMARAVATI AND JAGGAYYAPETA DESCRIBED AND ILLUSTRATED.

By J. BURGESS, C.I.E., LL.D., F.R.S.E., ETC.

With the Aśoka Edicts at Dhauli and Jaugada, translated by PROFESSOR G. BÜHLER, C.I.E., PH.D., LL.D., Vienna.

With 69 Plates of Sculptures and Inscriptions, mostly autotypes, and 32 Wood-cuts.

Super-royal quarto, half-bound, gilt top, 1887. 3 *Guineas.*

"Dr. Burgess has recently issued an admirable monograph on the Buddhist Stûpas at Amarâvatî and Jaggayyapeta, supplementary to the late Mr. Fergusson's 'Tree and Serpent Worship,' and has thus, to some extent wiped away the reproach of the Southern Presidency."—*Quarterly Review*, July 1889.

LONDON:—KEGAN PAUL, TRENCH, TRÜBNER, & CO. CALCUTTA:—THACKER, SPINK, & CO.
BOMBAY:—THACKER & CO. (*Limited*).

R

EPIGRAPHIA INDICA

SUPPLEMENTARY TO

THE CORPUS INSCRIPTIONUM INDICARUM.

Edited by JAS. BURGESS, C.I.E., LL.D., F.R.S.E., ETC.

Vol. I, super-royal 4to, 482 pages, with 35 facsimile Plates, and Vol. II, 518 pages, with 51 Plates. 21s. 6d. each.

A côté des diverses séries de 'Reports' dont la marche est forcément peu régulière, M. Burgess a créé un organe périodique, l'*Epigraphia Indica*, spécialement réservé aux inscriptions. L'épigraphie indienne aura ainsi son *Ephemeris* avant d'avoir son *Corpus*. Si M. Burgess arrive de cette manière à centraliser, ne fût-ce que dans une certaine mesure, les travaux épigraphiques actuellement éparpillés dans une infinité de recueils, dont plusieurs sont des publications locales absolument inaccessibles en Europe, il aura rendu une fois de plus un service inestimable aux études indiennes.—*Revue de l'Histoire des Religions.*

At the Congress of Orientalists lately held in London, the very highest praise was awarded to Dr. Burgess for his share in this undertaking as chief editor. No higher praise could be accorded here to Dr. Burgess than this statement of the value attached to his labours by so many of the highest Oriental scholars.—*The R. Inst. of Br. Arch. Journal*, Dec. 22, 1892.

CALCUTTA:—SUPERINTENDENT OF GOVERNMENT PRINTING, INDIA; THACKER, SPINK, & CO
LONDON:—LUZAC & CO.; BERNARD QUARITCH; A. CONSTABLE & CO.

MISCELLANEOUS PUBLICATIONS OF THE ARCHÆOLOGICAL SURVEY OF WESTERN INDIA.

4to demy.

No. 1. Memorandum on the Buddhist Caves of Junnar, by J. BURGESS, LL.D.: and Translations of three Inscriptions from Badami, Pattadkal, and Aiholi, by J. F. FLEET, Ph. D. 1874.

No. 2. Memorandum on the Antiquities at Dabhoi, Ahmedabad, Than, Junagadh, Girnar, and Dhank, with Appendix of Inscriptions, and 10 plates of facsimiles, by J. BURGESS, LL.D., 1875.

No. 3. Memorandum on the Remains at Gumli, Gop, and in Kachh, etc., by the same. 1875.

No. 4. Provisional Lists of Architectural and other Archæological Remains in Western India, by the same. 1875.

No. 5. Translations of Inscriptions from Belgaum and Kaladgi Districts, by J. F. FLEET, Ph. D.; and of Inscriptions from Kathiawad and Kachh, by HARI VAMAN LIMAYA, B.A. 1876.

No. 6. Notes on the Antiquities of the Talukas of Parner, Sangamner, Ankole, and Kopargaum, in Ahmadnagar, by W. F. SINCLAIR, Bo. C.S., with revised Lists of Remains in the Ahmadnagar, Nasik, Puna, Thana, and Kaladgi Zillas, by J. BURGESS, LL.D. 1877.

No. 7. Architectural and Archæological Remains in Khandesh, by W. H. PROPERT, Bo. C.S., Collector. 1877.

No. 8. Reports regarding the Archæological Remains in Sindh, with plans of Tombs; by District Officers. 1879.

No. 9. Notes on the Bauddha Rock-Temples of Ajanta, their Paintings and Sculptures; and on the Paintings of the Bagh Caves, Modern Bauddha Mythology, and the Sanskrit Inscription at Cintra, with 31 plates, by J. BURGESS, LL.D. 1879.

No. 10. Inscriptions from the Cave-Temples of Western India, with Descriptive Notes, a S'ilâhâra grant of Mârasiṁha, and three Sanskrit Inscriptions in possession of the American Oriental Society: with 52 plates, by J. BURGESS, LL.D., and BHAGWANLAL INDRAJI PANDIT, Ph.D. 1881.

No. 11. Lists of the Antiquarian Remains in the Bombay Presidency, Sindh, and Berar, with an Appendix of Inscriptions from Gujarat: pp. 340, by J. BURGESS, LL.D., C.I.E. 1885. Rs. 6.

No. 12. The Caves at Nâdsur and Karsambla, with 7 plates, by H. COUSENS, M.R.A.S., Archæological Survey of Western India. 1891.

Report on the Architectural and Archæological Remains in the Province of Kachh, with Inscriptions and 10 Native Drawings, by DALPATRAM PRANJIVAN KHAKAR; with five papers by the late Sir ALEX. BURNES. Edited by J. BURGESS, LL.D. 8vo, pp. 120. (*Selections from the Records of Bombay Government, No.* 152, 1879.)

Notes on Bijapur and Satrunjaya, with two maps. *Bombay Government Selection No.* 145 (*N.S.*),—by H. COUSENS, M.R.A.S., Archæological Survey of Western India. Price 12 annas.

BOMBAY:—GOVERNMENT CENTRAL PRESS.

THE SHARQI ARCHITECTURE OF JAUNPUR;

WITH NOTES ON ZAFARABAD, SAHET MAHET AND OTHER PLACES IN THE N.-W. PROVINCES AND OUDH.

By A. FÜHRER, PH.D., and EDMUND W. SMITH, ARCHITECT.

Edited by JAS. BURGESS, C.I.E., LL.D., *Director-General of the Archæological Survey of India.*

Illustrated by 74 Plates of the Sharqi Architecture of Jaunpur, etc. Super-royal 4to. Sewed. Price 21s. 6d.

The Government may properly be urged and expected to continue this survey in the North-Western Provinces, and to utilise the Architectural members of the Survey, moreover, in advising and controlling a reasonable conservation of Historical Monuments in the Indian Empire.—*Journal R. Institute of British Architects, 19th June* 1890.

The first volume of Dr. Burgess's new series is a scholarly and exhaustive monograph on a special and well-defined architectural period. It is published in the form of a handsome quarto. . . supplying a valuable and interesting record of the history and architecture of Jaunpur, a city which for nearly a century vied with imperial Delhi both in power and splendour.

Unlike the majority of the volumes in the former series, the Report is one of which the Government has no reason to be ashamed, and it may be safely recommended to anyone interested either specially in Jaunpur or generally in Indian architecture as an adequate and trustworthy source of information.—*The Pioneer.*

CALCUTTA:—GOVERNMENT OF INDIA PRINTING PRESS. LONDON:—LUZAC & CO.

List of Volumes constituting the New Imperial Series of the Reports of the Archæological Survey of India.

Number in New Series.	Title of Volume.	Author or Editor.	Date (passed or proposed) of publication.
I.	Report on the Belgaum and Kaladgi Districts	Burgess	1874
II.	Report on the Antiquities of Kathiawar and Kachh	Burgess	1876
III.	Report on the Antiquities of the Bidar and Aurangâbâd Districts	Burgess	1878
IV.	The Buddhist Caves of Western India and their Inscriptions	Burgess	1883
V.	The Caves of Elura and the other Brâhmanical and Jaina Caves in Western India.	Burgess	1884
VI.	The Buddhist Stûpas of Amarâvatî and Jaggayyapeta	Burgess	1887
VII.	Lists of Antiquarian Remains in the Presidency of Madras (Volume I)	Sewell	1882
VIII.	List of Inscriptions and Sketch of Dynasties of Southern India (Volume II)	Sewell	1884
IX.	South Indian Inscriptions (Volume I)	Hultzsch	1890
X.	South Indian Inscriptions (Volume II)	Hultzsch	1891
XI.	Report on the Sharqi Architecture of Jaunpur	Burgess, Führer, and Smith.	1889
XII.	Monumental Antiquities and Inscriptions in the North-Western Provinces and Oudh.	Führer	1891
XIII.	Epigraphia Indica (Volume I)	Burgess	1891
XIV.	Epigraphia Indica (Volume II)	Burgess	1893
XV.	South Indian Buddhist Antiquities	Rea	1894
XVI.	Revised Lists of Antiquarian Remains in the Bombay Presidency	Burgess and Cousens.	1897
XVII.	List of Architectural and Archæological Remains in Coorg	Rea	1894
XVIII.	Report on the Moghul Architecture of Fatḥpur Sikri (Parts I–IV)	E. W. Smith	1895–98
XIX.	List of Antiquarian Remains in the Central Provinces and Berars	Cousens	1897
XX.	The Jaina Stûpa and other Antiquities at Mathurâ	V. A. Smith	1897
XXI.	Châlukyan Architecture, from the Ballâri District, Madras Presidency	Rea	1896
XXII.	Bower Manuscripts	Hoernle	1894
XXIII.	Muhammadan Architecture of Bharoch, Cambay, &c., in Gujarât	Burgess	1896
XXIV.	The Muhammadan Architecture of Ahmadâbâd, Part I	Burgess	1900
XXV.	Monumental Remains of the Dutch East India Company	Rea	1897
XXVI.	Report on Explorations in the Nepal Tarai	Mukherji	1897
XXIX.	South Indian Inscriptions (Volume III)	Hultzsch	1899
XXX.	Moghul Colour Decoration of Agra	E. W. Smith	1899
XXXI.	List of Antiquarian Remains in H.H. the Nizam's Territories	Cousens	1900
XXXII.	Antiquities of Northern Gujarat, Baroda Territories	Burgess and Cousens.	1902